Introduction to the philosophy of social research

SOCIAL RESEARCH TODAY

Series editor
Martin Bulmer

Additional titles to include:

Introduction to the philosophy of social research

Malcolm Williams
University of Plymouth

&

Tim May
University of Durham

with Richard D. Wiggins

Routledge
Taylor & Francis Group

LONDON AND NEW YORK

First published in 1996 by Routledge

Transferred to Digital Printing 2005

By Routledge,
2 Park Square, Milton Park,
Abingdon, Oxon, OX14 4RN
270 Madison Ave,
New York NY 10016

The name of Routledge is a registered trade mark
used by Routledge with the consent of the owner.

British Library Cataloguing in Publication Data
A catalogue record for this book is available from the British Library.

ISBNs: 1-85728-311-2 HB
        1-85728-312-0 PB

Typeset in Palatino.

Contents

Acknowledgements

We were inspired to write this book because of our belief that an examination of the relationship between philosophy and social research is an important and useful one. At present, however, there often appears to be a polarization of interests that prevents fruitful discussions. As such, this has not been an easy project. Yet there are a number of people who have encouraged us in the writing of this book and provided us with supportive and critical comments on the text itself.

We would first like to thank Alan Bryman, not only for writing the Foreword, but for reading drafts of the manuscript and providing us with very useful comments. Thanks also go to Ken for reminding Malcolm and through him to Tim, that there are those who still believe in a "real world!" John Lewis also provided us with financial support in the search for new knowledge! Dick Hobbs was good enough to listen to the readings of his work that we have used in Chapter 6, and Dee, Mary, Lyn and Calum each provided support during the writing period. Finally, our thanks to Justin Vaughan for his encouragement.

Foreword

Alan Bryman

The Philosophy of Social Science is a field about which there seems to be a fair degree of consensus that it is an important and central area of enquiry. Even among those social scientists who do not dwell on the kinds of issues that typically form its subject matter, there is often an acceptance of its importance. In the UK, the Economic and Social Research Council has prescribed the Philosophy of the Social Sciences as a necessary ingredient of the postgraduate curriculum in Sociology.

It is with some trepidation, therefore, that I have to confess that it is a field that I find very unappealing, though I can appreciate its potential. One reason is that as an examination of the textbooks in the field, which are now fairly numerous, would reveal, there is a curious unwillingness to ruminate about what the area is actually about. Two writers who do open their books with reasonable clear statements about the area's focal concerns are Rudner (1966) and Rosenberg (1988). The former sees it as concerned with "the logic or the rationale for social theorizing" (Rudner 1966: vii). By contrast, Rosenberg writes, "The traditional questions for the philosophy of social science reflect the importance of the choices of research questions and of methods of tackling them" (1988: 5). These two formulations are fairly different: Rudner emphasizes the role of the Philosophy of Social Science in relation to the logic of theory construction; Rosenberg's vision is somewhat broader and embraces the selection of research problems. Far from being a device through which social scientists will be able to come to terms with the philosophical backcloth to their field, they will often find that the Philosophy of the Social Sciences is as uncertain about its domain as social scientists themselves are uncertain about theirs.

But my main bone of contention lies with the comparative lack of interest among philosophers of social science in the practice of social research. This reveals itself in a number of ways. One is that often they tend to lay stress on the structure of social theories (as implied by Rudner's concerns), rather than on the epistemological warrants of social research. Secondly, they hardly ever cite illustrations of social research. Whereas philosophers of natural science cite a wide range of case studies and examples deriving from experimental investigations (for example, Harré 1972), their counterparts fall silent when it comes to illustrations of social research. While Rosenberg's vision previously cited of the Philosophy of the Social Sciences looks as though it might be concerned with the practice of social research and so include copious illustrations, the reader would be disappointed in this connection.

There are a small number of well rehearsed illustrations. Durkheim's examinations of suicide and religious life receive frequent attention, for example by Bernstein (1976), Hollis (1994), Keat & Urry (1975), Rosenberg (1988), and Trigg (1985). His work on suicide, in particular, is often used to exemplify the nature and problems of a positivist approach to social research and as such almost becomes a lens (one might even say in some cases the lens) through which positivism is viewed. The other illustration that readers of texts in the Philosophy of the Social Sciences are likely to encounter is Zande witchcraft, which is routinely employed to examine the problems of rationality and relativism, and often acts as a route to discussions about interpreting behaviour in terms of people's own meaning systems (for example, Hollis 1994; Keat & Urry 1975; Pratt 1978). Of course, other illustrations are occasionally used, but these two are fairly continuously recycled. Yet whether these works warrant being treated as exemplars is rarely directly examined. The fact that Durkheim's research was based on official statistics whose status is nowadays known to be highly questionable seems not to be a relevant consideration. But it is also highly unlikely that two recycled illustrations, that were published many decades ago, can stand in for philosophical speculation about social research practice. It is to the credit of the authors of this book, that one of their central aims has been to confront a wide variety of philosophical issues relevant to social research and to deploy a wide range of recent and not-so-recent illustrations in the process.

One area where philosophical issues and modern social research practice have come together is with respect to discussions about the epistemological underpinnings of quantitative and qualitative research. This discussion is revealed in contrasts between different positions variously described on the one hand as positivist or naturalist and on the other hand as idealist, phenomenological, hermeneutic, or interpretivist. The former position is depicted as involving an attempt to apply the principles of the natural sciences (or at least one version of those principles) to the study of people; the alternative perspective rejects such a project because people have agency and are able to engage in reflection about themselves and their environment. Matters of social research practice rear their heads because in the eyes of quite a large number of commentators, research methods are locked into such philosophical concerns.

One of the few writers to attempt to relate philosophy to social research exhibits this standpoint when he writes:

> every research tool or procedure is inextricably embedded in commitments to particular versions of the world and to knowing that world. To use a questionnaire, to use an attitude scale, to take the role of participant observer, to select a random sample, to measure rates of population growth, and so on, is to be involved in conceptions of the world that allow these instruments to be used for the purposes conceived (Hughes 1990: 11).

Similarly, Layder writes that "specific methods are always saturated with methodological prescriptions and thus, theoretical assumptions" (1988: 459). Thus, a questionnaire is not just a questionnaire: its use carries with it a baggage of beliefs about the nature of society and epistemological views about how it should be studied regardless of what the questionnaire actually comprises. As Williams & May show, to elevate the significance of broad epistemological issues involved in the selection of research techniques and methods of analysis in this way neglects other, often tactical, factors that impinge on decisions about methods and analysis.

One of the chief problems with the suggestion that methods cling like leeches to the legs of epistemological presuppositions is the growing tendency for investigators to combine quantitative and qualitative research. I have explored elsewhere a number of forms that such attempts at integration can take (Bryman 1988; 1992). But what are we to make of these cases of mixed methodologies? Do they represent rapprochements that reconcile positivism and hermeneutics, or Lazarsfeld and Schutz? For some writers these unions are more like shotgun marriages and they object to them as attempts to combine the incompatible or as spurious exercises in integration at a purely superficial level (for example, Buchanan 1992; Guba 1985; Smith & Heshusius 1986). But such reservations only apply if we are convinced that methods are so firmly rooted in philosophical issues that attempts to integrate, say, a questionnaire-based survey and participant observation, are ersatz combinations of the uncombinable. In fact, such connections as positivism-questionnaire or phenomenology-ethnography are merely assumptions that have become conventions. Historical investigations rarely confirm the validity of such supposed connections between methods and their underpinnings (Platt 1985; 1986). Thus, everybody's favourite exemplar of participant observation, Whyte's (1943) Street Corner Society, shows little of the loftier epistemological commitments that are often ascribed to this method nowadays. His discovery of a relationship between individual bowling scores and group structure has all the supposed hallmarks of the mind-set of positivism. It is not surprising that for Whyte the

> issue should not be quantitative versus qualitative research methods but rather what is to be quantified and how the measurements are to be integrated with the descriptions and analyses of behavior (Whyte 1991: 236).

Researchers may legitimately choose a particular research method because of its apparent correspondence with their epistemological commitments, but that does not mean that use of the method concerned inevitably implies those epistemological commitments. In other words, philosophy has an important role in relation to social research in laying bare such putative connections, but as Williams & May make clear, those connections are contingent rather than determinative.

As an illustration of some of these themes, I shall draw on Sutton & Rafaeli's (1988) research on the display of emotions in organizations. As a result of their reflections, Sutton & Rafaeli hypothesized a positive relationship between employees' display of positive emotions to customers (smiling, friendly greetings, eye contact) and retail sales. This hypothesis was tested using data collected on 576 convenience stores in the USA. Data on the display of positive emotions were collected using structured observation; sales data were used for the other variable. In terms of their hypothesis, the authors anticipated that stores in which there was a greater display of emotions would report greater sales. An analysis of the data showed that there was a relationship but it was negative. In other words, the finding was the opposite of that implied by their hypothesis (sceptics who think that quantitative researchers always confirm their hypotheses should take note). To investigate this puzzle, a qualitative study involving unstructured interviews and observation was carried out in a number of retail outlets. This investigation prompted a solution – the relationship was negative but retail sales are a cause not a consequence in the relationship, that is, more sales engenders a lower level of displays of positive emotions. This was because greater sales were associated with greater time pressure on sales staff and longer lines at check-outs, so that positive emotions were less likely to be engendered. This reinterpretation of sales as cause rather than consequence was then confirmed through a reanalysis of the quantitative data. Although Sutton & Rafaeli had not planned to combine quantitative and qualitative approaches, their research shows how combining them can be powerful. If they had relied on their quantitative data alone, their conclusions would have been very misleading.

For writers like Smith & Heshusius, this is not true integration because it does not operate at the paradigmatic level; instead, the qualitative element has been transformed into a "procedural variation of quantitative inquiry" (1986: 8). However, as I have suggested, since the connections between epistemological position and method are far more problematic than they are implying, the issue of whether the integration is genuine or superficial is irrelevant. Instead, what we have is an article that won the award for the best paper of the year in the journal in which it was published and which was singled out by peers as an example of "exemplary organizational research" (Frost & Stablein 1992).

An interesting twist in the possible connections between philosophy and social research can be discerned in a position, which is attracting a growing band of adherents, that suggests that there is a fundamental unity between the natural and the social sciences. At first blush, this view seems to herald a return to the positivist world view with its assertion of the universal applicability of the methodological canons of the natural sciences, or at least the positivist version of those canons. But the point of writers like Knorr-Cetina (1981) is very different. Their argument is that observations of natural and social scientists at work reveal little difference in how they go about the task of producing knowledge. Among both types of scientist, "all knowledge production is seen as skilled craftwork requiring a heterogeneous mix of practical, political, and rhetorical resources" (Ashmore et al. 1994). Furthermore, the hermeneutic/idealist position, which posits the fundamental difference between the objects of the social sciences and of the natural sciences – in other words, people and everything else (though biology represents a potential problem with this dichotomy) – on such grounds as the notion that only people have agency, is being questioned. It is on the basis of this quality of humans that the hermeneuts and idealists maintain that methods are required for their study that are distinctively different from those of the natural sciences. Not only is the ascription of agency solely to humans difficult to sustain, as Knorr-Cetina (1981) avers, but also the whole question of who or what has agency can be viewed as a matter of ascription (Edwards 1994).

What is striking about these ideas is that in this case the philosophical issues of the distinctiveness of humans and the material of the natural sciences, and of whether there are divergent approaches to their study, is being informed by social researchers concerned with such topics of enquiry as what really goes on in scientific laboratories, how natural and social scientists think, and the ways in which agency is imputed to humans and to objects. The traditional role of philosophy is one in which it alerts social scientists to the nature and implications of their practices. The more recent work is squaring the circle that relates philosophy to social science and social research by deploying social research to question some of the assumptions and beliefs that underlie philosophical issues. This development may represent the beginning of a new period in which there is much greater dialogue between philosophy and social science (and social research in particular).

A further contribution of this book is its preparedness to take on board recent developments in philosophy, such as poststructuralism and postmodernism. In this respect, the authors are engaging with issues into which others have felt uneasy about delving. In large part, this unease can be attributed to a lack of transparency in the implications of some of the ideas covered in Chapter 7 for social research practice. But the implications of these perspectives are being worked through, for example, as Foucauldian ideas are applied to human resource management (Townley 1994) and to standard costing and budgeting (Miller & O'Leary 1987) or as postmodernist themes are considered in relation to Disney theme parks (Bryman 1995). One area in which the influence of postmodernism has already been felt a great deal is with respect to the problematizing of the ethnographic text. As a result of the attentions of postmodernist influences, the ethnography is nowadays viewed in many quarters as a rhetorical device and consequently the authority of the writer of the text is brought into question (for example, see Tyler 1986). I very much hope that Chapter 7 will serve as a springboard for these and further issues associated with the "post-critiques" to be related to social research.

Philosophy can have a beneficial role in sharpening our awareness of the broader context of our research plans and our findings and thereby in drawing attention to a wider variety of conceptualizations of our craft than we would otherwise have access to. It can alert us to poor reasoning or to illegitimate inferences from data. It can bring to our attention new ideas that can generate novel agendas for social research. But philosophy must also respond to what is going on in the social sciences, as I have suggested above. It is in connection with these many issues that Williams & May have injected new ways of thinking about the relationship between philosophy and social research. What they provide us with is an introduction to philosophical issues that is relevant to the conduct and practice of social research and as such it will be useful, not merely as a *rite de passage* for postgraduates and others, but as a way of sharpening their thinking about social research.

CHAPTER 1

Introduction

Despite our personal commitments to what we regard as the fruitful examination of the relationship between social research and philosophy, we approached the writing of this book with a mixture of fear and trepidation. Although we are convinced that a consideration of this relationship is not only important for the practical purpose of clarifying issues, as well as the more abstract but equally important motive of intellectual curiosity, we sit somewhat uneasily in a path between these disciplines.

In each of these disciplines there are those who would regard any examination of their interplay as a dilution of the distinct contribution that each makes to our understandings of the social world. As it stands this is an unfortunate state of affairs, for each, while often aiming to achieve different ends, has much to offer the other. It is this belief that motivates us to write this book. At the same time, we recognize that for many social science students the study of philosophy is viewed as anything from difficult to irrelevant. We wish to correct the latter view, although having considerable sympathy with the former.

Yes, philosophy is difficult. So is social research and cooking. If you will forgive the metaphor, we wish to introduce you to a recipe, involving the ingredients of philosophy and social research, that when put together will provide a pleasant, rather than unsavoury taste. Our aim is also to enable you to see the important relations between its parts. This will allow a consideration of the philosophical nature of the social sciences in general and research practice in particular. In turn, this discussion of what is normally regarded as the "background" to social research, has the potential to refine, through reflection, the decisions that are routinely made in the research process itself. To achieve these broad aims, the actual content of the chapters are as follows. The section below is devoted to clarification. Here, we consider the aims, content and relationship between the two disciplines in order that you have a foundation upon which to proceed through the book.

Chapter 2 seeks to clarify what seems like an obvious question: what is science? This, of course, reflects the very nature of philosophical inquiry: to ask the obvious and, in so doing, to cause us to reflect upon our assumptions. What science actually "is" and what it is capable "of", are questions so often taken for granted. Science is frequently seen to represent the production of a body of knowledge that is assumed, in one way or another, to represent the "truth" about the phenomena with which it is concerned. However, on what basis are such claims made and how does science proceed in order to produce the truth?

By asking such questions, philosophy shakes the foundations of scientific practice. However, this should not be seen as a negative endeavour, for it enables us to examine not only the nature of science, but the foundations and subject matter of the social sciences. This is the subject of Chapter 3. In this chapter, we consider the extent to which the social sciences are similar to, or different from, the natural sciences. This is an important debate. Quite simply, if the sciences are capable of producing the truth about the natural world, then the social sciences may achieve, in adopting their methods, the same end in relation to the social world. Nevertheless, there is a tradition within the social sciences which argues that their aims and subject matter are different, but this does not mean that they are inferior. Given these arguments, Chapter 4 is devoted to a discussion of these issues in relation to how it is that we can "know" and "understand" social phenomena and what strategies we may adopt for this purpose.

For many, to follow in the path of the natural sciences is to replicate what is assumed to be, along with explanation, generalization and prediction, a central feature of their practice: value-freedom. In the age of genetic research, nuclear technology and environmental concerns, this ideal has found itself under increasing scrutiny. The motivations that underlie scientific curiosity are not always "disinterested". Plus, as large corporations and governments increasingly control the purse strings of such research, value-freedom may be invoked as often as a means of protecting oneself from undue encroachments on the process of research, as an attainable and ideal mode of scientific practice. As a result, this question is at the heart of research practice and for this reason we devote Chapter 6 to a discussion of the issue of values in social research.

Chapter 5 seeks to turn around our examination of the relationship between philosophy and social research. In this chapter we seek to unravel the philosophical issues that emerge in the research process itself. This allows a more focused discussion of the ideas contained in the previous chapters. Of course, we do not suggest that this is exhaustive. However, we hope this enables you, the reader, to locate and reflect upon the routine ways in which our decisions may be informed by a consideration of philosophical questions. Therefore, we are seeking to clarify further the relationship between research practice and philosophical ideas.

Chapter 7 would, for reasons that will become apparent, seem out of place in any book that seeks some linear progression in fulfilling its aims. Here we examine the poststructuralist and postmodernist movements in social science and philosophy that have appeared over the last few decades. These are said to aim at the very heart of our assumptions and practices, with a growing body of literature appearing by the day on these traditions and their implications for the social and physical sciences, as well as politics and social life in general. Given this, its inclusion is necessary in order to complete the picture of the relationship between philosophy and social research.

While it is our contention that philosophy is centrally important to understanding social research, it is clear that a great deal of research is not philosophically informed, whilst philosophy itself could do more for this relationship by understanding the daily decisions and actual contexts of research practice. Quite simply, reflection can be a luxury if one is on a temporary research contract, or is working for a large corporation or agency who want what they call "concrete" or "relevant" results, not "idle speculations". These and other considerations must be part of a more complete understanding of social research in the contemporary world. However, before moving on to Chapter 2, we first wish to clarify what is meant by philosophy and social research and the potential nature of the relationship between these two disciplines.

What is philosophy?

The concerns of philosophy often underlie and shape other disciplines. It seeks to clarify our concepts, transcend the particularity of disciplinary boundaries and ask questions about those very things that we often take for granted: for example, the nature of "truth". Let us examine a little more closely what it is that philosophers do and why they do it?

We all philosophize whenever we attempt to handle abstract ideas (Emmett 1964: ii). What is meant by abstract ideas? The nature of beauty, the purpose of life and whether we have free will encompass such ideas. We could add more mundane items to this list such as: where do flies go in the winter and why do we lose single socks and not pairs? You might object, quite reasonably, that the last two examples are problems for entomology and probability theory and have nothing to do with abstract reasoning. You would of course be right in that both questions are potentially answerable in concrete terms. In other words, they can be explained "scientifically". The question then becomes: what divides the abstract thinking of philosophy from scientific investigation? In the first case, the activity consists of thinking and in the second case, there is at least some engagement, via our senses, with the social and natural worlds of which we are a part. Yet there are problems that begin with abstract thoughts and end up being concrete and soluble problems in science. For example, for centuries philosophers have speculated on what "space" – that which lies between celestial bodies – consists of. The idea that it consisted of nothing, a vacuum, was the product of scientific discovery. This scientific "fact" is now questioned (Kraus 1989), indicating that science itself may not be assured of its findings. Nevertheless, it would not be an exaggeration to claim that what is now thought of as science was once the province of philosophical speculation.

That point noted, not all philosophical problems become scientific ones. There remain scientific problems with a large philosophical content. Other problems, such as the nature of the origin of the universe, or the workings of the mind, while the subjects of science, remain deeply philosophical; not least because the theories that claim to "solve" these problems are highly speculative and often incommensurate with each other. From this point of view, can we say that philosophy is pre-scientific thought?

A key area of philosophy is that of metaphysics. Literally, this means that which is beyond physics. This is a form of abstract thought that attempts to establish some "first principles" as foundations for knowledge. Perhaps the most famous example of this is the work of Descartes (1596–1650). As our experiences can play tricks on us, according to Descartes, they cannot be considered a satisfactory foundation for our knowledge. For instance, how do we know we are not dreaming and that our dreams are not just the tricks of an evil demon? Descartes believed that as long as you believe you are "something", the demons cannot deceive you. Therefore, in believing in yourself, he said that something called an "I" exists. For Descartes, this is the basic "truth" and the foundation for all our knowledge. To put it into its famous phrase, we can make only one statement with any degree of certainty, "I think, therefore I am" (*cogito ergo sum*). Later on in his career, Descartes moved from metaphysical first principles of existence, to an attempt to establish the location of the mind or the soul in the pineal gland – which led to some rather dubious experiments on cats!

If Descartes' curiosity, and that of philosophers in general, gives rise to the curiosity of science, an important question then follows: on what basis may we conduct science or even the philosophy that might have preceded it? This centres upon questions of knowledge. Where does our knowledge come from and how reliable is it? These are the concerns of the branch of philosophy known as epistemology.

The status of our knowledge claims is well illustrated by Bertrand Russell (1872–1970). He asked how can we know the world around us has any physical reality? How can he know, for example, that when he sees a cat move from one part of the room to another, but pass from his view in its journey, that the cat has continued to "exist" while out of his gaze? The only sense data available are to see the cat at one point and later at another. Our working assumption is that the cat continued to exist, but how can we know that? As Descartes argued, the cat may just be a dream. However, if we assume that the cat exists whether we see it or not:

> we can understand from our own experience how it gets hungry between one meal and the next; but if it does not exist when I am not seeing it, it seems odd that its appetite should grow during non existence as fast as during existence (Russell 1980: 10).

In this example, we can see how Russell makes a knowledge claim for the existence of the cat. A less trivial and important concern of this book is what is the status of knowledge claims in social sciences and sciences in general? While we are concerned with metaphysical problems, we tend to be more concerned with epistemological ones. However, these are not our only concerns, nor those of philosophy. We can see the mechanism by which Russell claims that there is a continued existence of his cat, despite its absence from his gaze. Yet there is still the question of the nature of the cat's existence. Two possible states are offered by Russell. First, that the cat had no "real" existence and was a product of the mind. Secondly, that the cat does exist and the epistemological "proof" of this resides in its appetite. Such questions form a branch of metaphysical enquiry called ontology. While we promise that the nature of the existence of cats is now a closed matter, the book will be concerned with more serious ontological questions concerning the nature of assumptions that underlie scientific theories. Quite simply, if we make a claim concerning the social and natural worlds, what are the presuppositions that are built into our ideas regarding their nature?

By now you may have formed the distinct impression that philosophy can be likened to games that young children play with their parents. When told something the child will reply, "why"? A further explanation is then given and the parent believes she or he has answered the question, only to be confronted with another inquiry. The game continues until either the child or the parent become tired or the questioning has arrived at something that is imponderable.

"Don't hit your brother."

"Why?"

"Because its naughty."

"Why?"

"Because brothers should be kind to each other."

"Why?"

"Because the social fabric of the nuclear family and western civilization itself will collapse if we don't show consideration for others."

"Why?"

(Smack)

Descartes' method of "radical doubt" can be likened to the questioning child. Persistent questions may be annoying to parents, but asking them can help the child develop an enquiring and questioning mind. Likewise, awkward philosophical questions may seem irrelevant to the practitioners of, say, physics or social research. However, questions such as these "enlarge our conception of what is possible, enrich our intellectual imagination, and diminish the dogmatic assurance which closes the mind against speculation" (Russell 1983: 93–4). In this way, they possess the potential to make us better physicists or social researchers.

Finally we should note that philosophers are concerned with what it is that makes human beings what they are. Are there certain things that we should, or should not, do? Are there values that transcend history and different societies? Can we say what can counts as the "good life" is the same for all? These are moral questions. As we will see, they form a central part of research practice. Indeed, the philosopher John Stuart Mill (1806–73) described what we now call the social sciences as "moral" sciences. In all of those things that concern us as researchers, we will find epistemological, ontological and moral issues.

What is social research?

Although the spirit of curiosity motivates social researchers as much as it does philosophers, by necessity, the former are moved to address those questions that are of concern to their disciplines or to those organizations or institutions for whom they work and/or are funded. They must be technically minded in their search for the best ways of achieving their aims. Therefore, they are not usually in the daily business of asking philosophical questions about the social world. It is usually the process of investigation that defines something as being "research", rather than being driven by more abstract concerns.

The research process is made up of a series of steps and judgements that involve the application of techniques. For this reason, the methods of research can be used in the service of curiosity. These may be everyday concerns, like whether or not to buy a pair of shoes, or those that are of general social concern: for example, the issues of homelessness, crime or poverty. The first may require an examination of our current funds and the state of our shoes, whereas the second will require funded research programmes with clear policy objectives. Both involve curiosity and necessitate techniques peculiar to the questions being asked.

Research may be characterized as methodical investigations into a subject or problem. To "research" is to seek answers that involve understanding and explanation, whereas the credibility of its outcomes will rest heavily upon the conduct of the investigation. Those whose job it is to conduct research will, hopefully, apply systematic methods in their practice. Most social research is conducted through the following methods of data collection: social surveys, field observations, interviews and the use of existing data. The method chosen will depend on the resources available and the nature of the phenomenon we wish to study. Despite these caveats, we are usually concerned with the quantity or quality of a phenomeon and different research methods reflect these concerns. At the same time, they reflect a philosophically inspired debate about whether social research can successfully "quantify" human behaviour. While we will have more to say on this topic, let us first ask what are the main styles of "quantitative" or "qualitative" research?

Social surveys are quantitative. In the main, they are single "one-off" studies of specific "target" populations at particular points in time. They are carried out in order to describe and explain sets of circumstances, behaviours and attitudes. Although a complete enumeration of a population would tell researchers what they wished to know, time and resources do not permit this and so attributes are "counted" in a population by drawing a sample that is taken to be representative of the total population in which the researcher is interested. For instance, though it is common to claim "smoking causes cancer", this claim is based on the observation that a great number of people who smoke subsequently develop cancer.

There are cases where researchers will want to say with a great degree of certainty that X was caused by Y. In psychology, for example, experiments are designed to investigate the causes of particular phenomena. The cornerstone of classic experimental design is termed "randomization", whereby the investigator manipulates or controls some feature of the environment and then observes any resulting change in the behaviour of the subjects under investigation in order to ascertain the relationship between cause and effect. Exposed subjects are thus compared to non-exposed subjects and conclusions drawn. The difficulty for the experimenter lies in isolating what it is that "really" does cause something else to happen. In fact, such associations are not always obvious and the whole question of cause and effect in human behaviour is questioned by both philosophers and some social researchers.

The concern of "qualitative research" is primarily with the qualities of given phenomena and less with their quantities. Unlike experimental methods, there is no desire to isolate specific or certain causes. Qualitative research encompasses a range of strategies that allow researchers to "get close to the data". They are often characterized as being concerned with the daily actions of people and the meanings that they attach to their environments and relationships. They take various forms that include ethnography, case studies, biography and autobiography. As we shall see, there is a debate in the social sciences, which has methodological and technical implications, that revolves around the question of meaning in social life.

Ethnography lays appropriate emphasis on its anthropological origins by direct observation of behaviours in a particular society. Its method is principally that of participant observation, whereas case studies rely on intense observation, tape recorded interviews and the collection of documents: for example, records of speeches, photos, diaries, letters, etc. In qualitative research, the understandings of the action of participants is gained by placing emphasis on the way in which action arises from and reflects back on, individual experiences. Qualitative research, in its various forms, thus becomes a complex interaction between the researcher and the researched (see Hobbs & May 1993). It is thus concerned with a reflexive understanding of the process of research activity, as well as the technicalities of method.

Lastly, research that uses available data or secondary analysis, stands apart from experiments, surveys, ethnography or case studies. The data does not originate as a result of the research, but is the product of earlier research activity or some form of record-keeping. Here, the variety of data appears to be limited only by the researcher's imagination (Singleton et al. 1993). Examples of secondary data can be found in official records, public and private documents, the print and broadcast media, physical material (clothing, works of art), as well as vast data archives covering both quantitative surveys and qualitative material (see Dale et al. 1988, Scott 1990).

The relationship between philosophy and social research

Both philosophy and social research aim to improve our knowledge of the world. The ways in which they go about this may seem strange to those immersed in only one of the disciplines, yet there is actually a great deal of common interest between them. Whereas philosophy is concerned to know what kind of things exist in the world and what is our warrant to know them, social research is concerned with their knowable properties. In this sense, ontological and epistemological outcomes of philosophical investigations will have a direct impact on what we can say of social properties. Philosophy thus possesses the potential to construct a frame of reference for the researcher. Sometimes, however, the researcher must choose between frames of reference: for example, whether we regard social groups such as classes, or communities of different kinds, as "things in themselves" with particular analyzable properties, or whether we simply see them as a collections of individuals. The former British Prime Minister, Margaret Thatcher, once asserted that there was no such thing as society, just individual men and women and their families. This assertion had an enormous political impact and though, on the face of it, Lady Thatcher was not being overtly philosophical in her argument, her utterance was actually an articulation of a philosophical position that has both methodological and moral, as well as political and economic consequences.

It is occasionally said that social research could get along quite nicely without philosophy, or philosophical reflection. Yes, the practice of social research would probably continue, but it would still have philosophical implications. Take two researchers engaged in separate projects on the existence and nature of poverty. The first might be informed by the individualist assumptions of Lady Thatcher and the second may take an opposite, collectivist, viewpoint. Each could claim not to be touched by philosophy, yet the outcomes of the research would probably be very different simply because they began from different starting points that, in turn, were grounded in particular philosophical assumptions. Philosophy will not go away. While we would maintain that philosophy can be interesting and rewarding for its own sake, it underwrites our research activity and that is enough of a reason for engaging with its ideas and insights.

Philosophy also needs social research, though this relationship is perhaps not quite so obvious. The philosophy of the social sciences emerged out of the special considerations and problems associated with knowing the social world. As such, it needs to be relevant to the concerns of researchers in social science and the way this is achieved is via an awareness and appreciation of the key issues of research practice. This does not mean that philosophy must simply reflect the preoccupations of the social or the physical sciences, for that would undermine many of its insights, but that the questions philosophers ask should be informed by current debates in research. For example, there has long been a symbiotic relationship between probability theory and philosophy, whereby developments in the former have had implications for the latter – particularly in the area of statistics (see Chapter 4). Likewise, philosophical debates concerned with social causality have been shaped as a result of practical research experiences (see Chapter 3). Some of the most important work in both areas actually straddles disciplines to the extent that philosophers themselves now work within research programmes and research centres alongside researchers whose concerns are more instrumentally based.

The above noted, philosophy and social research do not just rely on each other, they are two different, yet complementary, views of the world. Methodological decisions are implicitly ontological and epistemological, whereas moral considerations underwrite everything we do as researchers, philosophers or citizens. Whether you send bibles, bread or both to the starving, will rest very much on whether you prioritize spiritual or material considerations, or a combination of these.

A note on reading this book

This book is not intended as a definitive statement on either philosophy or social research, but simply as a tool (maybe even a blunt instrument!) to aid an understanding of the relationship between the disciplines. Throughout you will find references to research and occasionally a highlighted illustration of a particular research project. The intention of the latter is to give some flavour of the philosophical implications of research. The examples are neither definitive nor detailed and in many cases simply reflect the authors' own research interests! Moreover by no means all philosophical questions raised in the text are addressed in the research examples. The challenge for the reader is to consider the philosophical implications for her own research.

At the end of each chapter you will find some recommended further reading and some questions for consideration. Once again the former are not necessarily definitive, but represent texts we have found interesting or useful, while the latter should be considered food for thought and not a whole meal!

CHAPTER 2

What is science?

In this chapter we seek to ask what appears, at first glance, to be an obvious question. Yet its investigation reveals an ambiguity over definitions of science, its procedures and hence what it is capable of attaining. We are concerned to problematize these issues for two reasons. First, it will enable us to see how the aims and practices of science rest upon taken-for-granted assumptions that, when subjected to critical scrutiny, are often found wanting. Secondly, this will provide us with a basis for investigating, in the next chapter, the nature of the social sciences where there is a dispute as to whether they should replicate or replace the methods of the physical sciences; methods which, as will be noted, are themselves disparate when examined under a philosophical microscope.

Social research is a child of the scientific age. As an investigative discipline, its origins are to be found in a nineteenth century model of physical science. Previously, social thinkers had often confined themselves to general observations about human nature. The seventeenth century had witnessed an emergence of thinkers who, in their attempts to better understand the physical world, began to place at least some emphasis on theory testing. Francis Bacon (1561–1626) and later Isaac Newton (1642–1727), were claiming an empirical basis for their statements about how the world was and how it might be investigated. Following this, there was a growing realization, particularly after Newton, that the "language" of science was essentially mathematical. In its simplest sense, an investigation of the world was a search for the existence or non-existence of phenomena. Things either existed or they did not. If they did, the measurable relationship to other phenomena involved an encounter with number (Losee 1980: 86–94).

13

If the "new" science had met with the level of success achieved by the alchemy or witchcraft of the middle ages, it would probably not have been emulated by those wishing to establish a method of investigating social life. As it was, the success of science lay in the workable technology that was derived from it. The inventions of the nineteenth century were the technological results of the successful scientific theories of that and the previous century. Given the status of the sciences at this time, it is not surprising that the founding figures of what were to become the social sciences were anxious to claim a legitimacy for their work by linking it to what they saw as the success of parallel research in the physical sciences. Thus, Sigmund Freud (1856–1939), an admirer of Newton, entitled an early manuscript of his, "A project for a Scientific Psychology" (Wollheim 1971). Similarly, Marx regarded his project as "scientific". Indeed, nineteenth century thinkers such as John Stuart Mill did not make any methodological distinction between investigations of physical and social phenomena. Mill believed such methods to be equally applicable to the investigation of diverse phenomena (Mill 1987), distinguishing between physical and social phenomena only by reference to the greater complexity of the latter.

The physical and social sciences thus share something of a common history. Although much of this is accounted for by the desire of the infant social sciences to emulate the methods of their successful physical counterparts, the two disciplines have a number of philosophical issues in common. There are, of course, crucial differences in the nature of some of the key problems encountered and we will point to these in the following chapter. For the present, a brief examination of the methods of the physical sciences is valuable for the two reasons we outlined above.

Science: a search for method

There are a number of ways a critical description of science could be presented. None would be entirely comprehensive and all would be controversial. Here, we have two aims. First, to present some prominent views of what scientific knowledge is, or ought to be, and secondly, to convey a sense of the controversy that exists in the philosophy of science. In furtherance of these aims, we will focus in this section on the idea of a search for scientific method.

For those previously unacquainted with such matters, the idea that there should be a search at all, that there can be anything other than a single scientific method, may seem rather surprising. However, what counts as *scientific method has long been the subject of dispute*. More specifically, controversy has centred upon how knowledge can be justified as scientific, which, in its turn, has been strongly linked to the question of how scientists actually discover things. Yet, why a concern with the attempt to identify the scientific method? Because most philosophers of science have argued that the method used is the only guarantee that the knowledge obtained is valid, reliable and thus scientific. By employing the correct method, the scientist may be sure that their findings are "true", "repeatable" and "generalizable". In this sense, science is method. It follows that if there is more than one method, then there is more than one science. For the majority of philosophers of science, that leads to trouble in terms of its knowledge status.

Let us first ask what is the difference between ordinary everyday knowledge and scientific knowledge? The popular view states that, "Scientific knowledge is reliable knowledge because it is objectively proven knowledge" (Chalmers 1982: 1). In turn, this is dependent upon the formulation of scientific theories, which are:

> derived in some rigorous way from the facts of experience acquired by observation and experiment. Science is based on what we can see, hear and touch, etc. Personal opinion or preferences and speculative imaginings have no place in science. Science is objective (Chalmers 1982: 1).

This view that scientific theories are derived from the facts of experience is controversial. Nevertheless, it has a long history as an explanation of how science discovers things. As such, we need to examine it in more detail.

Science and the role of experience

The view that scientific discovery is the result of our experience of the world, though traceable to the Ancient Greeks, has its modern origins in the work of the eighteenth century Scottish philosopher David Hume (1711–76). Hume's theory of knowledge (epistemology) is perhaps the best known example of the philosophical doctrine known as "empiricism". Empiricism may be defined as the idea that all knowledge has its origins in experience that is derived through the senses. Broadly speaking, Hume made a distinction between "impressions" and "ideas". The former, he argued, have more influence upon our understanding. Although complex ideas do not necessarily resemble impressions – you can imagine a mermaid without necessarily having seen one – the parts that make up complex ideas are themselves derived from impressions and impressions are derived from experience. Anything else is rejected as metaphysical speculation. Thus:

> Those perceptions which enter with most force and violence we may name *impressions;* and under this name, I comprehend all our sensations, passions, and emotions, as they make their first appearance in the soul. By *ideas*, I mean the faint images of these in thinking and reasoning (Hume 1911: 11. Original italics).

However:

> I observe that many of our complex ideas never had impressions that correspond to them, and that many of our complex impressions are never exactly copied in ideas. I can imagine to myself such a city as the New Jerusalem, whose pavement is gold and walls are rubies though I never saw any such. I have seen Paris; but shall I affirm I can form such an idea of that city, as will perfectly represent all its streets and houses in their real and just proportions? (Hume 1911: 13).

On the face of it, the assertion that we discover things by seeing, hearing, touching, smelling or tasting them seems unremarkable. How else could we come to know the world? On the other hand, the claim that reliable knowledge is derived from sense impressions depends on the assumption that we all use our senses in the same way. In other words, if the information received via the sensory organs is the same for two people, each will then possess exactly the same knowledge. This seems, initially at least, plausible. After all, chaos on the roads would ensue if each driver saw something different in the same road sign! However, what we see depends on what we are looking for. Observation is not a straightforward affair for it contains two dimensions which interact in complex ways. They are the cognitive and social dimensions. Let us briefly considered each of these.

From a cognitive vantage point, we select phenomena from the world on the basis of a learned classificatory system. For example, we are able to recognize and classify many different sizes, shapes and varieties of trees on the basis of learned "tree like" characteristics. The more we know about trees, the more sophisticated our classificatory system becomes. The characteristics that differentiate the species must be selected and what we select will depend on our knowledge of the phenomenon. Although most people in Europe and North America can distinguish an oak from a palm tree, distinguishing specific varieties of palm or oak requires prior, systematically accumulated, knowledge. Therefore, though we are all able to select and classify, the process of selection comes from us, not the object as such. For this reason, two people looking at the same object may not see the same thing. When it comes to images on an X-ray, for instance, person A may see an object that person B does not.

We have spoken of the above characteristics as learned. Now although we can learn many things from direct experience of the world – fire is hot, ice is cold, lemons are bitter, etc. – many of the determining mechanisms of the classification and selection process are the result of the social nature of human beings. Although it is logically possible to learn most things about the world through direct perception, much of what we learn and subsequently formulate views upon are social products. A medical researcher investigating the causes of heart disease would begin from the basis of an enormous amount of knowledge and a sophisticated classificatory system. She would not have been employed unless she had undergone a rigorous programme of training and had already amassed considerable experience and data in the area of research. When the observations are made, her selection criteria are based upon the end product of this training and experience. Not only is it likely her observations will differ from those of the lay person, but they may differ from those of an equally experienced colleague employing slightly different criteria of selection.

In recent decades physics, in particular, has become concerned with objects that cannot be directly experienced by the senses. These phenomena can only be known through the means by which they are recorded or, in the case of black holes and sub-atomic particles, reasoned from indirect evidence. The things that are experienced, the presence of a particular radio wave, or the reading on an instrument, are not the things we wish to make ontological claims about. At best, they provide evidence for that which we wish to know and can never, in themselves, constitute direct sensory experience of the phenomenon itself. Indeed, it might be argued that their very nature is the product of theoretical description. From this point of view there is no "neutral" way of knowing them and the way we know them will inevitably be a product of the way that they are described: for example, in cosmology and mathematics (see Ferris 1988, Penrose 1989).

We are now left with the idea that science does not begin from observation, but presupposes a theory to render its observations intelligible. Observations are thus said to be "theory laden". The philosopher Karl Popper (1902–94) recounts an experiment conducted with physics students in Vienna in the early part of the century. He gave them the instruction to pick up a pencil and write down what they observed:

> They asked, of course, what I wanted them to observe. Clearly the instruction "observe" is absurd . . . observation is always selective. It needs a chosen object, a definite task, an interest, a point of view, a problem (1989: 46).

All observations thus presuppose a theory of some kind. As Chalmers puts it in relation to a sentence uttered in commonsensical, everyday language:

> "Look out, the wind is blowing the baby's pram over the cliff edge!" Much low level theory is presupposed here. It is implied there is such a thing as wind, which has the property of being able to cause the motion of objects such as prams that stand in its path. The sense of urgency conveyed by the "look out" indicates the expectation that the pram, complete with baby, will fall over the cliff and perhaps be dashed on the rocks beneath and it is further assumed that this will be deleterious for the baby (Chalmers 1982: 28–9).

"Low level" theories such as these are the outcome of a complex relationship between our physical ability to observe and a cognitive selection process shaped through socially obtained knowledge. They only differ from "higher level" theories of science in terms of the complexity of the knowledge obtained.

The problems associated with the acquisition of sense impressions of physical objects are compounded by the non-physical nature of some concepts. How can it be said, for example, that we have acquired concepts such as liberty, honesty or utility through sense impressions? However, we do seem to have these without any corresponding images of things in the world. Similarly, as Immanuel Kant (1724–1804), the German philosopher argued, arithmetic is itself an abstract concept. Our idea of number appears to be quite separate to the things we are counting. Indeed, although we can have a concept of the number 23,468,098 it would be impossible to have simultaneous experience of that many objects. Therefore, Kant maintained that although sense impressions provide the raw material for our empirical knowledge, it is our ability to reason that is responsible for ordering and organizing that knowledge (see Scruton 1982).

It is not our intention to suggest that observation plays anything but a large role in science, it is merely to show that assertions about the prior nature of observation, upon which science is thought to base itself, is highly problematic. Discovery in science is not just about observing the world, as passive receptors of sense data, but is dependant upon the process of active and purposive selection. Therefore, there is a constant relationship between theory and data. This still leaves the question as to how observed and theoretically constituted phenomena are actually presumed to be related to one other. To consider this issue, we need to examine the ideas of "causality" and "association".

Causality and association

Scientific theories are not only about the nature of objects, but the relationships that exist between them. Therefore, theories about objects on their own are usually accompanied by theories about how objects are related to other objects. In particular, what caused an object to be the way it is? For example, the cause of a particular chemical reaction, the cause for a collapsed bridge and the causes of heart disease. From this, it might be said that if we know the cause of an event on one occasion, we will know the cause of an event in the future where the circumstances of its occurrence remain the same. We stake an awful lot on this proposition. A great deal of effort is expended to establish the cause of an aeroplane crash, so that the defect might be rectified. The reasoning being that if the fault caused one plane to crash, it might well be the cause of further crashes. As such, cause is commonly held to be necessary for an event. No events occur without a cause and to explain an event is to know its cause. In these terms, science may be characterized as the search for causes.

Hume (1911) argued that if all we know of the world comes through our senses, then what we know of causes and effects must come to us in the same manner. This being the case, there is nothing in the events themselves to warrant us claiming a necessary connection between them. According to this view, if we observe, for example, that the striking of a match is followed by its bursting into flames, all we can say is that flames ensued after the match was struck. We cannot observe what, if any, connection exists between the two events. However, we can counter this by saying that if objects themselves are not always observable, then it is unsurprising that the relationships between them cannot be observed.

At one level Hume is correct to say that all we see in a cause is what is known as constant conjunction: that is, when event A occurs it is followed by event B. When one pool ball hits another, we see the second move and the only warrant we have for calling this a cause, is that in our experience one pool ball hitting another is followed by movement on the part of the second ball. However, suppose you make the statement "my watch broke because I dropped it". On the face of it, this seems a perfectly good example of cause and effect and in making such a statement, you are actually holding that a causal chain of events occurred. Thus, the watch hit the ground and this impact caused the displacement of a component A that, in turn, stopped component B from working, etc. Similarly, to talk of pool balls hitting each other in a causal sequence could entail the citing of a causal chain involving air pressure, friction, gravity and so on.

One philosophical solution to this question of cause and effect is to employ the concepts of sufficient and necessary conditions. By sufficient conditions, we simply mean that the occurrence of A was sufficient for the occurrence of B. Therefore, a sufficient condition for the breaking of a watch was dropping it. A necessary condition is when B could not have occurred without A. However, A might be necessary, but may not have actually caused B. To take another example. If a match is struck, oxygen can be said to be necessary for successful ignition, but it is not the cause of the match lighting. Matches will not combust simply due to the presence of oxygen. In the case of the watch, a necessary condition might be cited as the disturbance of a crucial part of the mechanism. Given this, to talk of one thing causing another in a straightforward manner is not always helpful for explanatory purposes. Within any cause–effect sequence, we can identify a whole series of relationships that are both necessary and sufficient.

If employing these concepts may be viewed as one philosophical solution, which is still open to dispute, it is not a methodological solution. In order to identify a cause, we need to identify all of the necessary and sufficient conditions. However, at this point we encounter the practical problem of such identification and the logical problem of never knowing that we have identified all of these conditions. If we wish to claim that something caused something else, we may pursue a broad strategy: that is, we can attempt to identify as many as possible of the antecedent conditions of an event. The more we identify, the more we will know. Detectives do this all of the time. It is not enough to say that a murder was the result of a gunshot wound, nor that Joe Bloggs committed the murder. They also require to know who did it, how, why and when? This may involve pathologist's reports and the statements of witnesses. Thus, we can say that to know more about a cause, although accepting from a logical point of view that we may never known enough, is "sufficient" for the purpose at hand.

The problem with this pragmatic solution is that scientists are not always able to discover anywhere near the full range of antecedent conditions. In such cases, they must fall back on something like a Humean view of causality: that is, constant conjunction. For example, though the claim is made that people who smoke are more likely to develop lung cancer, a full causal description may not be possible even though more and more antecedent conditions are being identified on a daily basis. Although we can say that smoking appears to be sufficient condition for lung cancer, all we can actually claim is the strength of association between smoking and cancer. In itself such statistical associations might be powerful scientific tools, but they should not be confused with a causal description consisting of all necessary and sufficient conditions.

Hume's account of causality does not simply rely upon the idea that we cannot observe any necessary connection between events. This is only one part of his argument. A second part concerns our habits of projecting our past experiences into present or future events. In other words, when we say that the movement of the black pool ball was the result of the white ball striking it, our claim for this is based on past experiences of observing the behaviour of one pool ball when struck by another. This kind of reasoning is called "inductive" and forms a central part of the idea of "science".

Induction

Induction concerns expectations about the uniformity of nature. Each time we drink a coffee, we have certain expectations of taste based on prior experiences. In the same way, we expect rain to be wet, sea to be salty and the sun to rise tomorrow. We have no reason to doubt these things because, in our experience, they have always occurred. Hume regarded this as a basic psychological characteristic of human beings.

Induction can be defined as the derivation of a general principle (or possibly a law in science), which is inferred from specific observations. As such, it can be seen as an important basis for many justifications of scientific knowledge. Scientific experiments are of little value unless they are able to tell us about the world in general. It is also an important claim for scientific method in that it enables prediction of future circumstances. For example, if a scientist establishes that the breaking strength of a particular type of steel bar is 1000 kg, her experiment would have little point unless she can claim that a bar of the same composition and construction will have the same breaking strength under the same conditions in the future.

Long held scientific laws are actually based on inductive principles. Take two examples: acids turn litmus paper red and the larger a planetary body, the greater the gravitational pull and as bodies move further apart, the more the force of gravity diminishes. In both cases, we could take many examples of planets or litmus paper and each would produce the same effect if the principle holds. Indeed, most scientists will discover a single instance of a phenomenon via an experiment, or observation, and though they will repeat this under a variety of conditions to obtain confirmation of their hypothesis, what they are actually doing is reasoning from specific examples to general principles. How are these generalizations to be justified?

There are three conditions that must be satisfied in the process of induction. First, the number of observation statements forming the basis of the generalization must be sufficiently large. Secondly, the observation statements must be repeated under a wide variety of conditions and thirdly, no accepted observation statement should conflict with the derived universal law (Chalmers 1982). Once these conditions have been met and a "law" is said to be established, it is then possible for the scientist to both explain and predict phenomena. The explanation of a particular substance turning litmus red is that the liquid is an acid. Alternatively, if our scientist is given a sample of an acid she can predict it will turn litmus paper red.

Though Hume identified induction as a psychological process, he also pointed out its logical drawbacks. For Hume, all argument from experience was the attempt to create a "syllogism". A syllogism can be defined as a statement whereby something other than that which is stated necessarily follows. That such attempts must fail was vividly illustrated by Bertrand Russell in the story of the chicken who was fed every day of his life until the day he had his neck wrung (1980: 35). The expectation of food, which had hitherto arrived every day, was dramatically unfulfilled! Such a foundation for science appears rather shaky when we consider that no inductive argument is "safe". Not even the sun rising tomorrow is a certainty.

It might well be objected that these issues are pointless if the sun does not put in an appearance tomorrow. Induction as a problem in the philosophy of science is rather arcane. Despite this, it remains a real problem for all kinds of researchers. Inductive evidence can appear rock solid. Yet the history of the physical sciences is replete with generalizations that are found to be wrong, sometimes after hundreds of years of being considered "right". Consider just two examples. Though it has been known since Copernicus that a central Ptolemic principle of the heavens turning around the earth is false, Ptolemy's geocentric model of the heavens still works perfectly well as a means of navigation:

> For a system that we now consider to be entirely "wrong", it was spectacularly accurate. Ptolemy, for example, calculated the distance of the moon from the earth as 29.5 times the earth's diameter. Our figure is 30.2 (Appleyard 1992: 25).

Far from being "irrational", or "unscientific", belief in the geocentric model was backed up by good solid observation and even though an inaccurate representation, it accurately predicted phenomena; for instance, the earth's distance from the moon. Moreover, it had survived for over thirteen hundred years.

A more contemporary example concerns the role of stress in heart disease. Studies conducted in the late 1950s by Friedmann & Rosenman (cited in Golob & Bruce 1990) proposed that hurried, impatient, aggressive and hostile people were more likely to develop heart disease than those who were more relaxed, easy-going and co-operative. Though initially controversial, by 1981 the first kind of behaviour, known as "Type A" behaviour, was officially classified in the US as a risk factor for heart disease. However, studies conducted in the 1980s have concluded that there is no link between personality and heart disease (Shekelle cited in Golob & Bruce 1990). The variations in these findings were the result of different tests and procedures that overturned long and firmly held assumptions.

In the everyday world of science, on the other hand, the problem of induction is not usually confronted head on. Most researchers who make generalizations do so on the basis of the probability of their assertions being true:

> The fact that probabilities can in certain contexts be represented by numerical values led to the hope that one could assign values to the degree to which a body of evidence rendered a theory probable (Newton Smith 1981: 216).

If we toss a coin 100 times, we can reasonably expect that heads will come up about 50 times. Simply because there are only two possibilities, this expectation is a reasonable one though, of course, it is perfectly possible that heads may appear more or less than half of the time. Probabilities are usually expressed on much more complex matters. For instance, we could express the probability of a group of 18 year olds becoming unemployed in the next ten years. What is important to note here and in virtually all cases where probability is used, is that we can only arrive at the odds of something happening on the basis of past experience. Just as a bookmaker will offer 10/1 on a particular horse based upon its past form, so researchers decide on probabilities on the basis of what they already know. The probability of our 18 year olds becoming unemployed can only be arrived at on the basis of the odds of a similar group becoming unemployed in the past. Sophisticated models may build in other factors to try to account for changing circumstances, but unfortunately we can never know what these are or the effects they will produce. The inability of economists to accurately forecast growth or shrinkage in any economy is sufficient testimony to this observation.

In employing probability we are faced with two problems. First, like any form of induction we have no guarantee that what is true now will remain so in the future. Secondly, because we cannot know the future, we cannot be *sure* of the probability to assign to particular circumstances. As Chalmers points out:

> Given standard probability theory, it is very difficult to construct an account of induction that avoids the consequence that the probability of any universal statement making claims about the world is zero, whatever the observational evidence ... any observational evidence will consist of a finite number of observation statements,

whereas a universal statement makes claims about an infinite number of possible situations. The probability of the universal generalization being true is thus a finite number divided by an infinite number, which remains zero however much the finite number of observation statements constituting the evidence is increased (Chalmers 1982: 18).

That noted, let us not be too critical of probability. Logically and perhaps mathematically, probability may be flawed, but without it many sciences would be more difficult and some, such as quantum mechanics, impossible. That noted, alternative characterizations of scientific method still exist. One of these is the notion of deduction, as opposed to induction.

Deduction and logical positivism

Kant, as noted, held that there are ways of knowing the social and natural worlds other than through experience alone. At the heart of this argument is the distinction he makes between synthetic and analytic knowledge. Hume, in denying that there can be any necessary relations between propositions, overlooked what Kant described as analytic statements. In analytic statements the concept of the predicate is included in the concept of the subject. Thus, "All bodies (subject) are extended in space (predicate)" or, "All senators (subject) are citizens (predicate)." By definition, a body is something extended in space and by definition, a senator must be a citizen. Conversely, the statement, "Some bodies are heavy" though true, is not analytic because the idea of "heaviness" is not contained in the (subject) word "body". This kind of statement is described by Kant as synthetic.

Deductive logic depends on analytic truths. A deductive statement is where the conclusion must follow from the premiss. In other words, just as in the first two examples above, the truth of the conclusion is contained in the premiss. This is generally not problematic in mathematics, but when we use linguistic expressions the truth of the conclusion is not a matter of logical agreement with the premiss, but depends on the truth of those premisses. For example, "All pigs can fly, Porky is a pig and so, Porky can fly." Now, if all pigs can fly then it must be the case that Porky can fly; if he chooses to do so! A deductive statement, though logically correct, is not necessarily a true statement. Conversely, if something is true it does not mean that it is logical. Take the following, "French is the official language of France. This woman is a French citizen. Therefore, she speaks French." The conclusion cannot be derived from the premiss. It does not follow that if the woman is a French citizen she necessarily speaks French. She may be a monoglot Breton, Corsican speaker, or even the daughter of emigré French parents. Although she may speak French, this cannot be deduced from the premisses.

The above examples may seem trivial, but they serve to establish an analytic–synthetic distinction in everyday life that, in science, is very difficult to maintain. It can be illustrated by the everyday example of the boiling point of water. It is commonly held that water boils at 100° centigrade. It should follow that, by definition, a pan of water that is boiling is doing so at 100° centigrade. Not so. Water will boil at a lower temperature at higher altitudes. In scientific method, as elsewhere, deductive arguments are no guarantee of truth.

The role for, or the emphasis placed upon, induction and deduction has important implications for the process of justification in science. Concern about how this should proceed has dominated the philosophy of science for much of the twentieth century. Though the empiricists and their challengers place different emphases on the role of observation and theory in the process of discovery and where inductive and deductive inference might be appropriate, something of a consensus evolved concerning a model of scientific procedure. In this model, hypotheses, as speculations based on what we believe we know, are tested against data. Our knowledge takes the form of existing scientific laws. Thus, if it is a law that acids turn litmus paper red, then it might be hypothesized that it is the acidic nature of a substance that is responsible for turning litmus paper red. Laws can thus be deduced from specific instances and specific instances deduced from those laws. The justification for this form of explanation works only if laws hold for all times and places. The problem is, of course, that the laws themselves, as noted, are the product of induction. In other words, the "law" that acids turn litmus red is simply obtained from the evidence that all acids tested so far on litmus paper have resulted in it turning red.

Given the above, it is not surprising that the problem of induction has plagued scientists since the time of Hume. As a problem in logic, it was considered insoluble, for all logic can do for us is to specify relations between concepts and must be silent on any "real" nature of these concepts. These things were recognized by the Logical Positivists in the 1920s and 1930s. Their attempt to ground scientific knowledge in principles as sound as those of mathematics, may be characterized as one of the heroic failures of modern philosophy.

Logical Positivism was born out of the work of a group of scientists and philosophers collectively known as the Vienna Circle (Von Mises 1951). The logical positivists were the most radical of empiricists, denying not only that we could identify any form of natural necessity in the world but that, in principle, we could never come to know the *real* world. We can never get behind what is apparent to the senses. It follows that all we can describe is that which we can know through our observations of the world. Anything else is regarded as speculative metaphysics. This is a view known as phenomenalism. This led the logical positivists to advocate a way of "doing" science that was based on the validation of theories by the use of "elementary observation statements": that is, simple statements about direct and basic observations. Whether something was the case or not could only be verified through the observation of phenomena. On this basis, if something is not observable and therefore verifiable, then we are not entitled to make claims about it:

> we have to proceed from that which is epistemically primary, that is to say from the "given" i.e. from experiences themselves in their totality and undivided unity . . . The elementary experiences are to be the basic elements of our constructional system. From this basis we wish to construct all other objects of pre scientific and scientific knowledge (Carnap 1969: 108–9).

Logical Positivism did not so much ignore the problems of observation and induction. Instead, it recognized them and held them to be insoluble. If science cannot be based on observables, then what can it be based on? Moreover, verification through observation will give the most certain knowledge that it is possible to attain.

The expurgation of metaphysics from science was criticized most notably by Karl Popper. As he wrote of the logical positivists:

> in their anxiety to oust metaphysics, [they] failed to notice that they were throwing all scientific theories on the same scrap heap as the "meaningless" metaphysical theories (Popper 1989: 259).

Because of their speculative nature, theories always contain an element of metaphysics. Arguably, they only stop being metaphysical when a system of testing them is constructed. Thus, theories about Black Holes, for example, are inevitably metaphysical because they remain, at present, unverifiable from an empirical point of view. However, if and when means of testing the theories are found, then they will cease to be metaphysical. A demarcation between metaphysics and meaningful propositions, therefore, is the ability to define methodical tests. The problem is if we cannot admit of theories, such as those about Black Holes, because they are metaphysical, then we will never test them simply because we rejected them in the first place!

This latter issue is closely connected to a further problem. This concerns the logical positivist need to separate the language of observation from the language of theory. The language of observation must be neutral and "uncorrupted" by theory, if the verification principle is to hold. This can be illustrated by a simple example. The theory to be tested is that substances S1, S2, S3 are acids. It was observed that when litmus paper was placed in substance S1 and S3, it turned red. Therefore, substances S1 and S3 are acids. The language of the observation in this case only makes sense if acids are defined as substances that turn litmus paper red in the first instance. The observation is necessarily theory laden. For this reason, the way that we describe observations cannot be separated from our theories about them. This example is an oversimplification, but even when logical positivism was at its philosophical height, the complexity of sciences, particularly physics, made the separation between observation statements and theoretical statements a practical impossibility.

Logical positivist attempts to build a justificatory framework for scientific knowledge were killed off by a close associate of the Vienna Circle – Karl Popper. Here is his confessional:

> Everyone knows nowadays that logical positivism is dead . . .
> "Who is responsible?" or, rather the question "Who has done it?" .
> . . I fear I must admit responsibility (1986a: 88).

His murder weapon was "falsification" and his motive twofold. First, Popper was highly critical of verifiability and indeed any attempt at justification in science. Secondly, he wished to mark out that territory that belonged to science; a goal he shared with the logical positivists. For Popper these are interconnected:

> I understood why the mistaken theory of science which had ruled

since Bacon – that the natural sciences were the *inductive* sciences and that induction was a process of establishing or justifying theories by *repeated* observations or experiments – was so deeply entrenched. The reason was that scientists had to *demarcate* their activities from pseudo science as well as from theology and metaphysics (1986: 79. Original italics).

The need for justification was the need to show why science was special in that knowledge derived through scientific method was superior to other forms of knowledge. The actual problem of demarcation of science from pseudo science was the subject of Popper's first book in 1929, *Logik der Forschung* (published in English as *The Logic of Scientific Discovery* in 1959). Hume, it will be recalled, while noting that induction could not be logically justified, "explained away" our tendency to rely on it as a psychological pre-disposition. Popper claimed that this was mistaken (1979: 85–90). His solution to the problem of demarcation rests on the need to logically solve the problem of induction. He achieves this by sidestepping it. The core of Popper's falsification can be stated in the following terms: although any number of observations can never conclusively prove a theory, one disconfirming observation is sufficient to refute it. This is no more than Hume had already argued. However, what was unique in Popper's formulations was his insistence upon characterizing science as a search for *disconfirming instances*.

A scientific theory, as opposed to a "pseudoscientific" theory, is one open to falsification. Here, it is stated in the specification of the theory what will count as crucial tests. If the theory fails these tests, it is falsified. Now, the logical positivists had allowed that theories may be falsified. The difference between them and Popper lies in their idea that if a theory passes the tests, it is confirmed, whereas Popper maintained that all this meant was that the theory was not falsified on that occasion. As such, Popper maintained that all theories remain conjectures and are open to refutation. Incidentally, this leads Popper to maintain there is no logical distinction between a theory and a hypothesis. A traditional view that hypotheses are unproven theories is turned on its head when theories are considered as conjectural (Popper 1986a: 81). It follows from this that laws in science are conjectures and that no part of science is safe, not even the tests themselves which can also be falsified. One question, however, remains: how can science ever make progress in the absence of laws upon which to build new knowledge?

Popper answers this question in two ways. First, a theory that "survives" all possible tests may be considered better than the theories it replaces. Theories must always contain testable propositions and scientists who advance them should specify, in advance, what are to be the crucial tests. A competition between theories, or what Popper describes as "a kind of Darwinian struggle for survival" (1986a: 79), then ensues. This will produce the best theories available to science at a given time. Secondly, by eliminating "untruth" through the falsification process, science moves closer to the truth. Although "truth" may never be attained it follows, according to Popper, that the elimination of error must leave fewer candidates for this accolade. The aim of a good theory is "truth likeness", or "verisimilitude" and the elimination of error (1989: 228–38). Moreover, unlike the logical positivists, Popper is a realist, which for him means that conjectural statements are about things in the real world. Yet can we know this?

> the procedure we adopt may lead . . . to success, in the sense that our conjectural theories tend progressively to come nearer to the truth; that is to true descriptions of certain facts, or aspects of reality (Popper 1979: 40).

If things, therefore, were not "real" how could they confound us by showing our theories to be inaccurate? Falsification represents a head-on clash with reality and Popper maintains that progress in science must be through a process of learning by mistakes. A preparedness to do so marks out a scientific attitude, unlike inductivist approaches in which demarcation between science and pseudo science cannot be maintained on logical grounds.

Though himself never a Marxist, Popper moved in an intellectual circle in 1920s Vienna where Marxism and psychoanalysis (in the work of Freud and Adler) were regarded as scientific. Indeed, these theories appeared to be able to explain practically everything that had happened within the fields to which they referred. Nevertheless, a problem remained:

> The most characteristic element in this situation seemed to me the incessant stream of confirmations, of observations that verified the theories in question . . . A Marxist could not open a newspaper without finding on every page confirming evidence for his interpretation of history (Popper 1989: 34–5).

For Popper, this resulted from a reliance on inductivist approaches to the accumulation of knowledge. It was mistaken. If Marxism and psychoanalysis were sciences then what marked them out from astrology or religion? Popper's answer was that from a logical point of view – nothing!

Popper thus shifted the focus of science from justification to discovery through error elimination. His contributions to the philosophy of science were far from being any kind of definitive, or final statement, but more the key that opened a Pandora's box. This Pandora's box was less a result of his falibilism and more a result of the introduction of personally subjective and social psychological criteria into the process of science. It will be recalled that Popper had taken issue with the empiricists, not just on the question of induction, but also on the grounds that observation is not neutral, but is theory laden. Despite this, his ideas are often and somewhat mistakenly regarded as variants of logical positivism, or at least as being very close to this body of thought. Yet he accepts that theories may have their origin in personal psychological factors, or that they might appear in a flash of inspiration, but what is important is what is then done with them. If theories are to be tested on the basis of "clashes" with the real world, then at some point scientists must rely on observational evidence. Surely, however, observation statements are themselves suspect.

Popper's response to this question is to introduce a "social psychological" element into his argument. For him, "basic statements" (observation statements) are intersubjectively testable. Though he insists that these observations are themselves open to refutation (Popper 1983: 111), it remains that any decision on whether or not a theory is falsified is the product of agreement between scientists at a particular time. This, in turn, depends on their seeing the same thing, or at least agreeing that they saw the same thing. Popper always maintained that science was a discipline "without a subject". Nevertheless, by allowing that the theories of science may have been arrived at purely fortuitously he admitted of the existence of subjective criteria in the research process. Theories could have been derived after years of painstaking methodical work, but could just as easily have been dreamed up after the consumption of a large meal and several beers!

Aside from the entry of subjective criteria into his formulations, on closer examination falsification as a basis for science begins to look a little shaky. What can count as falsification is subject to the same problems as what can count as a verification. If a scientist proposes a critical test of a theory and the theory fails that test, can the theory be said to be falsified?

The test itself and the observations are just as fallible here as in traditional inductivist accounts. The scientist arrived at the specification for the test via the same set of cognitive and social processes that dogged the selection criteria for the poor inductivist. Additionally, the observations themselves might be wrong for exactly the same reasons. To claim, as did Popper, that the tests themselves are open to falsification does not help because to "falsify" the test we would need a further test and so on. The result is a regress to infinity.

Finally, there remains a logical problem in Popper's ideas. If induction relies on an unwarranted move from particular instances to generalizations, then so does falsification. Why should something falsified at time $T1$ remain falsified at time Tn? Chalmers offers the following example from the history of science:

> In the early years of its life, Newton's gravitational theory was falsified by observations of the moon's orbit. It took almost fifty years to deflect this falsification on to causes other than Newton's theory. Later in its life, the same theory was known to be inconsistent with the details of the orbit of the planet Mercury, although scientists did not abandon the theory for that reason. It turned out that it was never possible to explain away this falsification in a way that protected Newton's theory (1982: 66).

Science is littered with examples of instances where a "falsification" was later overturned, while scientists have persisted to hold on to theories even after they appear to have been falsified, only to be proven correct in the long term.

Science: a psychological and social process

The challenge to falsification, though initially from within a deeply conservative philosophy of science establishment, led to the questioning of science as a *rational* discipline. If falsification and induction must rely on observation statements that appear to be rooted in some subjective criteria, then the question of how science actually proceeds and therefore what it is becomes broadened.

The most influential of these challenges came from Thomas Kuhn

(1970). Kuhn claimed that the history of science offers little comfort to either traditional or falsificationist accounts. Science, he maintains, is periodically driven by crises. This has been the case since the emergence of a first scientific consensus from a "pre-scientific period". Science consists of periods of "normal science", where scientists engage in "puzzle solving" within the confines of a particular "paradigm". The paradigm is the mark of a mature science. It comprises the intellectual standards and practices of a scientific community, but more than this it is based upon shared metaphysical and philosophical assumptions. Laws are held to be axiomatic and puzzle solving within a given theoretical structure. Dissidence from the key tenets of the paradigm are not tolerated, although most scientists remain uncritical of the paradigm they are working within. However, in the process of puzzle solving, anomalies will occur. Key theories will appear to be falsified. When this happens frequently and particularly when key scientists themselves begin to challenge the orthodoxy, crisis occurs. The crisis then spreads and becomes a revolution where a new paradigm becomes established with a new set of laws, theories, intellectual standards, etc.

For a thousand years, until Copernicus, the geocentric model of the universe prevailed. We have mentioned above that Ptolemy had devised a complex and workable navigational system based upon these assumptions. Navigation, over this period, became sophisticated and accurate, but the geocentric basis of Ptolemy's work was questioned by Copernicus in 1514. Copernicus suggested that the stars were very much further away than previously thought. More controversially, the apparent motion of the stars at night and that of the sun by day, was the result of the Earth rotating on its axis. So controversial were his views that even after his death his work was banned by the Church and remained so for over 200 years. It was not just the Church that was critical; the celebrated astronomer Tycho Brahe dismissed Copernicus's revolutionary theories. However, within the space of 50 years the "Ptolemaic paradigm" was replaced by the "Copernican" one.

The above example illustrates how *sociological* factors – religious orthodoxy in this example – can be important considerations in the determination of the legitimacy of scientific claims. In this case, the "sociological content" came from outside the community of science, though it must be said that in the sixteenth century a separation between science and religion was less pronounced. If, as claimed above, theories are determined not only by what there "is", but also by that which is prioritized, then we

33

can see how various orthodoxies, whether they be religious or secular, can play a part in determining what the priorities of science will be. Until very recently, a challenge to the idea of mathematics as regular and deterministic would have been regarded as absurd; within a generation indeterminacy itself has become orthodoxy. To what extent the former "deterministic" view of science was the result of "rational" processes and to what extent it was a socially held convention, is now a matter of debate.

Paul Feyerabend went even further than Kuhn in claiming that historical, sociological and psychological factors determined how science progressed. His own reading of the history of science led him to conclude that the case studies examined

> speak *against* the universal validity of any rule. All methodologies have their limitations and the only *rule* that survives is *anything goes* (Feyerabend 1978: 295–6. Original italics).

For Feyerabend, science is a kind of "playful learning" where new meanings are grasped, just as a child grasps new meanings that they play with for a while and then abandon. The "play" process itself uncovers new meanings and is the method of discovery. It follows that there is not, nor can there be, any "one" method of science.

Unlike the inductivists who believed in scientific progress through the gradual accumulation of knowledge as a hallmark of science, Kuhn maintained that "progress" comes through revolutions. To think of science as gradually evolving misses the importance of paradigms in determining what science looks for and the manner in which it proceeds. Nevertheless, in his later work Kuhn offers some universal characteristics of a good scientific theory. These include accuracy and consistency (within the standards of the paradigm), broad scope, simplicity and fruitfulness (Kuhn 1977: 321–2). Feyerabend does not go this far and takes an anarchic view of knowledge. This is clearly of importance to the question, "what is science?"

Both Feyerabend and Kuhn have been accused of relativism. Relativism entails the view that there are no universal, ahistorical standards to which scientists might allude in justifying their methods and findings. In science, it means that no one theory is "better" than another. What is considered a true, or better, or worse theory, is the product of the community in which the theory is devised. Feyerabend gleefully accepted this accusation, whereas Kuhn responded with his definition of the characteristics of a good theory. Nevertheless, if as Kuhn claims, the certainties of an earlier paradigm cannot be carried over into a new paradigm, the implication is that the theories of each are not comparable.

Kuhn's conception of paradigmatic change has been criticized in a number of ways, not least for the inconsistencies in describing what comprises a paradigm and how paradigm shifts actually take place (Lakatos & Musgrave 1970). Space does not permit us to elaborate upon these issues. However, what is important here is that if relativism is right then any claim that science is superior to, say, astrology, witchcraft or voodoo, collapses. Science is just an historical manifestation of knowledge claims to be treated in exactly the same way as any others claims to knowledge, the result being that conceptions of science as a more accurate picture of the world are without foundation. In this respect the problems for "science" are twofold. There is, first, uncertainty about the status of what we observe and, relatedly, there appear to be not only difficulties in testing theories, but any number of theories can describe the same set of observations. In this sense, theories are said to be underdetermined. For example, Ptolemy and Copernicus both looked up to the same sky, apparently saw the same sun and stars, but arrived at quite opposite theories.

If it is the case that at different times incompatible theories are used to explain precisely the same empirical evidence, then we can never be sure that science is correct in its assertions. Scientific proof is a worthless currency that will be superseded by later scientific proofs. This is precisely the argument that one set of protagonists deploys in a controversy that has raged in rural England for several years. Since the mid 1980s, a series of "crop circles", patterns of intricate and sometimes beautiful designs, have been appearing in the ripening crops across several counties in the South of England. The "circles" invariably appear overnight and can be hundreds of metres in diameter.

Three explanations appear to be on offer for this phenomenon. First, a "scientific" inductive explanation whereby each new sighting is seen as evidence for an explanation of "plasma vortices" – a rather similar effect to that of "ball" lightning. The proponents of this explanation have needed to modify their theory many times to accommodate troublesome anomalies, to the point where the more recent theory is very different in form from the original. A second group has attempted to show that crop circles can be produced by hoaxers. Until a couple of years ago, this explanation was ruled out on the grounds that there were too many circles that were too complex to be "artificially" produced. Nevertheless, a group of academics from Southampton University did manage to convincingly fake some circles, fooling both the orthodox scientists and the "para scientists". This latter group favours some form of paranormal explanation that ranges from extra terrestrial visitations to various psychic powers. Not surprisingly, the orthodox scientists mock the latter explanations as "unprovable" or "unscientific". The para scientists' conjectures may well be unprovable, but then so are the orthodox ones. Indeed, in the gathering of data to support their own theories the para scientists have been equally as scientific as the orthodox ones. On the face of it, it is hard to see who is Ptolemy and who is Copernicus in this instance. Perhaps neither. The self styled "Wessex Sceptics" from Southampton University, despite the remaining objection from their opponents that not all the circles could be fake, may end up in the role of "Copernicus" in this dispute.

We end up with the implication of relativism being that one explanation is as good as any other. There is no one "truth", but many truths that are particular to time and place. On this basis, science becomes a social product that varies across time and is united in name only. We shall return to the question of relativism later. Relativism as a problem, or a solution for some, ends up being a question of what is regarded as truth. Therefore, we need to briefly digress and pursue this question.

In pursuit of the "truth"

We noted above that a statement that is logically correct is not necessarily "true". However, what do we mean by "true"? Any attempt to answer this question comes up against the problem that most things in the course of human history that have been regarded as true at one time, end up being seen as "false" at another. As such, it seems reasonable to suppose that those things we regard as true now will not be necessarily so in the future. This problem has led philosophers to arrive at different theories of truth. There have actually been many theories of truth, though we will confine ourselves to briefly considering three versions in order that some feel for the complexity of the topic might be obtained.

The first idea of truth is the most intuitively obvious. It is the *correspondence* theory. Quite simply, something is true if there is agreement with the facts. This definition has a resonance with logic. It requires an agreement between premiss and conclusion, yet it entails two important difficulties. First, there is the logical problem of sentences such as, "this statement is false". If the sentence is true then what it says must be true – that it is false, but if it is false then what it says must be false, so it must be true! The logician Alfred Tarski attempted to solve this problem by saying that the truth of a sentence can only be established in a further sentence(s) (Popper 1989: 116). Nevertheless, this requirement for a "meta-language" appears counter intuitive and complex. Secondly, most of the really important questions are matters of dispute about the constitution of the facts. It is all very well saying truth is agreement with the facts when we can agree what the facts are. A government may claim that its citizens are richer now than in the past and the facts offered to demonstrate this may seem to support it. However, this claim will always be dependent upon what is meant by "richer" in terms of the use of relative or absolute measures.

Dissatisfaction with the correspondence theory of truth has led many to adopt various "intersubjective" versions of truth. The commonest of these is the view that coherence between propositions is itself a criterion of truth. This does not just mean statements must be consistent. If it is said "ripe strawberries are red" and "Paris is in France", there is no disagreement, but there is no coherence either. Coherence is a stronger relationship. However, there is intersubjective agreement that ripe strawberries are indeed red and Paris is in France. There have been numerous reports that have confirmed these things to be the case. Reports have been coherent with each other and there have been no reports to the contrary.

This view of truth is also problematic. First, statements might be coherent, but this does not make them "true". Truth lies only in the veracity of a number of statements, not in the thing itself. There are millions of coherent reports that koalas are bears. Therefore, it is true that koalas are bears. Yet this says nothing about the koala itself that actually turns out to be a marsupial. All those coherent reports were wrong. Secondly, despite the reliance on coherence between propositions, what is intended is not agreement between statements, but to make a statement about the "thing" itself. Coherence collapses into correspondence simply because there has to be at least a perceived agreement with the facts. Thus, the thousands of reports of koalas as bears were coherent, but wrong, whereas a single report of koalas as marsupials was correct because of a better agreement with the facts.

Finally, the American philosopher William James argued for a *pragmatic* theory of truth, whereby something was true if it was useful and of benefit for it to be true. This was not just a matter of expediency:

> Grant an idea or belief to be true . . . what concrete difference will
> its being true make in anyone's actual life? How will the truth be
> realized? What experiences will be different from those which
> would obtain if the belief were false? What in short is the truth's
> cash value in experiential terms? (James quoted in Ayer 1982:
> 79–80).

In this version of truth, the focus shifts from the property of a thing to how
we think about a thing. In the correspondence theory of truth something
is true for all time. Although coherence definitions are still concerned
with the truth of a thing, though this may change, truth for the pragmatists is not fixed or immutable, but something that happens to an idea itself, not to the thing to which it refers. It becomes true if it can be
assimilated or validated in a community of experiences.

James suggests that our desire to eliminate error rather than seek truth
leads us not to choose between propositions, whereas if we choose one or
the other we have an even chance of being right. Many objections have
been raised to this definition of truth. In particular, it is often not a question of deciding whether something is true or false, but a matter of assign-
ing degrees of belief to the matter. For example, suppose you see a man in
a crowd who resembles the picture you have seen of a dangerous criminal
wanted by the police. The person you have seen may or may not be the
criminal but, all things being equal, it is more likely he is not. Further,
imagine now that your decision to believe must rest not on the degree of
probability you assign to the likelihood of the man being the wanted
criminal, but instead to the effects of your belief either way! If you are
right, society is safer and you reap a reward. On the other hand, if you are
wrong an innocent man is arrested. Your decision depends on what you
see as the "best" outcome. With a little imagination, it can be seen that the
moral dilemmas involved in adopting such a criterion of truth become
both complex and problematic.

The outcome of this short discussion of truth is not a happy one for
either the philosopher or scientist. Even what counts as truth is without a
consensus! Adherents of the correspondence and coherence view are ultimately concerned with "reality", whereas the pragmatists are equally
concerned with how we view reality. Although the correspondence
theory of truth claims to refer to reality it simply ends up being about
semantics – logical rules between statements. There is also a blur in the
pragmatists' argument between describing the production of truth as

taking place within a community of experiences and an advocacy of the notion of truth as expediency.

Social interests and scientific practices

At every stage subjective criteria enter into the scientific process. Indeed, even what counts as truth is not beyond dispute. Our choice of problem may be attributed to psychological or social factors as is choosing what is to count as a test. What holds as a solution to a scientific problem can likewise be socially determined. That social factors determine not just the subject matter of science, but also how science itself is done, has been the thesis of a particular group of sociologists of science in the last two decades or so. This view is associated with the work of Barry Barnes (1972, 1974, 1977), Harry Collins (1975), David Bloor (1976) and Steve Woolgar and Bruno Latour (1979). Much of their work was inspired by the emergence of psychological and social concerns to the debate about method in the 1960s (for example, see Lakatos & Musgrave 1970) and was much influenced by the work of Kuhn and Feyerabend.

For this group of scholars our understanding of science has been flawed by our reliance on the "internal accounts" of science that are themselves used to explain science. In other words, scientific rationality is itself a product of science and is just as suspect as those aspects of science that are seen as rational or irrational. To explain science, they argue, we need a sociology of scientific knowledge:

> The sociologist must ask what it is that guides the research of a scientific speciality, what makes it a coherent social phenomenon, and what makes its rapid rate of cultural change feasible. He must seek a description of normality and change within the speciality (Barnes 1974: 48).

Like Kuhn and Feyerabend, this work is located in the study of specific episodes in the history of science or, in the case of Woolgar & Latour (1979), studies of what actually goes on in the laboratory. These studies point to socially determined reasons for both the substantive and intellectual content of science. It is not just the agendas of what are interesting problems for science, or how results are seen, but also the actual process or method itself that is socially determined. Let us take some examples to illustrate this focus.

Foreman (1971: 109) maintains that the willingness of scientists in the German Weimar Republic to accommodate themselves to fashionable thought was such that they were prepared to abandon any principle of causality – one of the cornerstones of physics at that time. Now, although causality in the sense understood since Hume was to be later challenged by quantum physics, it was still used as a justification for the scientists' decision to "abandon" causality. Therefore, in this process science was reconstructed to appear as if the decision was scientific, but it arose from a desire among the physicists to win public acclaim in a climate where "spiritual values" and the "mystery of things" were fashionable (Brown 1989: 13). Similarly, Shapin (1975) claims that the enthusiasm for phrenology in the nineteenth century was not the result of the power of the scientific explanations of its "founder", the Viennese doctor, Franz Joseph Gall, but is explained through its adoption by influential people in the social reform movement, such as George Combe (Shapin 1975: 232). Given such examples, there are those who have argued that not only is "respectable" science wholly shaped by social concerns, but that the only difference between science and the "para" science of "ufology", for example, is that the former has attained its prominence only because it is favoured by intellectual elites (Blake 1979).

The implication of these forms of approaches to science is to "debunk" it as a form of enquiry superior to any other. Thus, an account of social science that rests upon claims to scientific legitimacy is appealing to a specious concept. However, it is not this simple (things rarely are in philosophy). Although on the face of it a sociological account of science may be appealing to social scientists in a quest for intellectual justification, the account has not gone uncriticized, even from those sympathetic to what is known as a "post-Popperian" philosophy of science. For instance, Chalmers has criticized a number of the accounts of these particular sociologists of science as being based on a misrepresentation of science, which emphasizes bad science and the extreme empiricism and rationalism of (what they term) the standard account of science (Chalmers 1990: 83). This is exemplified by the claim that scientific theories are underdetermined by the evidence available and that there is never enough evidence to make rational decisions (Brown 1989: 7). As a result, any number of theories can be used to explain the evidence:

Therefore extra-scientific social factors enter into the processes that lead to the selection of one among the perhaps many possible theories compatible with the evidence (Chalmers 1990: 84).

However, in practice, "scientists often struggle to find *any* workable theory compatible with some problematic evidence" (Chalmers 1990: 85). What is occurring here is that the chosen episodes are being made to fit the sociologist's own theory and are not representative of what actually happens in the day-to-day business of scientific practice.

In addition, if it is argued that scientific beliefs are socially derived, then so are all beliefs:

> if all beliefs are socially caused, rather than rationally well founded, then the beliefs of the cognitive sociologist himself have no relevant rational credentials and hence no special claim to acceptability (Laudan 1977: 201).

Thus, the sociologists of science are selective in their description of scientific practice and, according to Laudan, guilty of the same kind of universal justification for knowledge that they accuse science of possessing.

We are now left with a further issue to contend with in answering our question: is the production of scientific knowledge the result of rational scientific procedure, or is it socially and/or psychologically determined? If it is the latter, then scientific knowledge, as superior to any other, appears to be undermined. On the other hand, if the philosophy of science, or sociology of science, cannot explain science, why it is that we appear to know considerably more now than five hundred years ago? Quite clearly, there is something going on in the laboratory and something which has had and will have, an enormous effect on our lives. Moreover, it might also be said that to know science is to know of its dangers and potential excesses, thus allowing us to use it as a tool for the betterment of humankind.

The above question has two concerns at its heart. First, what is "rational belief" and is this a characteristic of science? Secondly, what is the ontological status of the things that science investigates? We shall return to the first of these questions later, for the tackling of this problem from a social scientific viewpoint offers insights that are of value in understanding the physical sciences.

The question of the nature of things that exist is a very old one in philosophy and the debate above is merely a new angle on an old problem. The problem is a metaphysical one at heart that can be reduced to a simple question: do the things that we know of in the world really exist? On the face of it this may seem to be a trivial question and for most of the time it is not really an issue. However, consider the problem of the quantum physicist. The objects she deals in are not just very small, they simply cannot be observed and the only knowledge she will have of them is the "effects" they produce, which are only known through very sophisticated means of measurement. Do these objects exist, or are they a product of the theories we have about them?

There are two views on these matters. The first is idealism, which is the view that the external world is the product of mind. This can take the form that all material objects consist of nothing but ideas, or those things that we perceive in the world are just appearances and have no independent existence outside our thoughts. The former view is associated with the eighteenth century Irish bishop, George Berkeley, and the latter (sometimes called transcendental idealism) with Kant. The second set of views are known as realism. As with idealism, they take different forms but can be summed up as claiming that things in the world have a real existence, independent of our thoughts about them.

Whether one adopts an idealist or realist view, will make a huge difference to what we can say about the social and natural worlds. The methods advocated often point to a view on the "nature" of things. For example, whereas empiricism is neutral on whether things exist or not, the view that all we can know of the world is that which we perceive through our senses is, by default, an idealist one. Contrast that with Popper's principle of verisimilitude as implicitly realist in its postulation of getting closer to the "truth" – to what is real – through the elimination of error.

In the debate over the status of scientific knowledge we must classify Kuhn, Feyerabend and the "sociologists" of science as idealists. Why? Because they are committed to the view that scientific theories are the product of minds, but more importantly, what counts as their verification, or falsification, is also a product of mind(s). Now this does not mean that such decisions about theories are produced by individual minds in isolation but, as is especially stressed in the above sociological accounts, social products. In other words, the scientist adopts or rejects a theory on the basis of a decision not made with regard to a "real" state of affairs pertaining to that which is being investigated, but on the basis of social and psychological criteria. Moreover, there is no "real" state of affairs to appeal to, but just so many theories that are themselves the product of mind or, in this case, collective minds.

The plausibility of this view has been questioned by a number of philosophers who point to important differences in the classes of things we want to make knowledge claims about. As Laudan puts it:

> There is an enormous amount of evidence that shows that certain doctrines and ideas bear no straightforward relation to the exigencies of social circumstance: to cite but two examples, the principle that "2+2 = 4" or the idea that "most heavy bodies fall downwards when released" are beliefs to which persons from a wide variety of cultural and social situations subscribe. Anyone who would suggest that such beliefs were socially determined or conditioned would betray a remarkable ignorance of the ways in which such beliefs were generated and established (1977: 199–200).

Nevertheless, Laudan goes on to point out that it does not follow from this that science may be characterized as wholly rational in its decisions and formulations. It may be bad science and there may be a lot of it, but it still remains the case that the studies produced by Feyerabend, Barnes, Bloor, Shapin, etc. were records of how science was performed. Here, Laudan proposes what he calls the "arationality assumption" (1977: 201). Briefly put, if we can explain a belief as being the result of the rational examination of the evidence, we should assume it to be the correct explanation. If, on the other hand, no such explanation is to hand, then we must look for social or other forms of explanation. To use a concept favoured by the sociologist Robert Merton, there are both "internal" and "external" accounts of science (1968: 516) and both appear to be necessary to its practice. On the face of it, Laudan's concept of arationality seems attractive, but it is open to a fairly obvious criticism: that is, what is going to count as the rational thing to do and is this the same for all times and places?

In the foregoing, we have characterized the "social" view of the derivation of scientific knowledge as idealist, but the problem does not end there. Even if we could divide the methodological decisions of science into the rational and the social, we would be left with the problem of how "real" some phenomena actually are. For example, the kinetic theory of gases involves the claim that gases are made up of molecules in random motion colliding with each other. Yet, no one has ever seen a molecule with their own eyes, so in what sense are they real? A version of empiricism, known as instrumentalism, attempts to get around the problem by saying that theories are just useful devices for connecting one set of observables with another. Gases can be "observed" – they can be seen, or smelt, or weighed. These observable properties need to be explained and it is the role of theories to achieve this end. In the instrumentalist view, if the theory adequately explains the behaviour of a particular gas, for example, then it is a useful theory, but does not necessarily describe any "real" world. Molecules are convenient theoretical fictions. Apart from the implicitness of a "pragmatic theory of truth" and its attendant problems, instrumentalism runs into the problem of the "theory laden" nature of observation.

Contrast this with the realist view that our theories actually describe things that exist. The kinetic theory of gases, for instance, is taken to refer to the behaviour of molecules as real things in the world. One principle often evoked in support of this view is that things can be taken to be "real" if they have real effects (Bhaskar 1975, 1989). This gets over the problem of the theory laden nature of observations by classing any "imprint" as evidence of reality. Thus, our direct observations of the world are real, as are those that result from the effects of phenomena on complex instruments. This does not necessarily mean the theories are "correct" and that an observation is always "correct", but that our theories and observations are records of real phenomena and not just illusions.

Most forms of realism depend on a correspondence theory of truth. Science, however, as Bhaskar (1975) notes, is often dependent upon experiments for its results. Experiments are themselves closed systems constructed by humans as appropriate to the test of their theories. The "footprints" of phenomena are in this sense brought about by the experimenter. In principle, she could never have known what would have happened had the experiment not taken place. The correspondence between the theory and that which it seeks to explain is the result of the scientist's intervention. A distinction can thus be made between the results of experiments and the way the world is. Although evidence of the latter might have been found and this may come to constitute a "law", this does not exhaust the characteristics of a phenomenon. As Chalmers points out:

> In general, systems in the world will possess other characteristics in addition to those picked out by a particular law ... For instance a falling leaf is at once a mechanical, chemical, biological, optical and thermal system (1982: 155).

If the experiment intervened in only one of those systems how can we be sure the "truth" it tells us is applicable to all of the other systems? After all, the systems themselves are not recognized by nature as distinct. If things are true, then they are true under all conditions not just those contrived by the experimenter working within one theoretical framework.

Summary

The whole *raison d'être* of the philosophy of science can be said to be the quest for a method of doing science and of defining its nature in the process. We have seen that, in their day, the logical positivists thought they had found this holy grail, as did Popper after them. Recent forays into questions of method have been more circumspect. Though the extreme relativism of some of the sociologists of science may not be any more desirable than the narrow prescriptions of logical positivism, it remains the case that "post-Popperian" philosophy of science has opened up possibilities and we should be wary of prematurely closing these down. New philosophies of science abound. For instance, in Chapter 4 we go on to discuss, in relation to social science, the "network" model of science of Mary Hesse (1974) and the "research programmes" identified by Imre Lakatos (1987). The debate is far from over and continues to produce new ideas and insights, many of which remain controversial (for example, see Brown 1994).

What is more certain is that any question about the scientific nature of social enquiry is parasitic upon what counts as scientific. Yet, if this is a difficult question to answer, it demonstrates that all forms of systematic enquiry are plagued by philosophical problems. Whether we call something "science" or not, it remains that there are questions that will always be present in the systematic pursuit of knowledge. These are philosophical problems concerned with what kinds of things exist and how we can know them. Moreover, many of these are shared by both social research and investigations of the physical world. For this reason, in the next chapter, we will examine the nature of social research and in so doing we will refer back to many of the philosophical issues that we have raised in this chapter.

Questions for discussion

1. What is the role of observation in science? Can there be a neutral observation language?
2. How sustainable is a falsificationist account of science?
3. Can science distance itself from social interests?
4. How well does Kuhn's theory of paradigmatic change account for the history of science?

Suggested reading

Chalmers, A. 1982. *What is this thing called science?* Milton Keynes: Open University Press.

Hospers, J. 1967. *An introduction to philosophical analysis.* London: Routledge.

Lakatos, I. & A. Musgrave (eds) 1970. *Criticism and the growth of knowledge.* Cambridge: Cambridge University Press.

Law, J. & P. Lodge 1984. *Science for social scientists.* London: Macmillan.

Woolgar, S. 1988. *Science – the very idea.* London: Tavistock.

CHAPTER 3

Philosophy, social science and method

In the last chapter we saw that the physical sciences face a number of difficulties in the search for a method that can provide certain knowledge. Despite these, there appears to be general agreement that the whole point of the exercise is the pursuit of universal explanations. Therefore, most philosophers of science tend to agree upon the ends of science, but disagree upon the means for the attainment of such ends. The social sciences do not enjoy such a level of consensus. A fundamental disagreement lies at the heart of social science about whether social phenomena can be subject to the same kinds of explanatory goals as physical phenomena. Doubters maintain that social phenomena are distinct enough to require not just different standards, but a distinctive conceptual framework upon which social investigation can be based. For those who believe there can be a "unity of method", there are not just the difficulties of justification and verification to be faced, but how to deal with the very obvious differences that social phenomena present in comparison to physical phenomena.

In their infancy, sitting in the shadow of the physical sciences, the social sciences experienced no such widespread crisis of confidence and were distinguished by an empiricist method. Indeed positivists, notably Durkheim, based their claim for the scientific nature of social science on the assertion that the methods used to study the social world did not differ in any important way from the methods used to study the physical world. The crisis of method was yet to come. As such, it was with some confidence that the positivists could make this assertion.

Given the strong emphasis on method, the actual nature of what was to be discovered was thought unproblematic. Only the subject matter itself distinguished one discipline from another and it was unthinkable that the subject matter might dictate the appropriateness of method. After all, physicists, chemists and zoologists all studied quite different phenomena, but it was held that this made no difference to the methods they employed. Though positivism appeared to be at the leading edge of social science, it did not have an epistemological monopoly. An important alternative tradition existed in the form of hermeneutics that held the view that there were crucial differences between the physical and the social worlds, although the *"verstehen* sociology" of Max Weber, in particular, offered a serious empirical alternative to positivism. Though Weber was equally as concerned as Durkheim to establish the "scientific" credentials of social science, he emphasized that human consciousness was a distinguishing feature of the social world. Quite simply, because human beings have the capacity for autonomous reflection, they cannot be studied in the same way as inanimate objects.

Today no-one seriously doubts that subject matter makes a difference to method. However, how these differences manifest themselves and what their implications are for the study of social phenomena, are matters of some controversy; all of which have important implications for research methodology. Therefore, this chapter is concerned with examining two very distinct views on the social sciences. First, the view that the physical and social sciences are constrained to share key logical, epistemological and methodological features. Although the subject matter is important, social research should be just as scientific as research in the physical sciences. It follows from this position that it is legitimate for the social sciences to pursue the same goals of explanation, generalization and prediction that characterize the physical sciences.

In contrast, a second position argues that the differences in subject matter are so important that any attempt to study them in the same way is doomed to failure. Those who take this view cite the inability of the social sciences to produce any "law" like statements such as those in physics and chemistry. This argument rests on the premiss that the nature of social life precludes both explanation, such as that found in the physical sciences, or any form of prediction that can hold true for all people at all times and in all places. In other words, if science necessarily is about explanation and prediction, then the social sciences are different, but not inferior to, the physical sciences. Thus, we begin our discussions by asking can social research share, with the physical sciences, the goals of prediction and explanation and if not, what are the alternatives?

Explanation, prediction and generalization

When a scientist investigates a phenomenon, the desired outcome might be an explanation of that phenomena. The explanation for a substance turning litmus paper blue is that it is alkaline. The explanation for a moon remaining in a particular orbit is the nature of the gravitational attraction of a nearby planet. In everyday life we seek explanations that will satisfy us and although what will satisfy the scientist is perhaps more rigorous than what will satisfy us, it remains the case that science and everyday life both seek forms of explanation. It is important to note, however, that philosophers of science differ in what kind of things can count as an explanation, or whether universal explanation is possible.

More disagree about the goal of prediction in science. As we have seen, the method and success of prediction is by no means settled in physics or chemistry. Some believe that our predictions can rest upon the principle that the future will resemble the past in important ways; others argue that we can only show what cannot be the case. Yet explanation can be said to presuppose prediction. Take, for example, our simple litmus paper example. If it remains true that an alkali turns litmus paper blue, then we can predict that all other alkalis will have the same effect. Even a falsificationist would agree that this prediction is legitimate because it may be subjected to continual testing. If an explanation is a good one then it will lead to successful prediction. The reverse also holds: a prediction, if correct, becomes an explanation. Our prediction is that if a substance is alkaline it will turn litmus paper blue. A substance is explained as alkaline if it does this, or an acid if it turns the paper red. Thus, "the logical structure of a scientific prediction is the same as that of a scientific explanation" (Hempel 1994: 45).

In everyday life we routinely predict and explain. Perhaps you will predict that on your birthday you will receive gifts from friends and relations; that one day of the year you are the sole recipient of gifts is explained by it being your birthday. On the other hand, predictions about birthdays and similar social events may turn out to be wrong. For instance, an incident may occur with the result that your relatives no longer speak to you. Alternatively, you may move to a society in which it is expected that you will give gifts to your friends and relatives on your birthday! Despite such possibilities we seem to get by with these sorts of predictions in our everyday lives. In the physical sciences, however, there is a desire for something stronger than predictions that are "quite likely" to be accurate. After all, a great deal of important technology rests on the success of scientific prediction. Science requires invariable laws of nature in order that our predictions about the tensile properties of steel, or the escape velocity of space shuttles, do not end in disaster.

Scientists can and do routinely and successfully predict events and produce explanations. Although Kuhn may be correct in his observations that, from time to time, whole paradigms are overthrown in science, prediction and explanation are still conducted with high degrees of success in "normal" science. Scientific laws tend to hold true. Disasters to do with bridges, or space shuttles, are the results of error or forces of nature that are beyond the control of human beings, not exceptions to laws as such. Though our understanding of the status of a particular "law" may change, as with the shift from Newtonian to Einsteinian physics, the empirical consequences remain, for most purposes, similar. For instance, the advent of relativity did not seem to make any difference to the odds of toast falling buttered side down!

Despite these observations, the question remains as to whether we can predict with such degrees of certainty when it comes to social life. As social scientists, the types of events that interest us are more like birthdays than gravity. Predictions and explanations concerning crime levels, for example, are fraught with problems. Even economics, often assumed to be the most "legitimate" of the social sciences, does not have a good record on prediction and explanation; the success of which will depend upon whether one is a neo-classical, Keynesian, or Marxist economist.

Three reasons, in particular, have been offered for the apparent lack of success in prediction and explanation in the social sciences (Scriven 1994). First, the generalizations made in social science are more complex than the physical sciences. More "standing conditions" must be specified in order to describe even the most simple of relationships. It follows that more variables must be measured to obtain the most basic data upon which to base generalizations. For example, a specification of the "standing conditions" needed to explain the boiling of water are pretty well exhausted once we know that under conditions C water will boil if heat is applied. Once we have this information, it is easy to predict in what circumstances water will boil in the future. Contrast this with the controversial attempts to measure intelligence in humans (Eysenck 1953: 19–40). Just one aspect of this seems to present insurmountable difficulties. Quite simply what it is that is being measured will be culturally specific. What it is to be "intelligent" in Western Samoa will be manifested in a very different way to what it is to be intelligent in the US, and in the UK there will be

---

RESEARCH EXAMPLE 1
European integration and housing policy predictions

Social researchers, particularly those engaged in quantitative research, routinely make predictions and such predictions often begin from explanations of past events. This can take the form of statistical analysis, and modelling prediction may arise from an examination of existing or newly implemented policies, or the research may seek to adjudicate between two or more differing viewpoints. Priemus et al. (1994), for instance, conducted analyses of the likely outcomes of the 1991 Maastricht Treaty on the European Community. The research question centred upon the consequences of European integration for national housing policies. Their work begins with a description of the key features of economic and monetary union and then moves on to examine the consequences of the liberalization of markets and the probable economic effects that will, in their turn, impact upon decisions at a national level concerning housing. Their conclusion was that whereas such decisions will continue to be made at a national level, economic and social policies made at a European level will produce a tendency towards similarities in the development of housing markets in European countries. The assumptions here are both inductive and deductive. It is assumed, from an inductive viewpoint, that certain economic conditions or trends will hold in the future. Given this, it can be deduced that particular consequences for housing will follow. A causal path is thereby implied. European economic and monetary union will lead to specific economic consequences that will lead to an effect on housing policies.

---

cultural variations in what is considered to be "intelligent" behaviour. To this we must add an even greater variation in the psychological and physiological states that an individual can occupy at any given time. Even an Einstein can have a hangover, or be worried about his tax returns. There are an awful lot more variables to measure in social life even to produce the simplest of explanations, or predictions.

A second difficulty relates to a perceived need to use the concepts of physics, or mathematics, for the purposes of describing the social world. Notwithstanding the problems described above in relation to intelligence testing, if we say that Garfield has a higher IQ than George, not only are we postulating the existence of an entity (IQ) that possesses certain characteristics, but we are implicitly or explicitly suggesting that they are measurable. In other words, to produce explanations that will count as "scientific" requires the use of scientific concepts; the very concepts over which there is disagreement as to their applicability for studying the social world.

Thirdly, in everyday explanation and prediction we tend to use "low level" laws, such as those related to birthday presents, that result from experience. The consequence is to "skim off the cream" from the subject. For instance, everyday life provides us with at least partial explanations that the social scientist, unlike her physical counterpart, must take into account in her formulations. There are no "everyday" explanations in spectrochemistry. The implication is that the social sciences must exhibit some congruence between everyday explanations and social scientific explanations in order that the latter are "valid".

The first of these above differences has given rise to both optimistic and pessimistic views about the possibility of explaining the social world. The optimistic view is that the social world is very much more complex than the physical world, but this is a matter of degree, not fundamental difference. Essentially, this was the view of Mill and that of positivism in general. The claim here is that improved explanations will result from more accurate descriptions of the constituent variables and these, in turn, will lead to more accurate identifications and descriptions of the relevant variables themselves. Pessimists might agree that this is true, but it is not very helpful in practice. It would take so long to arrive at levels of explanation as good as those in the physical sciences that humans beings would probably no longer inhabit the planet!

There is another view on this topic. Not only is the social world more complex than the physical world, but it is of a completely different nature (Rosenberg 1988). The very use of the concepts of science is merely the use of a special language that actually blinds us to the need to develop a different language to describe the social world. In taking this view, the second and third of Scriven's difficulties disappear because "folk psychological" concepts are the very topics that the social researcher should focus upon. The search for laws of social life is thus doomed to failure. Moreover, the use of the language of the physical sciences is singularly unproductive. Social researchers are not in the business of "predicting" or "explaining" and if the concept of "explanation" is to be used in the social sciences, then it will have a very different meaning. It is necessary that we investigate this view in more depth. However, we must first consider what makes the social world so distinct from the physical world according to this perspective.

Causality, meaning and reasons in the social world

If the goals of science are explanation and prediction, then this rests upon the notion of identifying relations of cause and effect. Indeed, we might characterize science as the search for causes. In order to predict, we must first identify causes. Similarly, an explanation of X relies on identifying the cause of X. As we suggested in the previous chapter, this is not always a straightforward matter. For Hume, causes were actually observed constant conjunctions between events. We noted, however, that often we can specify more about a cause than the simple observation of two events and that we can even point to a distinct set of conditions that govern whether or not something will occur. Along these lines, can we identify the "necessary" and "sufficient" conditions that comprise a cause in the social world?

There exists a view in the social sciences that approximates the Humean notion of "constant conjunction". Behaviourism takes the view that only observable and measurable concepts are appropriate foci for scientific study. The aim is to systematize observable behaviour. As such, underlying phenomena are regarded as unknowable and thus irrelevant to the study of social life. Systematization is achieved by "providing general statements that enable us to correlate observable environmental conditions with the behaviour they trigger" (Rosenberg 1988: 52). The environmental conditions associated with Sid hitting George might be that Sid was observably angry with George. In causal language, we can say that Sid's anger with George caused Sid to hit him.

The behaviourists' argument, like that of Hume, is that we cannot know any more than we observe. A behaviourist may then wish to generalize and say something to the effect that person A hitting person B is a manifestation of the anger of A with B. The problem here is that A and B may be boxers and hit each other for either pleasure and/or profit. All the behaviourist aims to achieve is a specification of the environmental conditions with which certain behaviour may be associated. Like Hume, they seek to establish the presence of constant conjunction.

In our boxing example, the behaviourist would either have to abandon his generalization about the causes of anger, or specify some necessary and sufficient conditions associated with it. Let us say, for the moment, that the outcome of certain types of behaviour results in physical confrontation. The problem is to know whether general manifestations of physical violence may be explained by the same causal mechanisms, or whether different ones are required according to time and place. In causal language, there is a need to specify both sufficient and necessary conditions. In terms of sufficient conditions, from a behaviourist vantage point, there is less of a problem. Anger, in this case, appears to be a sufficient condition for one person to strike another. However, in order for this to be generalizable it would have to be held that anger is a sufficient cause for striking another person. Clearly this may not be the case in all instances in which such behaviour is manifestly observed.

Necessary conditions are more difficult to specify. Clearly, one necessary condition will not cover all instances of people hitting each other. For this reason, the necessary conditions will rest upon other observables in the environment: for example, whether A and B were wearing boxing gloves. The core issue here is that those phenomena that we might observe will not exhaust the possible necessary conditions that are associated with the causes of people striking one other. Quite simply, there may be a surplus of observed causes that are indistinguishable from one another. To distinguish one from the other, we would need to know the full range of reasons that people invoke for striking one another. Proffered reasons imply internal mental states that are anathema to behaviourism with its analysis of external environmental effects on human behaviour. A may hit B because A is angry, but A may actually exhibit symptoms of mental imbalance. Despite this possibility, the outward manifestations of their mental states appear similar. Behaviourism ceases explanation at the level of observable relations with an external environment, because any other level of explanation or mode of understanding is thought to require unjustified imputations regarding a person's mental state.

For many social scientists, the reasons that people give for their behaviour are taken as a beginning, not an end point, to explanation. In everyday life, we explain our actions by giving reasons for them. Therefore, if there is to be a congruence between social scientific and everyday explanations, then the reasons people have for what they do, or say, become a legitimate area for investigation (Davidson 1994). In social science reasons are used to explain not just micro level individual interactions, but large scale social phenomena: for example, the rise of capitalism (Weber 1985). However, what comprises a "reason" for behaviour? When we attribute a reason to someone for doing something we are implicitly suggesting that a person had a belief about certain things in the world and, from this, desired certain outcomes. An explanation of Tamsin drinking a beer would require an investigation of her desires and beliefs. It may well be that she was thirsty and desired to drink beer in the belief that it would satisfy her thirst. But why beer and not water? On the other hand, perhaps she desired the effect that she believed the beer would provide. Clearly, the number of beliefs and desires that might inform possible explanations for Tamsin's action is as wide as her imagination.

Beliefs and desires appear dependent upon the attitude of a person toward his, or her, environment, as well as the actions of others in that environment. People attach meaning to things in the world, as well as the actions of others. From this point of view, social research is not just about behaviour, but about meaningful behaviour. Clearly, the action of gravity has no meaning in the sense that voting or drinking may have. Meaningful behaviour is the product of consciousness and experiences. It is this that is at the heart of the claim that human action is different to phenomena in the physical world.

As Popper (1966) has pointed out, the autonomous actions of conscious human beings produce open systems. From this point of view, we cannot logically anticipate outcomes for they are, it is claimed, indeterminate. Because the possibilities for individuals to take any number of different actions exist as an option, successful prediction in the social world will be limited. It is perhaps limited because of the difficulties we have in specifying causes. Our "causes", in social science, are therefore more properly thought of as reasons. The question must now be: can reasons serve as causes?

There have been numerous attempts to produce a form of words that will incorporate the language of beliefs and desires into something that might be said to provide a universal formula upon which to base explanation and prediction in the social sciences (see, for example, Papineau 1978: 78–84). They tend to take the following form: If agent X desires Y and believes that A is the best way to achieve it, then X will perform A. There are two possible classes of objection to this form of explanation. The first is that beliefs and desires are about future states and to specify them as being the same as causes leads to teleological explanation: that is, explanations that rest upon the specification of end states and thus attribute

---

RESEARCH EXAMPLE 2
Changing attitudes to cohabitation
in the British Household Panel Survey

The BHPS is a longitudinal study based on a cross-sectional sample of households who are interviewed at regular intervals over a period of years:

> [the BHPS]...shows how things follow from each other in the
> lives of real people. It allows us to see how our conditions and
> manner of life at one point in time turn us into the people (and
> kind of society) we subsequently become (Gershuny et al.
> 1994: 11).

Since the 1960s there has been an increasing tendency for people to live together outside of marriage. The BHPS found that 30% of women and 25% of men aged 21–24 had cohabited before marriage, whereas only 4.6% of women and 7.4% of men 60 years and older had cohabited. This indicates a change in attitudes between generations leading to a change in behaviour. Indeed, this is borne out by parallel findings which show that of those born since 1960 only 6.8% of women and 7.5% of men thought cohabitation to be wrong. However, changing attitudes are not necessarily reasons for these may be more complex. Thus, the cause of cohabitation may lie in factors such as a desire to live together prior to marriage, or as the result of the break up of a first marriage. Therefore, while disapproval may have been a reason *not* to cohabit in the past, the absence of disapproval is not likely to be a reason to cohabit now. Even if reasons can serve as causes, an exact specification of those reasons may not be an easy task.

---

purposes to actions or social systems. This is considered illegitimate because to specify an end state (a desire) as an explanation for action actually reverses cause and effect. The future cannot *cause* the past. This is sometimes answered by saying that in specifying the desires and beliefs of an agent, we are not talking about actual end states at time $t2$, but what it is that makes the agent act at time $t1$. Even if we said the explanation for Tamsin drinking beer was that she was thirsty and believed beer would quench her thirst, this would not imply any necessary outcome. Tamsin could have had precisely the same beliefs and desires, but have been thwarted by the fact that the bar was closed, or had run out of beer!

The second class of objections to this form of explanation, though more obvious, is also more serious. Agent X may desire more than one thing. Further, A may be one of two, or even more, equally good ways of achieving end state Y. There may be less of a desire to achieve Y than to avoid Z and so on. Now, although we can make numerous attempts to further specify what a universal formula should be by adding these possibilities, the difficulties never really go away. Thus, even if reasons (consisting of beliefs and desires) can be said to be the equivalent of causes in the physical world, there is still the need to attach many more caveats, or what are known as *ceteris paribus* clauses, to our universal formula. Eventually, we will have to attach so many that we end up saying that X will do A, all other things being equal. In scientific terms, this appears not to be anywhere near good enough and would seem to preclude successful explanation and prediction. If reasons are treated as causes we end up with n possible causes of a particular action. It would be as if we could identify plenty of sufficient conditions for combustion, but no necessary ones.

Rules and rationality

The foregoing has charted some of the difficulties in the search for causes in individual human action. However, much of social science is concerned to explain events at a macro level. For example, Wall (1990) used census data to explain the differences in the structure of English and French households. Such explanations rely on, for example, being able to differentiate norms within particular societies. Thus France has a higher proportion of elderly people living as couples than in England, and in the South of France households tend to contain more related members than in the North (Wall 1990: 18–19). A description of the differences between family and household structures in these societies therefore implies the existence of social norms, defined as shared expectations of behaviour that are deemed culturally appropriate.

Norms in society can be regarded as rule following. In social research the discovery of a social rule may count as a sufficient explanation of behaviour. If we wish to explain why it is that drivers drive on the right in the United States, but on the left in Australia, it would be unusual to seek an explanation via individual reasons and more usual to cite a rule that is subject to sanctions. In this way, rules may come to stand in for laws. However, not only are rules broken, but different rules apply in different times and places. In this sense, they lack the robustness of laws in the physical world. Nevertheless if, as researchers, we want to explain social behaviour then rules appear indispensable. What do we mean by rule following, or indeed rule breaking behaviour?

Rules imply something else central to social explanation – rationality. To behave rationally is to follow explicable rules. To break a rule does not necessarily imply that a person is behaving irrationally. The difficulty lies in deciding what counts as rational and what counts as irrational. We have seen the difficulty in attempting a universal specification of reasons for individual actions. Perhaps the implicit assumption behind such attempts is that human beings act rationally. This is a reasonable assumption, for social life would be difficult if we continually misunderstood the meanings others attached to their and our actions, or utterances.

An important area of microeconomic theory is that of rational action theory. This begins from the assumption that agents behave rationally in that they will always attempt to calculate the most effective way to achieve their ends (Elster 1986). Quite apart from the unwarranted assumption often made that the ends an agent will wish to attain are motivated by pure self-interest, this approach treats rational behaviour as a straightforward relationship between ends and means in individual actions. Social life is not that simple for it depends on our ability to anticipate the actions of others that themselves may be the product of our own actions. Moreover, goals may be benevolent and/or consensual.

To consider the above, let us take the hypothetical case of firefighters who are confronted with a burning building in which people are trapped. In attempting a rescue, the likelihood of severe injury, or death, is often considered less important than the desire to rescue the people in the building. These goals may be viewed as benevolent and contrary to self-interest. The rational choice theorist may wish to say that it is the individual who will decide her ends and the best means for their attainment. Nevertheless, this leaves us with a very narrow definition of what it is to act rationally and one that is not particularly useful to describe a myriad of actions in varied social circumstances. After all, what is thought to be a rational way to act will be dependent upon a variation in circumstances along the dimensions of time and place.

The difficulty in specifying what is a rational way to behave lies in the absence of ahistorical, or acultural standards that we might employ for the purpose of adjudication. It is not just that what is rational in Western Samoa may be different to that of the United States, but that within the US itself there may be difference. In other words, standards of rationality possess both exogenous and endogenous variations. Moreover, even within given societies what is rational changes over time. In Britain during the Second World War, the sound of church bells would have prompted the rational reaction that invasion was underway. Nowadays, it tends to signal that a religious ceremony is about to commence or has just finished.

In the English-speaking world, a very influential exponent of the view that rationality, and thus rule following, is a normative product of a given society is Peter Winch. Winch (1990) argued that an explanation of an action can only be accomplished by evaluating it against the standards current within that particular society. According to Winch, it follows that causal explanations of human behaviour are invalid. Unlike causal generalizations, rules admit of exception. In this way, rationality becomes the mode through which we understand the rules of the particular society in which we live. The statement that X was behaving irrationally is a product of local standards. Viewed from his vantage point, X was perhaps behaving perfectly rationally. For Winch, therefore, an investigation of a society requires an understanding of the normative behaviour of that society. We will return to Winch presently, but for the moment let us examine in a little more depth this alternative to "scientific" type explanations.

Meaning, language and understanding

We now turn to the second "position" that, for the sake of convenience, we will label the "interpretivist". The core of this position has informed many of the above critiques of causal explanations in social science. However, it is important to also note that the position itself has a distinct philosophical pedigree to positivism.

Interpretivism rests upon the philosophical doctrine of idealism. Although there are several variants of idealism, all hold the view that the world we see around us is the creation of mind:

Hunger, pain and anger in the human world cannot be described without investigating how individuals use language and symbols to construct what such states *mean for them*. For it is only by under-standing the individual experience of subjective interpretation that we will understand why human beings behave in the way they do; why, for instance, thresholds of pain, attitudes to death, and so on, differ so markedly from person to person, and from culture to culture (Johnson et al. 1984: 75. Original italics).

It does not follow that the world is considered "unreal", but simply that we do not have any kind of direct "one to one" relationship between us (subject) and the world (object). The world is interpreted through the mind. Indeed, our very observations of the social world depend upon a classificatory scheme that is filtered through our minds. Given this, we cannot know the "true" nature of the object world, separate from our perception of it.

Kant applied the term "transcendental idealism" to his view that the objects of our experience, those things that exist in space and time, are simply appearances and have no independent existence from our thoughts. This was a view that Weber took seriously in his analysis of the relationship between particular Protestant values and the ethos that underpinned the development of capitalism (Weber 1985). The Calvinist doctrine of "predestination" held that all were "saved or dammed", whatever their actions. Despite this, the early capitalists attempted to discern signs of their fate via their worldly success, or lack of it. This desire for salvation led to asceticism, thrift and good works, but particularly the desire to re-invest in enterprising schemes.

Prior to Weber's work, Karl Marx had explained the rise of capitalism as a result of material economic circumstances. However, Weber viewed this explanation as incomplete, for it failed to tell us why society A developed capitalism and B did not, even when the antecedent material conditions appeared similar in both societies. The missing part of the explanation rested on the meanings that individuals placed upon events and actions. It is quite irrelevant whether the Calvinists were correct in their beliefs about predestination, what is important is that their beliefs made them act in a particular manner. Only by knowing the meanings that agents attach to their actions can we hope to explain them. The social world thus becomes the creation of the purposeful actions of conscious agents. For Weber, no social explanation was complete unless it could adequately describe the role of meanings in human actions.

Weber was not the first to emphasize meaning in the study of social life.

RESEARCH EXAMPLE 3
Appearances and meanings
in studies of national identity

The contrast between appearance and intention is illustrated in studies of national identity. Kellas offers data from a survey of Scottish identity carried out in 1986 (Kellas 1992). Respondents were asked "how do you regard yourself in terms of nationality?" Possible responses included Scottish, British, equally both, more Scottish than British and vice versa. Clearly, no differentiation could be made on whether one asked "Scottish" or "non Scottish" people this question in the first place, because the aim was to find out how Scottish respondents felt. What of in-migrants? Even if they had begun to feel Scottish, we might still be justified in expecting quite different replies than from someone born and bred in the Highlands able to trace his, or her, ancestry back to the clans!

The problem in the above example lies in what the respondents themselves regard as "Scottishness". It is fine for the researcher to define what she means by "Scottishness", but unless this has some congruence with what the respondent means, the explanation will lack validity. In other words, social explanations must be derived from the meanings of the people we are investigating. For researchers, this is a problem of validity – can we be sure that the question asked is meaningful to the respondent and/or the reply we receive is meaningful in terms of the research question? In contrast, other more recent sociological and anthropological studies described by MacDonald (1993), place emphasis on learning about what counts as national identity via the way in which people construct those identities from the meanings they place on objects and relations in their social world. As she points out: "Identities [are] not merely relations which were present or absent, but actual phenomena which could be relatively strong, weak, confused disordered or in crisis" (MacDonald 1993: 7).

The key here is a German word that is often associated with Weber's methodology, *verstehen*, which means to "understand". Vico (1668–1744) was one of the first to insist on an ontological distinction between nature and human consciousness; a distinction born of the desire to understand the active processes of human history. Its practical significance in social science was the result of the work of the German philosopher Wilhelm Dilthey (1833–1911).

Dilthey's work occurred at an important time in the history of philosophy. Enlightenment reason, which had underwritten the burgeoning sciences, found itself under attack from a movement known as romanticism; a reaction against the increasing rationalization of human life. This reaction, which emphasized the centrality of the individual spirit and imagination, was typified in the writings of Shelley and Goethe. Dilthey's work was thus carried out against a background of the opposites of the rational and the empirical versus the metaphysics of the romantics. The romantics were philosophical idealists who emphasized the unknowability of what Kant called the noumenal world: that is, a world beyond appearances, the "thing in itself".

Dilthey, although wishing to emphasize a different set of philosophical assumptions for social science, still wished to rule out metaphysics as its basis. He took the view that in the physical world we can only study the appearance of a thing – the thing in itself (the noumena) remains hidden. On the other hand, the subject matter of the social sciences is human consciousness, which can be known directly (Manicas 1987: 121–2). Speculative metaphysics is unnecessary because in social science we are not dealing with "representations" of the unknowable, but with what Dilthey, following the German idealist philosopher Georg Hegel (1770–1831), called "objective mind":

> Every single human expression represents something which is common to many and therefore part of the realm of objective mind . . . the individual always experiences, thinks, acts, and also understands, in this common sphere (Dilthey quoted in Outhwaite 1975: 26–7).

In the pursuit of a new epistemological basis for the social sciences, Dilthey's work was to take this historical path. To understand society, we must understand history not just as a series of events, but as the outcome of human creativity. To say, for example, that the assassination of Archduke Ferdinand, in Sarajevo, "caused" the First World War is erroneous and misappropriates the language of the physical sciences in the social sciences. The search for cause and effect, in history, is as mistaken as the alchemists' search for gold. To understand history we must recognize that it represents a meaningful reality for those who "create" it. For this reason, the physical sciences are seen to represent a search for causal explanations, whereas the social sciences seek understanding.

As a method, understanding must begin from the presupposition that there is at least some common ground between the researcher and the person whom they are studying:

> Interpretation would be impossible if the expressions of life were totally alien. It would be unnecessary if there was nothing alien in them. [Hermeneutics] thus lies between these two extreme opposites (Dilthey quoted in Habermas 1972: 164).

Understanding thus begins from commonality; in particular, from shared experience that requires empathy on the part of the investigator. If we are to understand why Al Capone turned to a life of crime, we have to understand the meanings his world held for him. We have to understand the context and to do this we have to introduce our own lived experiences. Of course, life in London now (or even Chicago) is very different to Capone's day, so this process requires the exercise of imagination. Nevertheless, there would be enough in Capone's biography for us to imagine ourselves in his situation. Obviously, the more we are able to culturally situate people the better will be our understanding.

Weber, drawing upon the work of Dilthey, distinguished between modes of understanding. Not all modes involve empathy. Indeed, in history and sociology the search must be for what motivated a person to act in the way that she or he did (Weber 1949: 101–2). Here, Weber's search is a candidate for the pursuit of the "truth" that involves understanding. His work thus begins to look less like hermeneutics and a little more like positivism. Thus, he defines sociology as, "a science which attempts the interpretative understanding of social action in order thereby to arrive at a causal explanation of its course and effects" (Weber 1949: 88). Understanding becomes the starting point whose aim is the production of propositions that give rise to explanations that are adequate at the level of cause *and* meaning.

For Weber, the above was a necessary step to produce accounts of social, as opposed to individual, actions. For this reason, although an understanding of the social begins with an understanding of individual subjective meanings that are directed towards others, they are not the end of the story. Weber, though often thought to emphasize idealism,

---

RESEARCH EXAMPLE 4
Communist identity construction in Italy

The ethnographic strategy of participant observation is an attempt to get close to what is being studied by becoming part of that social setting. As with Kellas in the previous example, Chris Shore (1993) was concerned with the construction of identity. In this case, it was that of Communist identity in Italy, but more specifically, "the dialogue between communism and Catholicism in a city wide context" (1993: 33). Shore's research was carried out in an inner city area of Perugia and was an "account of the processes and relations observed . . . in the ethnographic present" (1993: 29). Though he was concerned to understand the lived experience of the people he studied this was inevitably from the point of view of a foreigner. Yet, as he notes, this was not always the most important factor in leading to acceptance or rejection in the community (the former being a prerequisite to obtain worthwhile data). Often the impression he gave about his political views was crucial. A rejection of capitalism and a particular view of the then British Prime Minister, Margaret Thatcher, was enough to win acceptance as a "comrade". Conversely, among the non-Communist Catholics his religion, or lack of it, became important to some of those with whom he spoke. To understand meanings is to understand context and to do this it is often necessary to become an insider – or at least to stop being an outsider. A central issue here is, can an an English non-Communist come to "know" the meanings of an Italian Communist?

---

considered the intentionality of conduct, alongside the pursuit of objectivity in terms of cause and effect. This was translated into an interest in both the meanings and the material conditions of action. In this sense, Weber's methodology appears iconoclastic for he attempts to form a bridge between the traditions of positivism and interpretivism. The question for social science then becomes: what motivates people to act in particular ways and where do their meanings come from in the first place?

To return us to our discussion of rules, there are those within the interpretivist tradition who argue that our actions are not governed by cause and effect, but by the rules that we use to interpret the world. In the phenomenological tradition of philosophical thought, "outer" explanations for human action based on, for example, the class position of an individual in society, are substituted by two different questions. It is these questions that should be the focus of social research. They are, "how does reality come to be constituted by mental operations as a known object?", and secondly, "how do we go about constructing our ideas of what reality is?" (Johnson, Dandeker & Ashworth 1984: 78). In this sense, Weber's use of *verstehen* towards the goals of social scientific explanation cannot be justified.

A number of responses to this issue have occurred, that either build on the work of people such as Dilthey, or the phenomenologist Edmund Husserl (1859–1938) who sought the basis of "true understanding". Among these, the work of Martin Heidegger (1889–1976) stands out. It is he who moved the focus of phenomenological inquiries from epistemology to ontology and in so doing posed a challenge to the ideas of Kant. For Heidegger, we are not simply observers of an external world that is mediated and sorted by our consciousness (Husserl), but are members of that world who exist as "beings-in-time". This moves social science away from Dilthey's neo-Kantian preoccupations with the question of appropriate methods for the study of social life, to an analysis of what Heidegger called *Dasein*. This is not an easy concept to grasp, but it may be considered as "pre-understanding":

> the *place* where the question of being arises, the place of manifestation; the centrality of *Dasein* is simply that of a being which understands being (Ricoeur 1982: 54. Original italics).

Importantly, Heidegger does not try to "solve" the question of the relationship between a subject (person) and the world (object) that they inhabit through the formulation of an appropriate method, such as *verstehen*. Understanding does not simply require the prioritization of human consciousness in the study of the social world, as it had for Husserl and Dilthey, because understanding is part of a "mode of being". Understanding actually emerges from a gap that exists between where people are located in history and the possibilities that are then made available to them in the future.

The point of this discussion is that ideas, such as *verstehen*, are not a method to be appropriated by the human sciences, but actually a fundamental part of human existence. Hans Georg Gadamer (1975) has been much influenced by the ideas of Heidegger. His concerns are ontological, rather than epistemological and in this focus three questions become of importance: how is it possible to "understand"; what kinds of knowledge can "understanding" give us and what is the status of such knowledge? Gadamer uses the hermeneutic language of "text" for this purpose, maintaining that understanding is made possible by grasping not just what the text says, but its cultural location. The text becomes an involuntary expression of a particular historic reality. The investigator can then access the meaning of the text through its context and the social context is accessible through the interpretation of the text. As such,

> Gadamer's position would require us to look beyond what is said to what is being taken for granted while it is being said, to the everyday meaning of both the language used and the situation in which the conversation occurs (Blaikie 1993: 64).

As with Heidegger and Gadamer, Paul Ricoeur emphasizes the ontological over the epistemological through his concern with the relationship between language and meaning. He agrees with Weber that meaning is the central concern of the social sciences. With Gadamer, however, he shares a concern with the interpretation of "texts". For Ricoeur, a text is a discourse fixed in writing, but social action itself does share some of the general features of a text. Although both employ language, the important difference is that speech forms a dialogue, whereas (and here he disagrees with Dilthey) a text does not. A text does not necessarily carry the intentions of the author; intentions that are present in dialogue. Quite simply, if two people are having a conversation the intention of the other is apparent, whereas there can be any number of interpretations of a text, each of which is equally correct. Ricoeur's aim here is to unite explanation and understanding. Language "has no subject" for it exists outside of time and it is this quality that allows for differing interpretations of texts. Two readings of texts are then possible. First, we can explain it in terms of its internal relations via the logical structure of languages or, secondly, we can treat it as speech and offer interpretations that lead to understanding.

The approaches of Gadamer and Ricoeur are essentially philosophical. In fairness to both, this is their intention. For this reason it is difficult to see how their prescriptions would "work through" in the world of research. However, their emphasis upon the centrality of language is important. Language offers us common horizons in which investigation becomes possible simply because meanings are shared and understood. As

Gadamer argues, even the worlds of other languages can be grasped from our own, because we have the capacity to broaden our insights to know other social realms. This optimism needs to be tempered with a logical point implicit in Ricoeur's work. If it is the case that we really cannot know the author's intention from the text, then how can we know we have achieved an understanding, or an explanation, consistent with the meanings that the author intended? On this basis, we cannot know whether we can know other social worlds!

This appears to be an overall problem when meaning is used as a "resource" in investigation. Dilthey believed hermeneutics could bridge the gap between the known and the alien. At a superficial level, this is clearly correct. However, the method ultimately relies on the philosophical assumption that we can know other minds. On the face of it, there seems little evidence to support this. After all, our best guesses as to what others are thinking are based on evaluation of their thoughts from our viewpoint. Maybe as a child you played a game whereby you had to guess what your friend was thinking and vice versa. The temptation is always to change your mind to thwart the person guessing! As social researchers who wish to *understand* social groups we are required to find meanings for action; a tall order in such circumstances. What we are actually constrained to do is to link actions and utterances to interpretations of meanings. We are back to Ricoeur and the inevitability of different interpretations.

Summary

In this chapter we have contrasted two "traditional" views of how we can investigate the social world. Through behaviourism, we have demonstrated the limits of traditional, naturalistic, approaches to social life. The failure of behaviourism lies in its sole reliance on observation and not accounting for the same kind of behaviours being generated by quite different motivations. Further there is no one-to-one correspondence between reasons for action and the action itself. This, in turn, casts doubt upon whether causal explanations are valid in social science, simply because they offend the principal characteristic of causal explanation: that is, the same cause should produce the same effect.

Such problems open up possibilities for the position we have characterized as interpretivism. Interpretivism is not without its difficulties; not least those arising over the issue of "knowing other minds". Social investigations, in order to be more than introspective examinations of one's consciousness, must rely on claims about knowing other minds. Moreover, if they are to produce findings that are anything other than trivially interesting, claims about their representativeness, validity and potential for generalization must hold.

Implicit in the debate between those who wish to find causal explanations for social life and those who argue this to be mistaken, is a fundamental dispute over the nature of knowledge itself. Philosophical naturalism, for the most part, depends on a correspondence theory of truth. Theories of causality, whether they are Humean or of the more complex kind we described, are also dependent in this way. Yet, if meanings are to be intersubjectively held, a coherence view of truth must operate whereby the agents sharing the meanings agree on the "truth" of the matter.

Difficulties exist in both naturalist and interpretivist explanations. Despite these, social research is still commissioned on a daily basis for the purposes of describing and explaining social phenomena. Therefore, if we are to render justice to this topic, we need to move beyond the arguments in this chapter, to examine the nature and practice of social science from other perspectives. In the next chapter, we examine a range of approaches that either regard the problems noted here as unimportant, or resolve them by starting from a quite different sets of assumptions.

Questions for discussion

1. Can reasons be causes?
2. Must the findings of social science be generalizable? If so what (if any) are the limits of generalization?
3. Should explanations be adequate at the level of cause and the level of meaning?
4. What is it to be rational?

Suggested reading

Hage, J. & B. Foley-Meeker 1988. *Social causality*. London: Unwin Hyman.
Manicas, P. 1987. *A history and philosophy of social science*. Oxford: Blackwell.
Papineau, D. 1978. *For science in the social sciences*. London: Macmillan.
Rosenberg, A. 1988. *Philosophy of social science*. Oxford: Clarendon.
Ryan, A. 1970. *The philosophy of the social sciences*. Basingstoke: Macmillan.
Wilson, B. (ed.) 1970. *Rationality*. Oxford: Blackwell.

CHAPTER 4

Knowing the social world

In the previous chapter we described some of the difficulties associated with causal explanations and interpretations in social science. In this chapter, we focus upon various philosophical justifications and methodological strategies that inform the practice of social research. Though some of the approaches we discuss imply views on problems such as those associated with causality or meaning, it is not our intention to offer "solutions" to the problems we have raised, other than to say that for some philosophers or researchers these are not the right questions to ask in the first place. For this reason there exist views about the nature of the social world, and how we can know it, which circumvent the difficulties discussed so far. Sometimes, these lead to new kinds of problems and though we will illustrate some strategies and justifications, we will not shrink from pointing out some of their more obvious shortcomings.

The first half of this chapter is concerned with the nature of social reality through the examination of various perspectives on the social world. In the process we will be asking: what kinds of things are social phenomena? All philosophical positions and their attendant methodologies, explicitly or implicitly, hold a view about social reality. This view, in turn, will determine what can be regarded as legitimate knowledge. Thus, the ontological shapes the epistemological. The second part of the chapter deals with a number of characterizations of the ways in which we come to know the social world. Here, we wish to demonstrate how epistemological, and sometimes methodological, views actually shape ontological claims. As such, the division of this chapter into two parts is a heuristic device. If the reader is left thinking that this is an artificial divide, we would not disagree.

Perspectives on the social world

Broadly speaking, there are two principal and opposed views about the nature of the social world and the world in general. The first of these we touched upon in the last chapter. It is the claim that the external world consists simply of representations and is a creation of the mind. The existence of common objects, such as cars or ice creams, is a condition of their perception. This idealist doctrine does not deny that things have a real existence, but maintains that all we can ever know is the world of appearances, or that material objects are a product of mind, or that all there is one mind to which all phenomena belong. These latter two views are attributable to George Berkeley (1685–1753) and Hegel respectively. Although Berkeley's idealism is not quite so odd as it sounds, it will not detain us here. The first and last kinds of idealism, however, underlie some examples we will use in this chapter. For instance, a close relative of idealism is empiricism. Empiricist assumptions about the nature of the world enter social science explicitly via positivism, and implicitly through a collapse into phenomenalism exhibited in some interpretivist approaches (Bryman 1988: 119). The opposite view to that of representation is that the phenomena we see in the world consists of "real" things. Here, although it is accepted that reality is not always directly known it is, in principle, knowable. So, first, let us consider representation in more detail and we can then move on to consider what is known as "realism".

Social reality as representation: the idealist path

The philosophical justification for idealism can be illustrated by a simple experiment. Next time you are in a room containing a table, or a desk, look at it from above and note its descriptive characteristics. Now get down on your hands and knees and look at it from underneath, now look at it sideways on. Does it not look very different? Which was the "real" table? Each of the tables you perceived was the same one, but if the experiences had been separated you could not have known this. Can we ever know the real table? This argument can be extended into the social world. However much we "carve up" social interactions, or social structure, we can never claim to have found out what is "real" about it. It follows from this that the search for the authentic, or the "real" in the social world, is a misguided venture. In contrast to this we have a series of representations that are equivalent to Kant's "phenomena". The representations of the "social world" are thus created by individual minds. Important consequences flow from these arguments.

Previously, we discussed the contention that all we can ever know are the meanings that individuals attribute to their social situations or the utterances of other people. This, you will recall, leads to the problem, how can we "know" the social, or to put it another way, what "is" the social world? If knowledge is a product of mind, then knowledge can only come via introspection. There are those philosophers who argue that this leads to solipsism: that is, the view that the world is only an object of personal consciousness and there is nothing outside of the individual mind. Berkeley's idealism led him to this view (see Emmett 1964: 156–81). Introspection and the solipsism that follows, become a blind alley for any kind of investigation that requires a degree of intersubjective agreement about what is observed.

Weber was a neo-Kantian. Given this, he maintained that the only way we can hope to know the social world is through a refinement of our instruments for observing it, rather than being able to "know" reality itself. Therefore, the best that social scientists can achieve is to describe the social world by employing "ideal types". These are, "the sum total of concepts which the specialist in the human sciences constructs purely for the purposes of research" (Freund 1968: 60). Ideal types are not averages, or even a summary description of phenomena found in the social world. Rather, they are a reflection of how an individual might come to know the world from their own viewpoint or value orientation. Crucially, it depends on a shared rational faculty, implying that ideally we can come to know the real world.

Ideal types may be characterized as a way of rescuing a programme for social investigation that rests on the philosophical assumption that "reality" is mind dependant. However, for Weber ideal types were not a rescue operation. Almost by definition, social life is rational. If we could not depend on others acting rationally, then there would be no social life, simply a collection of atomistic individuals. Quite simply, human actions are goal oriented and depend upon abilities to interpret the meanings of other goal oriented agents. Crucially and controversially, Weber's ideal types assume a congruence between the meanings of the investigated and the investigator. According to him, ideal types are "scientifically formulated pure type of phenomena" (1949: 96). In effect, they are testable hypotheses formulated to account for the action being investigated. They can be verified, or following Popper, falsified (Rex 1974).

From this point of view, Weber's work may be characterized as by-passing the problem of how we can know the social by employing the methodological strategy of ideal types. He turns an ontological problem into a methodological solution. Other approaches have utilized the philosophical starting point as a justification for statements about the nature of the social world. In particular, those that begin from an Hegelian, rather than a Kantian, idealism.

Hegelian idealism shares with the Kantian variety the view that the world is a product of mind, but disagrees with the view that the "thing in itself", the Kantian "noumena", is unintelligible. As noted, the Kantian "solution" to this is to seek to refine the instruments through which we gain a knowledge of reality in the first instance. It is this idea that forms the basis of Hegel's critique of Kant's epistemology:

> We ought, says Kant, to become acquainted with the instrument, before we undertake the work for which it is to be employed; for if the instrument be insufficient, all our trouble will be spent in vain . . . But the examination of knowledge can only be carried out by an act of knowledge. To examine this so-called instrument is the same thing as to know it. But to seek to know before we know is as absurd as the wise resolution of Scholasticus, not to venture into the water until he had learned to swim (Hegel quoted in Singer 1983: 51).

Therefore, the starting point for knowing reality is our ontological connection with reality. A close examination of our consciousness will thus enable the development of increased form of consciousness and so on . . . until "absolute knowledge" is reached. We do not need to be content with a Kantian "appearance of reality", for knowledge of reality itself may be gained in this manner.

Despite this revolution in philosophical thought, we are still left with a problem. If everything is just in the mind, then how can we distinguish the true from the false, the objective from the subjective? Hegel's solution was to take a "holistic" view of the world. The truth is the whole. Anything less than the whole is contradictory and only by knowing the whole truth can the contradictions be removed. This leads Hegel to a coherence theory of truth, whereby the progress of knowledge is seen as a journey towards one complete system. The process through which we move towards truth consists of contradiction and resolution – dialectics. The latter, of course, has been extremely influential on many approaches to social science; in particular, Marxism. However, although influenced by Hegelian idealism, Marxism tends to exhibit materialist and realist tendencies. We shall return to these views shortly.

Representation and the linguistic turn

Ludwig Wittgenstein (1889–1951) has been highly influential in the development of a linguistically based approach to social investigation. Through the work of Peter Winch (1990) and from there to ethnomethodology, this linguistic turn sees meaning becoming a topic, rather than a resource, in social investigation.

Throughout his career, Wittgenstein had a preoccupation with the scope and limits of language (Monk 1990). Though he first emphasized a "picture theory" of reality along the lines of a correspondence theory, his latter work was given over to the view that language was a social instrument. This involved the replacement of a search for hidden meanings and explanations with a description of the "use" of concepts in everyday language. It is this connection between language and social life which makes Wittgenstein's work of such importance. Language, he contends, actually makes us social. He compares it to a game for which there are set rules and criteria of success and failure. Activities employ different "language games" with different sets of rules. For example, in Western society if a stage compere says "let's give a big hand to X", we tend to clap. We do not throw large hands onto the stage where the person or group is performing. We know the rules of the game and how to play it. It follows that there are no external criteria of assessment that are capable of transcending all language games.

The idea that language is social gives rise to an argument that there cannot be any such thing as a "private language". Language, far from being the expression of inner consciousness, is actually publicly available and exists by virtue of our ability to use it and even a tendency to make mistakes in its use. If language really were simply a reflection of inner thoughts, the notion of a mistake would be irrelevant. Now we are forced to re-consider the view that we cannot access other minds because there exist publicly available linguistic forms of expression.

Peter Winch employs the analogy of the language game in his approach to social investigation. The task of social investigations is to elaborate the "forms of life" of a particular society (Winch 1990: 40–65). Thus, as we have seen, rule following behaviour is of central importance to Winch's formulations. Language implies rules and the rules of societies are apparent through its language games. Different societies will exhibit different sets of games. It follows from this that no ahistorical, acultural framework can be used to adduce the meanings agents employ in different societies. The only method through which we can know society S, is via an examination of its forms of life. This view, however, was extremely controversial and is now of interest due to its influence on a tradition of social thought known as ethnomethodology. Before turning to this position, it is worth elaborating on some more common criticisms of Winch's position, because these criticisms imply an alternative view of how we may come to know the social world.

In considering Winch's work, Steven Lukes argues that no matter how culturally different a society is from that of the investigator's, there has to be a mechanism from which we can begin to understand. Thus to understand the language of society S it:

> must have our distinction between truth and falsity if we are to understand its language, for if *per impossible* it did not, we would be unable even to agree about what counts as the successful identification of public (spatio-temporally) located objects (Lukes 1994: 293. Original italics).

It follows from this that any society that has a language must minimally possess concepts of agreement and negation and number: for example, there either is an X here or there is not, or there are *n* Xs here. Lukes's criticism seems to offer some support for Dilthey's view that there is enough in common between people to allow for an understanding of what, at first, appears to be an unfamiliar social situation.

A second criticism of Winch's ideas is that they are relativistic. His work echoes Feyerabend's insofar as Winch is saying that investigators are not able to employ evaluative, transcultural, comparisons. Indeed, as we noted earlier, Winch takes the view that rationality is specific to different societies. However, this begs the question as to whether societies are easily defined entities. The societies of the Winch–Lukes debate were often referred to as "primitive"; whereas we would prefer to say different from our own. Such hermetically sealed societies, if they still exist in the age of globalization (Spybey 1995), are hardly helpful illustrations in the evaluation of methodological procedures. Though we talk of "Western" society, there are no sharp demarcation points with non-Western societies. Within each, cultures blend and overlap.

In the "Global Village", we would be hard pushed not to find cultures that shared at least some conceptual notions with our own. Therefore, if societies cannot be sharply distinguished, what are we to make of rationality? Quite simply, defining rationality in a given society requires, at minimum, an identification of that society. We are thus left with two choices. First, we can arbitrarily define the boundaries of rational behaviour or, secondly, leave it to the individual to decide whether she, or he, is behaving rationally. The first route would take us back to Weber and would be antipathetic to Winch's project. The second route, on the other hand, renders the concept of the "rational" meaningless.

As noted, Winch's views translate in social science through the ethnomethodological tradition. Ethnomethodology brings together an emphasis on the importance of language with a particularly "philosophical" view of social life derived from the phenomenological writings of Alfred Schutz (1899–1959). Phenomenology holds that consciousness is the only phenomenon that we can know with any degree of certainty. All of the things we perceive in the world are the objects of our consciousness. Within this school of thought Schutz's overall aim was to take Husserl's philosophical problematics and translate them into a phenomenology of the social world which rendered them amenable to sociological study.

In *The phenomenology of the social world* (1972), Schutz describes how undifferentiated experience is constructed into meaningful social objects through the creation of "models". Repeated experiences become meaningful to us; they are "typical" to us and might be said to serve as markers to help us negotiate social life. These "models", which Schutz calls "typifications", are our stock of knowledge of the social world that we continually expand and modify. Typifications can be typical types of people, situations, objects, behaviour, etc. It is these meaningful typifications that must become the topic of sociology and a corollary of his argument is that typifications (and thus meaning) would then become the topic of all social science research.

The central doctrine of phenomenology is that of reduction. Here, we attempt to rid ourselves of prior understandings in order to grasp an experience in its unadulterated form. Thus, for example, to perceive the "essence" of triangularity we would need to examine the concepts of "triangular" that we hold in our mind. The aim of this strategy is to discover the "ideal" objects of consciousness. In this case, ideal refers to that which remains the same in repeated experiences. This introspective examination of the objects of our conscious mind is called "bracketing". In the social world, ideal objects do not exist in the same sense and the nearest we can get to discovering their essence is to discover what are the meanings that agents attach to them via their actions and utterances. Meanings, unlike, for example, ideal geometrical shapes, change. Therefore, the process of reduction is context dependent and partial.

From the above derives the claim that agents' meanings can be prioritized as the topics of social investigation. For example, in Egon Bittner's (1967) study of the police on skid row, "peacekeeping" was identified as the area of interest. Concepts such as "police", "skid row", as well as other social typifications – "arrests", "middle class morality", along with the physical objects encountered such as houses, cars, streets, truncheons – were taken as given. Only pre-judgements on "peacekeeping" and "law enforcement" were bracketed as the concepts of interest. In general, Bittner was concerned to understand the distinction between these concepts as employed by the police themselves. This work, however, lies within the tradition of ethnomethodology.

Ethnomethodology is an example, *par excellence*, of "folk psychology". Here, the common sense views and expressions of people in their everyday lives are taken as the subject matter of social science. The term ethnomethodology was coined by Harold Garfinkel in the 1950s and can be translated as "peoples' methods". If the imposed meanings of traditional sociology are to be rejected, then it follows that the "grand" explanations and generalizations that it produces are likewise inaccurate and irrelevant. The topic for sociology, Garfinkel argued, must be the everyday meanings people use to account for, or make sense of, theirs and other peoples' activities (Garfinkel 1967). This necessitated taking a very different route from that of Weber as the following quote from Garfinkel's earlier work illustrates:

At least two important theoretical developments stem from the researches of Max Weber. One development, already well worked, seeks to arrive at a generalized social system by uniting a theory that treats the structuring of experience with another theory designed to answer the question, "What is man?" Speaking loosely, a synthesis is attempted between the facts of social structure and the facts of personality. The other development, *not yet adequately exploited*, seeks a generalized social system built solely from the analysis of experience structures (Garfinkel quoted in Heritage 1984: 9. Italics added).

In order to perfect this analysis of "experience structures", ethnomethodology needed to move beyond phenomenology towards a linguistic focus upon social life. For this reason, Garfinkel maintained that social life is not just to be described through language, but is actually created by language. There are two ethnomethodological concepts that are of importance to this focus of social inquiry: reflexivity and indexicality. First, let us consider reflexivity.

Social life is created through talk. When we give an account of an event we usually consider that we are providing a description. However, Garfinkel argues that this process is creative in that it helps to make the social world. A friend describing a football game to another will be active in creating the culture of interest that surrounds the sport of "football". The reflexive nature of conversation itself helps us to grasp agents' meanings. To give an account of behaviour is to seek to make it intelligible to others. The sociologist can then take seriously the accounts given by those in whom she is interested, for those accounts will be an attempt to make behaviour meaningful not only to the person themselves, but also to others. It follows that the issues of rationality can no longer be considered a problem. If an agent can provide a situated account for his actions through an explanation of the context of those actions, then it follows that he is behaving rationally. Reflexivity thus becomes a routine part of social interactions that

> Members know, require, count on, and make use of . . . to produce, accomplish, recognize, or demonstrate rational-adequacy-for-all-practical purposes of their procedures and findings (Garfinkel 1967: 8).

Secondly, there is the notion of indexicality. Ethnomethodology embarks upon a refusal to differentiate between everyday theorizing in social life and professional social theory by invoking this idea. Indexicality, taken from Charles Peirce's semiology, states that everyday language and actions cannot be understood without being situated within the social context in which they are performed or uttered. In social life, unlike in the physical sciences, there is no one fixed definition of an event or object, for meaning is seen in relation to social context.

The implications of this position are far reaching. First, there can be no privileging of agents' or investigators' accounts. The accounts that agents give of their actions are indexed to particular situations and though similarities may exist, they tend to conceal complex, situationally specific, meanings. The similarity is the product of "glossing", whereby in everyday life we employ a range of taken for granted rules which have the effect of "avoiding the issue" – talking around a topic without giving a true specification of its content (Cicourel 1973: 109). Secondly, this leads to a complex relationship between meanings and rules in ethnomethodology. On the one hand, it is accepted that agents employ rules but, on the other, it is maintained that those rules are just the product of glossing. The application of social rules requires agents to make judgements about meanings. However, there can be no definitive or unambiguous means by which one can arrive at such judgements. Indexicality effectively rules out generalizations because there can be no privileged accounts and undermines explanation because rules cannot be said to have an objective existence. Rules do not place limits on action, or provide yardsticks against which actions may be judged. Instead, they are resources upon which people routinely draw in the situated nature of their activities.

The prioritization of agents' meanings as the topic of research takes interpretivism to its limits. There are many critiques of ethnomethodology. Here, we are concerned to examine briefly those that have implications for any investigative project in social science that seeks to prioritize individual meaning and in so doing deny the possibility of social explanation.

The first observation that may be made is that the insistence on the indexical nature of expressions leads to an epistemological and moral relativism. A principal property of indexical expressions is that they are considered to be unique events. Nevertheless, if they are unique events then it follows that the investigator should not generalize from one event, or set of events, to another. Each event will have a different meaning. Of course, it is permissible to report on the generalizations agents make themselves (their typifications), but the investigator should not attempt to produce her own typifications.

This injunction to investigate the "how" of social life, leads ethnomethodologists to adopt a stance of moral indifference toward those investigated:

Ethnomethodological studies of formal structures are directed to the study of such phenomena, seeking to describe members' accounts of formal structures wherever and by whomever they are done, while abstaining from all judgements of their adequacy, value, importance, necessity, practicality, success, or consequentiality. We refer to this procedural policy as "ethnomethodological indifference" (Garfinkel & Sacks 1986: 166).

If there can be no universal statements about the nature of rational action, then there can be no universal statements about the morality these actions represent. This appears to render social science pointless. If on reporting situation S, nothing is to be learnt about S-like situations, then why bother reporting on it at all? Also, a stance of indifference is not tenable. Ethnomethodologists, like all researchers, investigate those things that interest them (or others if they are commissioned to conduct research). As such, there is a process of selection whereby some things are considered worthy of attention and others are not. As we noted in the previous chapter, no investigation begins from a "theory neutral" vantage point. Indeed, as will be noted in the next chapter, arguments exist to the effect that social science must rest upon moral values.

What may be called "moderatem generalizations" about similar social events appear to be unavoidable. If researchers are unable to say that if X occurs in situation S, it is likely that in a situation resembling S, X may well occur again, then there seems little point to research. It seems impossible not to produce, as investigators, typifications about those we are investigating. The latter take the form of theories based upon the typifications of those investigated. To accept that we can be wrong about our theories is much the same as to accept that in everyday life we may be wrong in our typifications.

At this point, it might be helpful it we made some links with our prior discussions. For a long time, empiricism appeared synonymous with science. If science did not give us an insight into reality, then what could? In the social sciences empiricism has been associated (and sometimes confused with) positivism, yet it and idealism, as exemplified in the above formulations, share much of the same pedigree in the work of John Locke (see Russell 1984). Like Hume, Locke argued that our understanding of the world arises from our experiences. Unlike Hume, however, he emphasized that the way we classify objects in the world must be based on our view of the essential qualities of those objects. Therefore, with Kant, he is

---

RESEARCH EXAMPLE 5
The phenomenon of the "radical lawyer"

Max Travers was concerned to focus upon how "radicalism", in the legal profession, is "displayed, recognised, accomplished and constructed as a publicly visible cultural object by ordinary members of society going about their everyday working lives inside the legal profession" (Travers 1994: 245). The methods used by Travers in his research were ethnographic and consisted of the reporting of conversations with him and conversations between lawyers and others to which he was able to listen. He reports on the views of the lawyers themselves and those others, in order to build up a picture of what "radical" meant to those who viewed themselves as radical and those who saw the lawyers as being radical. Two distinct views thus emerged. For the lawyers, their radicalism was a conscious moral position, but for those opposed to their views (often non-radical lawyers), the lawyers were putting on an act to please the clients and to raise the profile of the firm. "Radicalism" thus became a contested phenomenon.

The research highlights the problematic nature of the term "radical lawyer" and how it is indexical upon the meanings of the different groups.

---

saying that we do not have any privileged access to things in themselves, but we do have access to their properties: for example, colour, shape, feel, etc. Indeed, such properties are perhaps more "real" in their actually being perceived (Emmett 1964: 177–9). Hume, you will recall, was even more sceptical and believed that all we could talk about was appearances. Yet Hume's views rested upon the assertion that we cannot base any knowledge of the external world on appearances, because we cannot know anything beyond them.

Given the above, empiricism may be viewed as a form of representation closely allied to idealism. If appearances are apprehended through sense experiences and we make sense of these experiences in our minds, or even via language games, then the question of separating out "truth" from "falsity" comes back to haunt us. For this reason, the empiricist emphasis shifts from statements about what the object world actually is, to statements regarding strategies for knowing the social world. However, there is another route available to both the natural and social sciences in considering their philosophical foundations. It is to realism that we now turn.

Beyond idealism: a realist theory of science

Realism, as a philosophical doctrine, has a long history. It is a complex body of ideas that, like idealism, takes many forms. Unlike idealism, however, it can be usefully summed up in one phrase: the world has an existence independent of our perception of it. It is then a "common sense" position. As Roy Bhaskar puts it:

> Normally to be a realist in philosophy is to be committed to the existence of some disputed kind of being (e.g. material objects, universals, causal laws; propositions, numbers, probabilities; efficacious reasons, social structures, moral facts) (1993: 308).

The kind of things that can be "real" present philosophers with problems. Although it is relatively unproblematic to discuss the reality, or otherwise, of everyday objects such as cats and aeroplanes, the difficulties begin when we want to say, for example, whether or not light is "real". Debates over the nature of light lead directly to the science of quantum physics and the attendant philosophical difficulties encountered in deciding whether or not elementary particles are "real" (for example, see Rae 1986). The reality, or otherwise, of light is far from unproblematic. Even if agreement about its existence can be reached, there is the problem of whether our ideas about these things are "real" or not.

It is possible to be a realist at a number of levels. The most moderate of realists, who are all but indistinguishable from idealists, maintain that there has to be a "reality" because if there was no "reality", then its negation would in itself be a reality! Furthermore, it is possible to be a realist about the "physical" world, but not about the social world. Here, the justification is that the social world consists of ideas that cannot be treated in the same way as physical objects. This view is, of course, held by many of those described above who view the social world in terms of representation. The difficulty with this subject–object dualism is that it entails the metaphysical belief that "mind" is somehow different from, and not reducible to, "matter" (Dennett 1991). If mind is not reducible to matter, then the difficulty arises in saying exactly what it is and where it divides itself from the physical world? Although such discussions are important, our focus on realism will be confined to those who argue that the social world is "real" and exists independently of the ideas that we have of it. How is this view sustained?

The first thing to say is that realists, like the empiricists and positivists, are philosophical naturalists. In other words, they take the view that the structure of explanation in the physical and social sciences are not fundamentally different, though each must elaborate its explanations in ways appropriate to its subject matter (Bohman 1991). This means that realists believe that concepts such as causality, explanation and prediction are just as appropriate in the social sciences as in the physical sciences. In the previous chapter, we noted Hempel's idea of explanation and prediction as isomorphic: one implies the other. As Outhwaite notes, however, this is an unsatisfactory position taking the form of: X has happened because it has always happened!

> If I ask why my train is late, I may be partially reassured to be told that the 8.55 is always late, but even British Rail would hardly dare offer this as an explanation (Outhwaite 1987: 21).

Given this, realists want more from an explanation. Empiricist concepts of explanation ultimately rest on a Humean view of what you see is what you get. This, of course, is exemplified in the idea of causality as constant conjunction. Yet, as we have pointed out, constant conjunction really depends on the level of description: that is, what you look at and how you look at it. Roy Bhaskar sums this up with clarity:

> Things exist and act independently of our descriptions, but we can only know them under particular descriptions. Descriptions belong to the world of society and of men; objects belong to the world of nature . . . Science, then, is the systematic attempt to express in thought the structures and ways of acting of things that exist and act independently of thought (Bhaskar 1975: 250).

There is a problem here. Empiricist critics of realism maintain that we have no business to go around saying things are "real" when we have no way of demonstrating their existence. The empiricist can say if we claim our description of things, for example atoms, are real, how do we then change our descriptions? Surely, descriptions can only be derived from our experiences?

There are two responses to this issue. First, we can admit that science changes its formulations, but they are simply hypotheses that have been refuted. These hypotheses are what Bhaskar calls the "transitive objects of science" (1989: 18–21) that are created to represent reality. Secondly, it is possible for philosophers to deduce that the world is structured and differentiated, but the kinds of structures and the way they exist are the subject matter of science. In this sense, recall Russell's argument about the existence of cats. The question of its existence is the province of the philosopher; the scientist focuses upon the properties of that existence.

Realists are saying that things have a real existence. Furthermore, this may be demonstrated by uncovering underlying causal mechanisms. However, the idea of causation employed here is different from that which we have come across before. For empiricists, causality amounts to a description of singular events, from which generalizations are built up via induction. Thus, if the 8.55 train has arrived late on a number of occasions, the explanation for it arriving late on a particular day is that it always does. Here, the explanation is built up of singular, but alike events. Yet the explanation is likely to be much more complex and dependent upon (perhaps) numerous causes that are dissimilar. For instance, on the first day the driver overslept. On the second day there were leaves on the line and on the third day, a signal failure at a station on a different line meant trains from that line were diverted, thus holding up normal traffic. In other words, things happen in open systems and causes are usually underdetermined. When the scientist in the laboratory carries out an experiment she is isolating a part of the world – or at least aims to. Observed regularities are the result of such isolation.

Add to the above discussion what we have noted in Chapter 3: that is, a core issue in the social sciences, and one for the physical sciences, lies in the difficulty of determining all of the conditions that comprise a cause. For realists, causes are regarded rather differently. If different sequences of events can produce the same outcome – for example, the train arriving late – then they are not, contra empiricism, dependent upon empirical regularities. Instead, causes must be understood as "tendencies". These "tendencies" may, or may not, react with other "tendencies" to produce effects. This does not mean that causes cease to exist. Causes are seen as necessary, but that necessity is not easily identified. This means that realism requires a sophisticated methodology that allows the investigator to postulate "transitive" objects. These are postulated in such a way that their mechanisms can be revealed in order to refine the original postulation; the overall aim being to achieve a correspondence between the "transitive" objects of science and the "intransitive" objects of reality.

The above process has been described in a realist methodology for science (Harré & Secord 1972: 125–47). This consists of empirical studies, whereby critical descriptions of non-random patterns are produced through observation and experiment, together with theoretical studies that aim to produce rational explanations of the non-random patterns in the data. On first glance this does not sound so very different to more traditional methodologies. Nevertheless, what is different are the underlying assumptions about the entities being studied. Some of these might be hypothetical entities and some of these may be candidates for real objects, or processes, in the world. Through a process of critical inquiry, the rest are eliminated.

In a similar fashion, Bhaskar's view of scientific discovery is based upon the identification and description of effects, from which hypothetical mechanisms are postulated that, if they existed, would explain the effect. From this, attempts are then made to demonstrate the existence and the mode in which the mechanism operates via experimental activity and the elimination of alternative plausible explanations. It is important to remember at this point that ontological assumptions about the world drive the process of discovery. As such, while realists are naturalists, they are not reductionists. Therefore, they do not claim that human behaviour can be explained biologically for a mode of explanation that is suitable to social phenomena is required. Despite this, it still follows that social objects can be studied as scientifically as physical objects (Bhaskar 1979: 26).

To admit that forms of explanation must be appropriate to the phenomena under consideration allows for an ontological differentiation between the social and physical sciences. Between these, Bhaskar notes three important differences. First, social structures, unlike natural structures, do not exist independently of the activities that they govern. Secondly, social structures, unlike natural structures, do not exist independently of the agents' conception of what they are doing in their activities and thirdly, social structures, unlike natural structures, may be only relatively enduring (1989: 79). Therefore, social structures only exist by virtue of the activities they govern and cannot be identified independently of them (1989: 78). People are "produced" by the structures and in turn they reproduce structures, or "transform" them. For example, national economies cannot exist independently of people who experience their effects and contribute to them.

From this, we can say that if a substantial proportion of the US population refused to recognize credit cards, or dollar bills, the economy would cease to exist in any recognizable form. As such, social structures are social products that are less enduring than "natural" structures and social systems are more "open" than physical ones. Nevertheless, it is claimed that social objects do have an independent existence of subjects while having real effects on their lives. At the same time, agents are able to act upon (transform) them. That said, the question remains as to whether we can successfully generate the transitive objects that represent aspects of social structures. In other words, how realistic are the methodological maxims of realism? This question also has an epistemological dimension to it.

Marx certainly thought it was possible to generate the transitive objects of realism. For this reason, he is often cited as the first realist social thinker (Keat & Urry 1975: 96). Marx's aim can be said to analyze the dynamics of capitalism in order to expose its underlying mechanisms that, in turn, give rise to particular social relations. To talk of the causes and effects of political economy without identifying the underlying mechanisms is to elaborate a fiction. As Marx says:

> [political economy] explains nothing; it merely pushes the question away into the grey nebulous distance. The economist assumes in the form of a fact, of an event, which he is supposed to deduce – namely the necessary relationship between two things – between, for example, the division of labour and exchange (Marx 1977: 62).

The form of explanation of which Marx complains is the same kind as that offered for the late train in Outhwaite's example; it is taken as fact without the need for further elaboration. Marx maintains that in order to understand the relationship between, say, exchange and the division of labour, it is necessary to understand the historical processes that have led to the current mode of production. Within capitalism, we can only account for the accumulation of capital when we understand the relationship that exists between constant and variable capital. These things are real because they have real effects on people. Capitalists and workers are the prisoners of these mechanisms. Capitalists must continue to accumulate if they are to remain in business. Workers, on the other hand, must sell their labour if they are to continue to live! The underlying mechanisms of political economy have real material consequence for people in their everyday lives. Yet not all of these things are visible. Just as the effects of sub-atomic processes are not visible but require particular procedures to make them known, alienation is a condition not visible to the proletariat and requires a particular class consciousness to make it visible. Despite this, alienation is seen to have real consequences (Marx 1977: 61–74).

Of course, Marx has been declared a realist *post facto*. Though we briefly describe one of the few recent research projects that are self declared as realist, for those who wish to find insights into just how a realist programme can be operationalized in social research, there will be some disappointment. Bhaskar lays out some ground rules for what a realist social science might look like, while Giddens's theory of structuration might be seen as an example of a realist social theory and Willis's *Learning to labour* is sometimes cited as an example of critical realist ethnography (Willis 1977, see also the example from Porter 1993). For Bhaskar, reality consists not only of events that are experienced, but also of events that happen even when they are not experienced. This has implications for the nature of the social scientific endeavour. Methodologically, we are led to an interpretative social science, but one based on what Bhaskar terms "retroduction" (Bhaskar 1979: 15). This is necessary because a full explanation requires us to separate the meaning of an act and its intention. Meaning is social, whereas intention is personal. Social scientists are in the business of discovering social reality and this will have antecedents in individual realities, themselves shaped by social meanings. Retroduction then requires the construction of a hypothetical model that:

> if it were to exist and act in the postulated way would account for the phenomena in question (a movement of thought which may be styled "retroduction"). The reality of the postulated explanation must then, of course, be subjected to empirical scrutiny (Bhaskar 1979: 15. Original italics).

This suggests that the strategy of a realist social science involves not only a description of social relations, but also accompanying explanations and re-descriptions; the overall aim is to uncover layers of social reality.

Giddens's structuration theory rests on the dynamic relationship of the agent with society. This he describes as a "duality of structure" (1976: 121) in which social structures are constituted by human agency, but at the same time are the very medium of this constitution. Therefore, his views are similar to Bhaskar, but he would not accept the dualism of Bhaskar in

RESEARCH EXAMPLE 6
Racism and professionalism in a medical setting

Sam Porter's research (1993) was directly informed by Bhaskar's critical realism. The focus of the study was on, "how racism affects occupational relationships between nurses and doctors, and how its effects are mediated by professional ideology" (Porter 1993: 591).

The theoretical assumption of the study was that human action is both enabled and constrained by social structures, but in turn action will reproduce or transform those structures. Porter argues that racism involves enduring relationships between individuals, thus qualifying as a "structure". Two hypotheses were postulated. First, that the relationships between white health workers and members of racialized minorities would be informed by racism. Secondly, the way in which the racism was expressed would be affected by the occupational situation of the health workers. The study itself took place within a hospital and consisted of observations of interactions between nurses and doctors. It was intended not just to describe the events, but to explain their occurrence.

Six of the 21 doctors were from what Porter describes as racialized minorities. While there was little change in the nature of the balance of power between the "six" doctors and nurses, the latter expressing deference to the former, later "backstage" conversations between the nurses (out of earshot of the doctors) were found, on occasion, to be racist. Why, Porter asks, was this racism not more openly expressed in challenges to the doctors' authority? Citing Bhaskar (1989), he notes that, "the actual outcome of a tendency will generally be co-determined by the activity of other mechanisms" (Porter 1993: 604). In this case, the other mechanism is professionalism. In other words, the structure of racism is being transformed by agents as a result of their being constrained by another structure – that of professionalism. Additionally, the doctors themselves used the strategy of occupational advantage to ensure that "the disempowering effects of racism were minimised" (Porter 1993: 607). The complexity of the relationship between the structures described, and the actions of the nurses and doctors in transforming them, leads Porter to comment on the inadequacy of a causal model based upon constant conjunction. There is no straightforward one-to-one relationship between racism as a structural phenomena and its manifestation. Rather, it is a tendency that is realized under some circumstances, but not others.

which social structure is said to have an existence that is potentially independent of its daily reproduction in everyday social relations. In Giddens's particular ontological focus, society is intentionally produced by agents who draw upon the rules and resources of social structure and, in so doing, their actions have unintended consequences; one of which is to reproduce society. Therefore, with Marx, he agrees that human beings make their own history, but not in the circumstances of their choosing (Giddens 1984). As such, social structures clearly have real consequences for individuals. Moreover, though these consequences are real, the mechanisms that produce them are not necessarily recognized by those experiencing their effects.

Knowing the social world

The emphasis in the first part of this chapter has been on the ontological suppositions underlying research strategies. So far, we have illustrated these through the strategies that ultimately rely upon such assumptions. However, the actual distinctions between the ontological, epistemological and methodological, are hard to sustain. The same is true when one shifts focus towards the epistemological. Here, we will find epistemological assumptions accompanied by existential implications and claims regarding social reality.

The approaches we examine in this section are not exhaustive, but serve as illustrations of philosophical and methodological views that place primary emphasis on the question of how we come to know the world – as opposed to starting from suppositions about what the world is actually like. All of the following belong to, or are informed by, the naturalistic tradition of philosophy. Implicit in all of these are the perennial questions we have found in philosophy: verification, falsification, induction and causality. For each approach it is a question of emphasis. For example, probabilists don't get too concerned about causality, for they would maintain it is not a soluble problem, whereas followers of Popper would claim that falsification renders the problem of induction harmless.

Critical rationalism

This view is usually associated with Popper and has, in its essentials, been described in Chapter 2. Popper's starting point was a desire to provide demarcation criteria between science and non-science. Although, unlike the logical positivists, he did not want to deny the role of metaphysical speculation in science, he did want to establish a more "rigorous" basis for scientific knowledge. Scientific knowledge must be testable. The best knowledge we can attain is that which is able to pass the most rigorous tests available to the researcher. As far as Popper was concerned, the principle of falsification was equally applicable in any area of investigation that called itself science. Clearly, then, the problems identified with this principle will occur equally in both the physical and social sciences.

As we have seen, falsification either collapses into induction, or is simply a very narrow view of science. Indeed, there is a tautology in Popper's idea of science. For claims about the world to be scientific, they must be falsifiable and if they are falsifiable then they are science. The process of falsification is enacted by the scientist who can then decide upon its criteria. It is simply a matter of adopting a convention, or set of conventions, as to what will count as a falsification. Furthermore, in the messy day-to-day business of science, or social science, test situations are enormously complex. In the latter, in particular, it is hard to conceive of any test situation as simple as "all swans are white", for example. In addition, scientists and for that matter social scientists, do not abandon a theory because of one disconfirming instance. Usually, modifications to the theory are made in the light of new findings and although this is "forbidden" by Popper's methodology, the history of science tells us otherwise.

Imre Lakatos (1970), although working within the Popperian tradition, recognized the tenacity with which scientists hang on to the key elements of their theories. He offers a conception of the growth of knowledge that might be described as midway between Popper and Bhaskar. He proposes, under what he calls "research programmes", that what actually happens is that researchers hang on to a "hard core" of theories that are not open to refutation. Around the hard core is a protective belt of auxiliary hypotheses, that are falsified and rejected, or modified (see Lakatos 1970: 131–7). Research programmes are then assessed on the basis of how productive they have been. If they continue to make novel predictions, they are maintained. Alternatively, if they do not live up to expectations, they are said to be degenerative and are abandoned by scientists. On

RESEARCH EXAMPLE 7
The Frankfurt School as a research programme

There are few examples in social science of the kind of research pro-grammes as described by Imre Lakatos in physics. One approximation, perhaps, is that of the Frankfurt School of social research during the 1930s and 1940s. The Frankfurt School was very eclectic in both its areas of interest and the style of its members. It could be said to include the psychoanalytic work of Erich Fromm, to some extent the literary criticism of Walter Benjamin, as well as the sociology and philosophy of Theodor Adorno, Herbert Marcuse and Max Horkheimer (Honneth 1993). Yet, in Lakatosian terms, it was defined by a hard core of theory. Though strongly influenced by Marxism, it was held that capitalism had succeeded in overcoming a number of contradictions and the working class had been incorporated into its dominant cultural and material mechanisms. Despite this pessimism, the School was moti-vated by a desire for political and social emancipation. In one form or another, these assumptions motivated its members:

> although there were marked differences in the way Horkheimer and the others conceived the political implica-tions of their work most of the Institute's members hoped that their cumulative efforts would contribute to the making of his-tory with will and consciousness. They intended their findings to become a material force in the struggle against domination in all its forms (Held 1990: 35).

However, implicit in Lakatos is at least the spirit of Popperian falsifica-tion, if not its substance. Whether or not falsification should inform our research was, as we will note in Chapter 5, at the heart of the debate between Popper and Adorno. In the Frankfurt School the hard core might be said to have withered away as history unfolded, rather than being systematically, or decisively, refuted. Indeed, though critical theory lives on in the work of Habermas and others, it is doubtful if enough of the "hard core" remains for it to qualify as the same research programme.

occasion, discoveries of great magnitude will serve to damage even the "hard core". More usually, however, the programmes will wither and die.

As a means of describing what happens in science, or for that matter social science, "research programmes" may have some merit; although we should note that Lakatos was mostly concerned with physics. Marxism and psychoanalysis, for example, both condemned by Popper as unscientific because their central propositions were not falsifiable, can be seen to have a hard core of theory. In the first case, these can be seen as the central propositions of historical materialism. In the second, the role of unconscious processes as the underlying motivations of behaviour (in this sense Freud may be characterized as a realist). While a challenge to the "hard core" is not permissible, hypotheses within the two traditions are challengeable.

Operationalism

In critical rationalism, emphasis is upon the status of theories. In the case of Popper, each of these is falsifiable, whereas for Lakatos science is constituted by interlocking theories, some of which are challengeable and others are not. One of the difficulties, particularly in the social sciences, is that of definition. Even if we could think of critical tests of social scientific theories, we first would have to agree on what it is those theories describe. The difficulty, for example, of devising a test for class would lie in coming up with an adequate definition of class in the first instance. Different definitions would lead to different tests, some of which may falsify the theory, while others might not.

These definitional difficulties and their proposed solution underlie the aims of operationalism. Operationalists place emphasis back onto verification and observation by saying that, "every bona fide scientific concept must be linked to instrumental procedures that determine its values" (Losee 1980: 175). For example, what counts as temperature is the measurement of it and what counts as class is what we use to measure it. This was a view, within social science, originally associated with the American sociologist George Lundberg (Blalock & Blalock 1971: 8). He maintained that sociologists are mistaken in believing measurement can only be carried out after things are appropriately defined; for instance, the idea that we must have a workable definition of alienation before we can measure it. The difficulty in producing definitions of concepts such as alienation has discouraged researchers from even attempting to measure them. Lundberg insisted that definition comes about through measurement, "A space is that which is measured by a ruler; time *is* that which is measured by a clock." (Lundberg quoted in Abrahamson 1981: 256. Original italics). In this view, alienation would consist of measurable variables.

Lundberg illustrated this view by examining the notion of "values". He argued that values can be inferred from people's behaviour; they are empirically observable. Thus, if people attempt to obtain more of a thing – power, wealth, etc. – then that is because they value it. Therefore, the extent to which they have values can be known through an examination of the extent to which particular things are valued. Do people value X? If so, how much do they value X?

The methodological difficulty here lies in how we translate concepts, such as alienation, or values, etc. into operational indicators. Paul Lazarsfeld described a four stage process towards this end (Abrahamson 1981: 257). A researcher begins with a vague concept. The concept is then further refined and specified in terms of components or dimensions. Next, indicators for each dimension are specified and these stand in for a probabilistic relationship to the concept. Finally, the researcher should formulate indices from the observed relationships among the indicators.

Offered as a methodology in its own right (Blalock & Blalock 1971), operationalism is very much associated with the positivistic tradition in social science. Its ontological premises are diametrically opposed to realism. Realists, in particular Rom Harré (1972), have criticized the "operationalist" aspect of positivism for its inability to recognize entities other than those that are observable. The credo of operationalism may be summed up as, "if you can't measure it, it doesn't exist". Operationalism is fundamentally empiricist. At the very least, it leads to a division of labour between the task of theory construction and measurement, with those involved in the latter reducing theories to concepts in order to operationalize them; the defence being that in empirical research, operational definitions are unavoidable. In order to measure the amount of X, or to postulate its relationship to Y, it is necessary to define X and Y (Bryman 1988: 22–3). Power, alienation, class and poverty will remain theoretical entities, with each just as good as the last, unless they can be translated into testable propositions.

The social scientist faces three difficulties in following an operationalist programme of research. First, there is a problem that is shared with the physical sciences, which is best described in the form of a question: how do we know the testable propositions fully operationalize the theory? For example, if our theory is that the domestic division of labour is becoming more equitable between women and men, how can we know that questions about household tasks, or attitudes towards them, fully represent the theory? If the theory is about equity, do such questions form a suitable measurement? Secondly, as the phenomenologists have claimed, just how meaningful are our theories to those we research? Social scientists struggle to understand the concepts and ideas of the social world and convert them into sociological theories. However, there is a "slippage" between the discourse of sociology and that of the social world, which Giddens (1976) seeks to encapsulate in the idea of the "double hermeneutic". The solution to this difficulty lies in a hermeneutic approach to social research, whereby to understand a particular social group it is necessary to employ the same techniques to know that group as members of that society. Operationalism does not so much solve the question as side-step it. Finally, we should note that "there might be as many concepts of, say temperature, as there are methods of measurement" (Tudor 1982: 59). Indeed, there are several – fahrenheit, celsius and kelvin. For the social scientist,

---

RESEARCH EXAMPLE 8
Studying homelessness

In recent years, homelessness has become a major social problem for Western governments (Hutson & Liddiard 1994). One of the difficulties arises, however, in defining what is meant by homelessness. This can range from the very narrow definition of literally sleeping "rough" to a complex description such as that devised by Glen Bramley (1988). However, researchers must opt for one or other definition and by opting for that definition, they then set the parameters of "homelessness". In some studies, notably by Anderson et al. (1993), this definition was established by defining all those who were clients of hostels, those who were sleeping rough and attending day centres and users of soup runs, as "homeless". In other studies, such as that of Fisher et al. (1994), the definition is achieved by the adoption of categories in local official statistics. Operational definitions thus appear unavoidable. Nevertheless, the process of definition can be said to "create" what shall count as "homeless".

---

this task is complicated by the degree of definitional disagreement.

Ironically, the latter point could be taken up by advocates of operationalism as evidence for its inevitability. Researchers must operationalize concepts in particular ways, where there is little agreement as to the form this should take in specific instances. While physical scientists may wrestle with three different definitions of temperature, there is no operational debate of the type or scale of that in social science around, for example, absolute versus relative poverty (Townsend 1979). Nevertheless, if research on poverty is to take place, researchers must define what they are to mean by poverty within a given study. In quantitative research this will take the form of a close specification of the meaning of a concept and although in some qualitative approaches this specification may be subject to modification, or be less specific in the first instance, it is still present.

Probability

Each of the above approaches are testament to the obsession in science with the pursuit of truth; mostly defined in terms of a correspondence with reality. Though in operationalism the reality becomes that which is measurable, the march towards truth is at least implicit. Probabilistic approaches also seek a correspondence with reality, but it suffices that this correspondence is "probably", rather than absolutely, true. Probability, because it relies on induction, can be seen as the opposite to critical rationalism. Quite simply, the probability of X being true is derived from the fact that X was true in the past, or put another way, the probability of a characteristic existing in a given population is derived from the fact of it existing in a large enough sample of the population.

We have noted the difficulties that this approach entails; in particular, that the prior probability of any generalization is zero (see Newton Smith 1981: 49). Yet probability, in the form of inferential statistics, has played a central role in the social sciences. It is often held that an antidote to the more "open" nature of systems in the social world is to assign probabilities to an event occurring. The problem with open systems, it will be recalled, is that of linking causes with effects. In contrast, inference in social science rests upon association between events. Thus, it is not claimed that unemployment causes poverty, but that unemployment is associated with poverty. In other words, if instances I are taken to be representative of a population P and in this sample "poverty" and

RESEARCH EXAMPLE 9
Probability

1 – Sampling

A fairly straightforward example of how probability is used in research can be found in survey sampling. One of the commonest forms of sampling in quantitative research is that of the "random" or "probability" sample. Most large scale surveys, such as those commissioned by government (other than censuses), rely on some form of probability sampling. Rarely do researchers study a whole population, but instead require a sample that is "representative" of the population. A probability sample accords to each person in the population the same probability of being selected. The size of the sample proportionate to the population will determine its accuracy. In a sample size of 10,000, we might expect a sampling error of 1%, whereas in a sample of 100 this could be as high as 10% – assuming a 95% confidence interval (i.e. we are 95% confident that the results we get from the population will be the same as the sample plus or minus the sampling error (DeVaus 1991). The strategy is inductive and depends on the sample sufficiently resembling the population. The "sufficient resemblance" therefore takes the form of the probability we attach to the sample being accurate.

2 – The survey

Probability in surveys will often take the form of the likelihood of an association between two variables occurring by chance. A null hypothesis is adopted that two variables are not related and that this occurred by chance. The statistical significance of the finding is then determined by using a test such as chi-square. The chi-square test allows: "the researcher to ascertain the probability that the observed relationship between the two variables may have arisen by chance" (Bryman & Cramer 1990: 158). The null hypothesis is expressed as the expected frequency of something happening and this is compared with the actual observed frequency. The larger the latter, in comparison with the former, the larger the chi-square statistic and the greater the likelihood that the finding is statistically significant.

"unemployment" are associated and the strength of that association can be established, then it is inferred that such a relationship will exist in P.

Probability appears to entail incompleteness, or even randomness. We do not know if X causes Y – the chain of causality may be much less direct. However, we can say that they are associated. It follows that if we knew more about the X – Y relationship, the less would be the need to make statistical inferences (Sayer 1984: 174). This, in turn, begs the question of how we assign probabilities. The manner of assignment must depend ultimately not on definition, but ignorance. The more we know about the X–Y relationship, the better we will become in predicting outcomes. Of course, this is exactly what one wishes to achieve, but it remains that in terms of knowledge claims, statistical inference will remain a substitute for something better.

The kind of probability we describe here is objective probability. In this there is the assumption that, "a hypothesis or other proposition descriptive of the world has either a logical probability or a propensity of being true, or a relative frequency of truth" (Hesse 1974: 105). In other words, a toss of a coin entails only two possibilities: that it will fall heads, or it will fall tails. When there are more than two possibilities and it is known what these are, then it is possible to talk of the propensity of one possibility, or another being true. The relative frequency of truth of past events can lead us to assign probabilities to future ones. This kind of probability, however, takes place in a closed system. Given n number of throws of two dice, it would be possible to elaborate all of the possible combinations that could ensue, though you could not know *a priori* which of these would be the actual combinations thrown.

The world is not like a die. As we have often remarked, it is "open" in character. This is reflected in another form of probability called "personalist" or "subjectivist". This often takes the form of "Bayesian theories" of probability. Thomas Bayes was an eighteenth century English cleric. He devised a theorem that was a statistical expression that describes the effect of some new evidence on the degree of probability of a hypothesis that had been allocated a previous probability on the basis of old evidence (Howson & Urbach 1989: 26). Bayes's theorem is a form of personalist probability theory; it is essentially subjectivist in the assignment of probabilities. The philosophical claim is that human beings assign probabilities to events occurring and change these in the light of new evidence. In this way we learn from our environment. When we walk under ladders, we assign probabilities to the paint not being dropped on our head and as we collect new evidence, we change the assignment of our probabilities.

The principal difficulty of Bayes's theorem is that it depends on how probabilities are assigned *a priori*. We can say that (a) new supporting evidence relates directly to the probability of original hypothesis *h* by making it more likely; (b) the new evidence is in itself more likely given its agreement with the old and (c) the new evidence will increase the probability of *h* if it was not anticipated, but if it could have been anticipated without *h*, then it will decrease it. Therefore, personalist probability measures degrees of belief in an event being true. It can be said to rest on the assumption that no rational person would accept betting odds on the assumption that they will lose. Clearly, you would not back a horse that you knew had no chance of winning a race. Similarly, you would not put to sea in a leaky boat. However, suppose you are being chased by a mad axeman and you reach a river where two possibilities present themselves. Either you fight it out, or you try to cross the river in a leaky boat. You will weigh the odds and assign a probability to your chances of success in each course of action. Suppose you then found the boat also contained a bucket for baling out. This changes the odds in favour of taking to the water. Nevertheless, suppose, further, that you find a suitably heavy branch that might be used in your defence. The odds now change again.

It is on the basis of the accretion of new evidence changing probabilities that advocates of a Bayesian approach say hypotheses are amended. Hypotheses are rarely shown to be conclusively true or false – depending on whether you are a verificationist or a falsificationist – but we do alter our degrees of belief about the relative frequency of events occurring and this, in turn, will change our views about the hypothesis. Thus, notwithstanding the difficulties in operationalizing the concept of homelessness, if in a given set of circumstances we observe only 12 cases of homelessness when 50 were expected, we do not say that an original hypothesis about there being homelessness is falsified, but we might say the odds of someone being homeless in these circumstances is less than we thought.

Despite these insights, an important difficulty remains with Bayesian probability. Although from an intuitive point of view we might accept that we subjectively calculate the probability of an event occurring, it is hard to translate that into prior possibilities, or degrees of belief, that have some comparative value. If these "priors" cannot be successfully assigned, then, of course, the effect of new evidence cannot be shown either. Bayes' theorem as an expression of the relationship between statistical terms is uncontroversial, but its operationalization is highly problematic.

For this reason, it is sometimes described as working back from an effect to a cause. This can be illustrated by a simple example.

If a group of people are defined as living in poverty and we wish to establish causes, working back to redundancy, or reduction in salary at particular points in their working life, would increase our confidence in the belief that we were closer to establishing causal relations. However, suppose that we discovered that this group had won the lottery. On the face of it, this would be much less likely to be a cause of poverty (it could of course have indirectly contributed, but it would not be an obvious candidate). Yet we can think of these putative causes as being part of a "network" of events, in which each event is strongly linked, or weakly linked, to the others. In this sense, poverty would be unlikely to be directly caused by redundancy, though the relationship between these two states is likely to be a strong one. From this we can note two points with regard to probability. First, the probability of links between some terms may actually be zero. Secondly, the strength of the link may depend on the direction one "moves" in the network (Law & Lodge 1984: 56–7). In relation to the first point, Law & Lodge give an example in zoology whereby there is a zero chance of fishes breathing air, or being warm blooded. In terms of the second, again employing their zoological example, it is certain that a mammal will be an animal, but we would need to assign a probability to an animal being a mammal.

Network theory

Probability theory intersects with what has become known as "network theory". In the above examples, concepts, it is maintained, are linked by the probability of one causing another, or in Law & Lodge's zoological example, by virtue of their relationship within classes, or between classes. Exponents of network theory hold that the same may be said of theories, the language we use to describe them, or any other concept in the world.

It will be remembered that one criticism of naïve falsification was the idea that a theory could be falsified by one discomfirming instance. Naïve falsification would appear to propose a world in which the theory and its test somehow exist without linguistic, conceptual or logical connections to any other part of the world. The French philosopher Pierre Duhem and the American logician W.V. Quine both advanced arguments about the holistic nature of theories. What is now known as the Duhem–Quine thesis, holds that scientific theories form an interconnected web. From this, it follows that any claim to have falsified a theory has implications for the rest of the web, or network. As Quine put it, "our statements about the external world face the tribunal of sense experience not individually but only as a corporate body" (1953: 41).

From these insights we are left with a question: how can we be sure that it is the particular theory that is falsified and not the background or auxiliary hypotheses that the theory entailed? If, for example, we find that in a given society the direction and rate of mobility between classes was different to that envisaged by our theory, it may not be the specific theory that is wrong, but our background assumptions of what constitutes mobility in the first instance! Conversely, our negative findings may have implications for the assumptions we have about how our measuring instruments actually behave. At this point, it is important to note that the Duhem–Quine thesis is predicated on the view that theories are simply heuristic devices that help us to describe the world. In this sense, they are linguistic in content in that they do not refer to the "real" structures existing in the world. For Quine, it follows from this that single sentences in themselves have no meaning, but acquire meaning only in relation to other sentences. Rather like Wittgenstein, this leads him to the view that sentences can have many meanings and that context is all.

The implications of the "network" view are important to both the physical and social sciences. The most radical interpretations come from the ethnomethodologists and the sociologists of science. Steve Woolgar (1988), for example, argues that the existence and characteristics of objects will be determined by the *social* network within which they are defined. Thus, scientific theories are not simply social products with a discrete existence, but social products with complex and possibly diverse origins within the network. Because the social network is linguistic in its nature, theories, or descriptions, are practical expressions of phenomena that recreate and establish anew the phenomenon itself (Woolgar 1988: 73). The conclusion, of course, is profoundly anti-realist and relativistic. The objects that theories describe exist only by virtue of the theories themselves existing and they are constructions of the social network. For this reason they can only be said to be true within the context of the network itself without reference to any "exterior" set of conditions. From this vantage point, we appear to have travelled from a correspondence to a congruence theory of truth as characteristic of the actual practice of science.

The relatedness of phenomena is so obvious that it seems hard to

---

RESEARCH EXAMPLE 10
Identity and networks
in small scale enterprises in Mexico

Gerard Verschoor (1992) has conducted ethnographic research on the proliferation of small scale business enterprises in Latin America. He describes the relationships that exist between the network of, "friends, patrons, clients, compadres, transport operators or politico administrative authorities" (Verschoor 1992: 184–5). In particular, the *tratada* networks are a diverse range of actors participating in a "deal" to purchase and subsequently resell a commodity outside of the network. He summarizes the complexity of the *tratada*

> the individual in question . . . makes a reasonable offer and pays cash for the good. Simultaneously word is spread informally about the characteristics of the commodity, and the possible amount of money that has to be put down for it. Meanwhile the item is sold . . . for a slightly higher price to someone else in the network. The second buyer never pays the full amount in cash: it is only a *trato* (deal). The new owner then speedily makes a deal with another member of the network and so on. This goes on until someone from outside of the *tratada* network gets wind of it and pays cash (Verschoor 1992: 184–5).

Thus, for the researcher to understand the causal patterns in small scale economic enterprises of this kind, a knowledge of the diversity and complexity of the networks is required. He rejects what he calls the "totatalizing discourses" of the determinist and reductionist assumptions on small scale enterprises. Such discourses, it is maintained, reify the assumptions of economism and evolutionary necessity within a modernizing society. The argument is that single mono-causal theories produce inadequate understandings of the strength and direction of relationships within the networks.

---

conceive of a philosophy of science, or social science, that would ignore its implications. Indeed, Woolgar's talk of "networks" in science is not radical enough, implying that the networks themselves are discrete. Quine's conclusion and it is one hard to avoid, is that the "unit of empirical significance is the whole of science [or social science!]" (quoted in Harding 1976: xi). Nevertheless, it does not follow from this point that any decision, or view about a proposition, is as good as any other, or that we cannot focus on one part of the world and learn of its characteristics. All theories entail presuppositions and these presuppositions may or may not be affected by what happens to a theory. As Alan Ryan notes, it is quite one thing to say that the facts of any case involve some presuppositions (thus implying a connectedness with other parts of a network) and quite another to say this prevents us from deciding between two theories (1970: 236). While the falsification, or indeed conclusive verification, of a complex theory is difficult, or even impossible, it should not blind us to the possibility of being right, or wrong, about the world at a much simpler level.

Pragmatism

In the journey from "objective probability" across to network theory, there has been an important shift in what can count as "truth". We have moved from a correspondence theory of truth over to one of pragmatism. Truth is not fixed or immutable, but is something that happens to an idea itself, not the objects to which it refers. Thus, Quine's "web" of theories is informed by a pragmatic view of truth. For this reason we need to consider the idea of pragmatism as a strategy for knowing the social world.

Pragmatism stems from, and might be said to be reducible to, a view of truth. It has been viewed as a radical form of empiricism (Russell 1955). Such was the reaction to its ideas that Emile Durkheim perceived in its formulations an attack on the rationalist tradition and the possibility of discovering the "truth" (Durkheim 1983: 1). These ideas may be found in the work of three American thinkers: Charles Peirce (1839–1914), William James (1842–1910) and John Dewey (1859–1952):

> the basic idea of pragmatism, namely that it is actions rather than consciousness which are the foundations of thought, was developed in the 1870s by a group of young thinkers in Cambridge, Massachusetts, and was first publicly voiced by Charles Peirce in 1878 (Joas 1993: 95).

The influence of these ideas on social science has been and continues to be, very important, informing, via the work of George Herbert Mead (1863–1931), the development of Chicago School sociology and the tradition known as symbolic interactionism, as well as the work of the German philosopher and social theorist Jürgen Habermas (see May 1996). Another intellectual line may be traced to the work of the contemporary American philosopher Richard Rorty who, in turn, has influenced what has become known as anti-foundationalist views (see Chapter 7).

Peirce's epistemological starting point was the subject–object dichotomy in social and philosophical thought. Thus far, this has manifested itself as the idea that either reality is mind-dependent, or that the mind itself simply discovers an order that is already present in reality. Peirce's position is a rejection of the subject–object dichotomy and of an epistemology based solely on reason, or solely on experience. Although we do rely on our senses for an apprehension of the world, we are also creatures of habit who live in communities. To this extent, we need to adapt to the world, but at the same time produce meanings that orientate our conduct towards that world. Therefore, although we cannot be absolutely sure of our knowledge, we do not doubt it all simultaneously. What we are seeing here is a displacement of the relationship between thought and reality and how truthfully one may represent the other, to view thinking as a social, not solitary act, that takes place within a "community of others".

Rather like Lakatos, a generation after him, Peirce is describing a "core" of knowledge that is amended, but rarely refuted as a body of ideas. Unlike Lakatos and more like Duhem or Quine, he is describing a "web" of knowledge within a community. This community of, say, scientific inquiries, pursues an ideal, but it is one that they will never reach. That ideal is truth. Its pursuit requires honesty, integrity and self-discipline that has not only an intellectual, but also moral content. In this sense meaning is as important as truth. However, William James became more concerned with the psychological process of knowledge production. For him, "self correction" might be seen in an idealist sense of experience as a product of the mind's structuring activity. This psychologism takes him a step further to end up insisting upon the function of thought in scientific discovery being to satisfy its indigenous needs and interests. It is this that leads him to his controversial view of truth as instrumentalism which states that, "knowledge should be judged as more or less 'useful' rather than as true or false" (Sayer 1992: 70). In response, Peirce was to call his latter work "pragmaticism" in order to differentiate it from such formulations.

We are left with an understanding of how people and societies construct truth from a pragmatic viewpoint. Of course, in terms of our chapter division, pragmatism is both a strategy and a perspective. For instance, Mead talks of a stone as having a number of objective perspectives that depend upon its social use, or how it is viewed, that will, in turn, have a strategic component to it. A stone becomes a chemical, thermal, gravitational, visual system as well as perhaps being an object of play for a child (Hammersley 1989: 60). Similarly, the pragmatism of W. I. Thomas, though not the end of this intellectual journey, is certainly an important part of this tradition. However, Thomas's perspective was that of a realist who held that the world is experienced as a reality by those who comprise it, but who maintained a separation between the subjective nature of social experience and the objectivity of science. His methodological writings thus reflect both a subjective and objective view of the social world (see Thomas & Znaniecki 1958).

Summary

In this chapter we have been driven by the aim of clarifying what are a series of complicated views on the nature of social reality and the most appropriate strategies for coming to know that reality. To the first set of questions we appear to be left with idealism and materialism or a synthesis of the two, as represented by realism. The world is either taken to be a product of the mind and the meanings that people attach to their social circumstances or, alternatively, it is their social circumstances that structure the mind. Each of these positions finds itself buried deep within, but exemplified by, different perspectives on the social world that, in their turn, inform the programme of social investigation that each undertakes. Thus, ethnomethodology is concerned to render explicit the methods through which people construct social reality. Add to its phenomenological lineage the insight of ordinary language philosophy and we find that the social world may be treated as a series of language games that are inextricably linked to a social context. This, in its turn, opens up the possibility for the study of everyday conversations in order to reveal their reality producing properties. In this case, we travel from philosophy to methodology to method, ending up in an empiricist programme of investigation.

We also found an ontological realism that, contrary to idealism, asserts the existence of social structures independently of our perception of them and at the same time views such structures as ultimately dependent upon their reproduction in human actions. To this extent we should not confuse action and consciousness, as if the latter has some prior existence to the former. Actions may be informed by, but also produce, consciousness. Furthermore, our actions may not have the outcomes that we intended. It is for this reason that Anthony Giddens speaks of the unintended consequences of social action. In drawing upon the rules and resources that exist within society, we both produce, and reproduce, society. This is not an idealist formulation, but one that seeks to take account of the durability of social institutions across time. Material relations thus become of consequence in his ontological focus upon human being and doing in everyday life.

Our division certainly began to break down when we came to consider, in the second part of this chapter, the epistemological underpinnings and methodological strategies for knowing the social world. Here, our old friend the dualism in social thought comes to plague us once more. On this occasion, however, it is in the form of nominalism versus realism. For our purposes we can say that the former refers to the view that there is no arbitrator to the meanings of a concept, theory of word, etc. that unambiguously lies within an "external" world. The latter, on the other hand, holds to a modified correspondence theory of truth through its fusion of the theoretical and empirical. Empiricism is not sufficient in itself for there are underlying relations within society that are not amenable to simple observations. If this were the case, then what is the point of science? Therefore, and this is where we link directly into our discussion in the first part of this chapter, we require theoretical concepts that penetrate a given reality in order to reveal its underlying properties. This strategy necessitates a fusion of the perspectives of critical rationalism and empirical, but not empiricist, work.

In this second section we also found some sophisticated versions of the actual strategies that characterize science at work: from probability to network theory through to pragmatism, all perspectives having strategic consequences. Probability, as discussed, rests upon induction that, from the point of view of Popper's critical rationalism, is not an adequate form of science. However, it does have pragmatic connotations insofar as it can be viewed as a systematic attempt to apply those very principles that are used in everyday life.

Questions are thus begged as to the neat distinction that may be made between science and non-science. If the former is characterized as being more systematic in its formulations, then the manner in which it actually conducts itself is of primary interest. Here, network theory brings a social aspect to its practice by seeing concepts, theories and ideas as part of an overall framework. The idea that the concept–indicator link is adequately dealt with through operationalism is problematic according to this idea. It may not be our theories, of which concepts and indicators are a part, that are proved to be wrong, but the very foundations upon which our ideas are based. Yet, according to the Duhem–Quine thesis, these are only self-referential. In other words, once again, this contains the Wittgensteinian position that the correspondence theory of reality is no final arbitrator and in the hands of those such as Steve Woolgar, it is the social network that is responsible for concept formation, testing and the dissemination of results. Science, therefore, is a social phenomenon whose justifications do not reside in its appeal to accurately represent an object world separate from its practice, but whose practitioners appear as judge, jury, defence and prosecution.

Finally, the tradition of pragmatism represented a search for truth within a community of like-minded others, as well as the need for meaning in human affairs. To this extent the idea of objectivity, defined as a value-free scientific practice based upon universal principles of rational inquiry, is rendered problematic. Truth is an ideal that, for Peirce, was an orientating principle for scientists and one which they pursue, but will never attain. This opens up the whole question of the relationship between values and scientific practice. Can science free itself of value content? Aside from the technical issues that this question poses, there are also moral components. For example, is it desirable that science should be distinct from values? Traditional views have held onto the possibility of objectivity as defined in this manner. However, there are those who would regard a science in the service of human betterment as necessarily being informed by values. Therefore, we now turn our attention to this important issues in scientific practice.

Questions for discussion

1. Is it possible for explanations to be adequate at the level of cause and meaning?

2. Can we "know" other minds? To what extent is social research dependent upon our ability to do so?
3. To what extent can it be said that all social research is a form of operationalism?
4. What is the relationship between "truth" and social research?

Suggested reading

Blaikie, N. 1994. *Approaches to social enquiry*. Cambridge: Polity.
Bohman, J. 1991. *New philosophy of social science*. Cambridge: Polity.
Bryman, A. 1988. *Quantity and quality in social research*. London: Unwin Hyman.
Law, J. & P. Lodge 1984. *Science for social scientists*. London: Macmillan.
Outhwaite, W. 1987. *New philosophies of social science: realism, hermeneutics and critical theory*. New York: St. Martin's Press.

CHAPTER 5

Objectivity and values in social research

It is often claimed that the social sciences are value laden, that unlike their physical counterparts, their starting point is both subjective and normative. This claim is not a simple one, nor is it universally accepted. The result is a large body of literature on the question of values in social science. Because so much has been written on this topic, this chapter is necessarily selective. Our aim is to provide an overview of the debate and to show how the position one then takes will inform our assumptions about what research can achieve.

There are three questions that will inform our discussion. First, can, or should, social research be value free? Secondly, is social research able to distinguish facts from values? Thirdly, although value freedom implies objectivity, the reverse may not be the case. Therefore, is it possible to be objective about the social world but, nevertheless, pursue such objectivity from a value-oriented position? Clearly, an answer to this last question is related to the position adopted towards the first.

Many early social scientists, such as Mill and Durkheim, maintained that if the social sciences were to become true sciences then they must aspire to the value freedom exemplified by the physical sciences; the assumption being that the physical sciences were value free. That the physical sciences were value free was held without question. Their very method of detached observation and hypothesis testing, underwritten by the canons of formal logic, were presumed to be its guarantee. What Mill called the moral sciences were seen as value laden, but this was simply a mark of their immaturity, as opposed to the nature of their practice and subject matter. Mill's view on this was influential:

the principal reason why the moral had lagged behind the natural sciences was not that men's thoughts and feelings and motives in any way escaped the rule of [scientific] law, but that the ultimate laws which they obeyed were excessively remote from their concrete instances (Ayer 1987: 10).

Thus, once we are able to uncover the mechanisms of human consciousness, it should be possible to reduce values to law-determined facts. Indeed, the laws of physics were often cited as exemplars of the domain of facts. Mill's claim is a "strong one" and one that is not often articulated today. In essence, it was that facts and values are separate and that social science possessed the capacity to demarcate between them.

This kind of reductionist claim about values gave rise to two criticisms. First, values might be said to constitute the very subject matter of the social sciences. Values are what social science studies, and any research programme that attempts to eradicate the language and concept of value, would produce a pointless and sterile discipline. The proponents of this view have often been prepared to "render unto Caesar", thereby allowing "facts" to be the appropriate foci of the physical sciences.

The criticisms of a second group are more radical in their implications. Here it is held that what are referred to as "facts", in both the social and physical sciences, are always subject to revision. Indeed, as many in the "post Kuhnian generation" of philosophers have shown, such "facts" were not just straightforward representations of reality, but (at least partly) were the product of a theoretical viewpoint. Within a generation of Mill, the "immutable" laws of Newtonian physics were to be fundamentally challenged by the findings of Einstein, Bohr and others. Yet even those who contend that facts always turn out to be values, often draw a distinction between values that are merely neutral descriptions and ethical, or normative values such as might be expressed through political programmes (cf. Popper 1986a: 193–6). The opposite view is also held, such that all values are ultimately based on a subjective perception of the world and there is no clear distinction to be made between facts and values. However, for the purposes of clarifying exactly what we are talking about, it would be helpful to understand these two terms in more depth.

Fact and values

In philosophy it is often said that facts correspond to "is" statements, whereas values correspond to "ought" statements. In other words, to state a fact is to describe the way something is. Ought statements ascribe a value to something, or prescribe how someone should act. For example, if we know the following to be true we can say it is a fact (an "is" statement): "Garfield has three houses, six cars and £2 million in the bank." On the other hand "Garfield is a miser" can be seen as an "ought" statement. On the face of it, this all seems quite straightforward. However, what of the statement, "Garfield is rich." Leaving aside the possibility that we have made a mistake, the first statement appears to be a statement of fact. Conversely, the second statement is a matter of opinion. Garfield might well dispute the appellation "miser", whereas relatives and friends disappointed by his lack of munificence may well view him in this way.

The distinction between "is" and "ought" seems to pose few problems in characterizing the first two statements. Yet what of the description "rich"? At first sight, it appears to be a factual description of a person. When we describe Garfield as rich we may be prepared to be challenged on a number of grounds: for example, we have confused Garfield with another person, or that he recently lost all his money in an unwise investment. Yet we do not usually expect a challenge on a point of view. Likewise, when we describe someone as "short" or "tall" we intend a factual description. Yet each is a relative. In some societies to own just a few head of livestock would qualify someone to be described as rich. In Western societies, on the other hand, such a person may well be regarded as relatively poor.

Does the above make "rich", "fat", "short", or "tall", a series of nonfactual descriptions? We certainly use them without intending to impute value. If we describe someone as "tall", this is a factual statement equal to describing someone as having two arms and two legs. The plot then thickens in terms of using the vocabulary of value to describe factual things. If one painting is described as being of more value than another, this may be verifiable in monetary terms. However, what of the aesthetic dimension to a painting that may not be reflected in its price? The term "value" may therefore be used in different ways.

In terms of the different uses of the word "values" Nagel (1961) suggests a distinction between characterizing and appraising value judgements. He demonstrates this distinction with an example from biology.

The term "anaemia" is meant to indicate a situation where an animal has less than the "normal" number of red corpuscles present in its blood. This cannot be precisely defined because what is normal depends not only on the individual member of a species, but the state of its health at a given time. Thus:

> to decide whether a given animal is anaemic, an investigator must judge whether the available evidence warrants the conclusion that the specimen is anaemic (Nagel 1961: 492).

For this reason:

> When the investigator reaches a conclusion, he can therefore be said to be making a "value judgement", in the sense that he has in mind some standardised type of physiological condition designated as "anaemia" and that he assesses what he knows about his specimen with the measure provided by the assumed standard (1961: 492).

This is described as a "characterizing" value judgement that is then compared with an "appraising value judgement". When employing this form of judgement an investigator decides that, "since an animal has diminished powers of maintaining itself, anaemia is an undesirable condition" (1961: 492).

Nagel's distinction appears to rest on the difference between a description and an opinion. From this point of view it is another way of formulating the is–ought distinction. Though the reformulation may have some merit, it is not without its difficulties. The language of social science, as Nagel himself notes, is replete with value terms such as "cruel", "mercenary", "kindly", "truthful" (1961: 494). However, he regards these as equivalent to descriptions such as "inaccurate", "inefficient", or "unstable" in the physical sciences. Is this the case? In describing a pump as inefficient the engineer has recourse to an agreed specification of efficiency for a given pump. If, on the other hand, a social scientist described the workforce of a factory as inefficient, it is unlikely that there would be agreement over such a characterization. Individual workers, trade unions and management may all possess differing views on the matter. In other words, there is a larger measure of intersubjective agreement that seems to be available with regard to descriptions in the physical sciences. It may

110

well be that the social scientist, in our example, thinks she is making a characterizing judgement, but if significant numbers of other people see it as an appraising judgement, then there is clearly something wrong with this distinction. After all, it is open to anyone who wishes to describe another as wicked, stupid or ugly to claim that their judgement is a characterizing, not an appraising one.

This problem is also apparent for those who wish to produce a fact–value demarcation on the basis of scientific testability (for example, see Hempel 1965). A statement such as "this beer is better than that beer" is untestable, because what is "better" is a matter of individual taste. As such, it is a value. However, "this beer has a higher specific gravity than that beer" is a testable proposition; the problem is that the criterion of testability is more likely to hold for the physical sciences than for the social sciences.

Karl Popper's definition of facts may be one way around this difficulty. Facts, he suggests, are, "something like a common product of language and reality" (1989: 214). Those things that we hold to be true and hence beyond dispute, will ultimately depend upon the relationship between language and reality holding. Thus "specific gravity" is more easily defended as a fact simply because the agreement between language and reality is more likely to hold – or does it? Quite simply, our perceptions of reality change across time and cultures. Facts are "theory impregnated". What we see as factual is a product of our theories and an agreement between them and reality itself. The history of science, however, is replete with changing theories that alter the ways in which we "see" reality. This, in turn, leads to new theories. Everyday description is also subject to revision. Our first description of Garfield's wealth may have been wrong because it changed between the point at which we accumulated our knowledge and the time when we made the statement. Alternatively, our description may have been based on faulty knowledge in the first instance.

Not surprisingly, we are left with yet another question: does this mean that there are no facts, but simply descriptions and opinions that are not easily demarcated? Although the above seems to point in that direction, it is not the whole story. What we call facts are very often supported by a complex framework of belief about other facts. Now, although parts of this framework may change, it is rare for there to occur at the same time a change in all of the things about which we hold beliefs. Take a researcher who is interested in patient satisfaction. We can say that what counts as satisfaction may be open to dispute. However, the existence of nurses, doctors, hospitals, beds and ambulances are not usually open to dispute in the same way. Judgements such as "this is a nurse", or "that is an ambulance", are usually considered as characterizations, not appraisals, and are not usually subjected to test. It does not follow that they may not be appraisals, simply that life is too short to question all of the beliefs that we hold at any one time. As such, Popper's definition of a fact seems a useful one, with the caveat that the firmness, or strength of a fact, will depend on the level of intersubjective agreement concerning its existence.

Having clarified the nature of values and facts and dealt with a few issues regarding their relationship, we now turn to some specific approaches to their interplay and role in social research. Four positions, in particular, are useful for characterizing the scope of this debate: these are, the positivist, Weberian, critical and feminist standpoint positions. Once we have summarized the basic arguments of each of these, we will then be in a position to consider the relationship between value freedom, objectivity and method in the practice of social research.

Perspectives on the fact–value relationship

Positivist research and value freedom

The strategy of enquiry adopted by the early positivists was a Cartesian one of separating the knower from what is to be known. Contained within this was classical empiricism, represented in the idea of neutrality in terms of what can be known. The method, it was believed, guaranteed objective enquiry and was valid for the investigation of any sort of phenomenon. For example, the observance of regularities in religious ritual will reveal rules, themselves evidence for societal organization. The observer is "separate" from those observed and is required to be neutral about the nature of the ritual. This approach, positivists claimed, allowed the investigation of the subjectively – and in the case of Durkheim, collectively – held views of society without the investigator being influenced by them. For Durkheim, the objectivity of sociological enquiry was guaranteed as long as the investigator concentrated on social and not individual phenomena. Legal rules, moral regulations, social conventions have just as much factual existence as physical objects. As he argued:

Let us suppose we wish to classify the different sorts of crime. We would have to try to reconstruct the modes of life and the occupational practices that are followed in different worlds of crime. One would then recognize as many criminological types as there are forms of this organization (Durkheim quoted in Giddens 1972: 122).

Despite the replication of a natural scientific methodology, this separation fails. Take our example of "richness" and "tallness" noted earlier. It is certainly possible to name a characteristic, but the naming process itself is a normative act, as are the characteristics so described. Durkheim actually claims that his method of investigation not only allows, but must insist upon, separating the pathological from the normal. However, what counts as pathological and what counts as normal can only be a product of the investigator's decision. These categories are not pre-given to fall as if manna from a positivist heaven. Despite this fairly obvious failing, value freedom of such a "naïve" kind continues to be a claim in the actual practice of social research. British Home Office research on crime can be seen as an example of such an approach (see Chapter 6). Similarly, many argue that the government's censuses are examples of value neutral research. Although census data, in Britain as in many countries, are commonly used for research that takes a "position" on matters such as migration patterns (Stillwell et al. 1992), women's employment (Ward & Dale 1991), or housing deprivation (Dale et al., in press), the census data themselves are often regarded as neutral. Despite the usefulness of census data, the categories chosen for which data are collected, are themselves far from neutral. For example, in Britain there has been considerable criticism over the years about how the census should approach the question of ethnicity (Silitoe 1987). Even the most factual questions, such as those about the accommodation in which one lives, have value laden antecedents and vary from country to country. From the French census, for example, it is possible to determine whether or not a person lives in high rise housing. In Britain, this is not possible.

Max Weber and value free social research

Despite the persistence of naïve concepts of value freedom, attempts to devise a more sophisticated "value free" methodology have a long his-

RESEARCH EXAMPLE 11
Gendered statistics

Ginn & Duggard (1994) have focused on how patriarchal values have influenced the development of statistical methods and the production and use of statistics. They note that while there has long been a tradition of critique of official statistics in sociology, it remains the case that sexist assumptions in statistics either render the lives of women invisible, or distort their realities. They describe "professional statisticians at work" as existing in an environment where technical ability is often measured through obscurity, a "male" environment that values competition, but not good communication. The result can be bias in a number of areas of official statistics that arise from the concepts and definitions applied. They cite a number of examples in women's health and women's poverty to reinforce their point:

> less than a quarter of women dying between 1979 and 1983 had their occupations recorded making it impossible to use this data to discover whether women's mortality is more closely related to the nature of their employment, to their standard of living as indicated by their husband's occupation or neither of these (Ginn & Duggard 1994: 7).

In addition:

> Because their income is aggregated with their husbands' for means tests, the proportions of married women with a personal income below subsistence level is nowhere to be found in official statistics (Ginn & Duggard 1994: 9).

tory. Actually, the expression "value free sociology" was coined by Weber (1949). He, unlike Durkheim, was prepared to concede that in social science debates will exist about ends. However, this is not to be seen as a fault in the discipline:

> The distinctive characteristic of a problem in social policy is indeed the fact that it cannot be resolved merely on the basis of

purely technical considerations that assume already settled ends. Normative standards of value can and must be the objects of dispute in a discussion of social policy because the problem lies in the domain of general cultural values (Weber 1974: 75).

Despite this admission, Weber's starting point is similar to that of the positivists. A fact–value distinction must be maintained because they are different kinds of phenomena. From knowing the facts of something, we cannot determine its value. Similarly, knowing of the value of something cannot lead us to a factual description. Social science should only deal in questions of facts and remain ethically neutral on the question of values.

How does this argument fit within his general strategy of *verstehen* sociology? Weber's answer is, on first glance, a simple one. An adequate description of a social practice requires us to understand the meaning of the practices to the agents involved. Moreover, this strategy necessitates an understanding of values. However, it does not follow from this that the investigator must take sides on those values. To understand deviance, it is not necessary to be deviant. For Weber, the values of other agents become the subject matter of social science that necessitates the strategic employment of *verstehen* sociology. We can, it seems, make reference to values without making value judgements. In this way, social science remains distinct from those values.

Weber, unlike Durkheim, insists that we must understand the values of agents and not simply observe societal practices; to consider, therefore, both the subjective and objective dimensions to social life. Yet surely the very act of understanding requires us to decide between values? A sociologist of religion must be able to distinguish between a religious activity and an activity which comprises elements of religious practices. Weber's work, much of it historical in character, is replete with value judgements expressed in the language of praise or blame, i.e. "grand figures", "incomparable grandeur", "perfection that is nowhere surpassed" (Strauss 1963: 433). As Strauss points out, most of Weber's work would be fairly meaningless without such value judgements. It is probably this aspect of his work that still provide his insights with such a contemporary resonance (Ray & Reed 1994). His work represents not only a value concern with the future of the individual in the face of the increasingly impersonal forces of modern society, but the continual struggle between the views of the individual social scientist against those of the investigated whom they should faithfully represent in the production of their findings.

How are we to assess the actions of those whom we investigate "factually"? Weber maintains that this should be done through an assessment of the internal logic of a situation. Did the agents' ends arise directly from the means and were the appropriate means chosen for those ends? In other words, rational behaviour is the yardstick for a factual description of a situation (Weber 1974: 73). In this way, value freedom involves not taking sides with those whom we investigate, despite the existence of our own value positions. It is within this tension that the best social science is produced. The standards of "rational action" were central to Weber's own world view and ones that, as he was only too aware, were historically and culturally specific.

So, Weber espouses value neutrality on the one hand and on the other, he seems to be saying that values are unavoidable in the practice of social science. The resolution of this paradox may be described in the following manner. The objects of social science are constituted by values and this presupposes an appreciation of the values peculiar to the part of the social world being studied. Without this, the researcher cannot evaluate the phenomena under investigation and their research is without relevance. However, it is appreciated that the investigator will be motivated by her own presuppositions that will shape her evaluative framework. This is inevitable and even desirable. However, to admit of this need not compromise "value" neutrality, for the researcher is able to objectively describe the values under investigation. Even the choice between values under investigation need not compromise neutrality. A researcher may evaluate something as "sacred" or "profane" in relation to a particular culture, and while making a value judgement on the assumptions about those terms, this does not commit them to any kind of preference. As Alan Ryan puts it:

> We cannot describe the world independently of *all* assumptions, and if this were required for objectivity, then we should indeed be unable to achieve it; but we can certainly describe the world independently of any particular assumptions we wish to question (Ryan 1970: 237. Original italics).

This kind of approach maintains the fact–value distinction by accrediting the values of the researcher, relevant to the investigation, as facts. In other words, the initial conditions of the investigation in part consist of values. In Example 12 the initial conditions are that discrimination consists of certain characteristics (though they are not stated) and is a bad thing. Unless

116

RESEARCH EXAMPLE 12
Ethnic monitoring:
a study of employers' experiences

The Department of Employment commissioned the Ethnic Minority Employment Research Centre at Leicester University to investigate the experience of a range of employers in implementing ethnic monitoring. The project aimed: "to identify and evaluate best practice in respect of monitoring, including the identification and evaluation of benefits (or otherwise) perceived by monitoring organisations" (Jewson et al. 1992: 3).

The research report begins by describing what ethnic monitoring is and sets out a number of reasons for monitoring, as well as the debate for and against monitoring. The researchers thus began from a position of value neutrality with regard to the practice itself and any decision on whether or not ethnic monitoring was a valuable exercise would be reached as a result of the findings.

Nevertheless, though not stated, a set of consensual values did inform the research. These values might be broadly described as a commitment to a view that whether or not ethnic monitoring was worthwhile, its intention as a means of combating discrimination on ethnic grounds was laudable. So, while there could be disagreement over the benefits of ethnic monitoring, or a particular form of monitoring, there would still be a consensus over the desire to eradicate discrimination in work practices or modes of recruitment.

discrimination was considered a bad thing, then there would not have been much point in the researchers even accepting the commission to do the research, or the Department of Employment considering the question in the first place. This kind of strategy appears reasonable when we consider the impossibility of any neutral algorithm to describe the world. As Thomas Nagel points out, there is no "view from nowhere":

> We rightly think that the pursuit of detachment from our initial standpoint is an indispensable method of advancing our understanding of the world and of ourselves . . . But since we are who we are, we can't get outside of ourselves completely (Nagel 1986: 6).

117

The lesson here seems to be that our own biographies are an unavoidable part of the research process. We can go further than this and say that our own biographies are not an individual creation, but the result of a complex history of interaction with the physical and the social worlds. An investigation of the world that maintains a fact–value distinction by accrediting certain values as "facts", is an acceptance that knowledge is a view from somewhere. That it is a view from somewhere, as in Townsend's studies of poverty in Britain (Townsend 1979), presupposes that it is a more desirable vantage point than others. Indeed, Townsend's view has long been unpopular with Conservative governments who see his research as an inaccurate representation of the extent and nature of poverty in Britain. Here, the argument concerns the relationship between ideology and values. It is to this subject that we now turn.

Ideology and values

Marxism

Thus far we have considered the notion that values appear to be unavoidable in any investigation, whereas even the most solid of scientific facts may be disproven. For many, values and objectivity are bound up with questions of ideology. The term ideology is used in many ways, which range from that which pertains to ideas, to meaning something close to political brain washing (see McLellan 1986). Here, we are principally concerned to use the term in its Marxist, or neo-Marxist sense. Marxists and those methodologically influenced by Marx, while accepting that knowledge has social antecedents, also argue that the views of those who are powerful in society come to be regarded as the truth. In other words, in capitalist societies, what appears as the truth is symptomatic of ideological distortion. For those that believe truth is shaped by such ideological considerations, objectivity depends on particular groups transcending a state of "false consciousness". Implied here is an ability to reach the "truth" having transcended and/or overturned those social conditions that serve to mask its attainment. Within this very broad notion, there are the ideas of Marx, the critical theorists and standpoint feminisms. We will consider each of these in turn.

At the beginning of one of the most famous passages in the *German ideology*, Marx and Engels state:

> The ideas of the ruling class are in every epoch the ruling ideas, i.e. the class which is the ruling material force of society, is at the same time its ruling *intellectual force* (1970: 64. Original italics).

Although Marx (and Engels) were at pains to stress the material basis for ideas, there is an implicit assumption that knowledge is socially produced and there exists a dialectical interplay between ideas and material circumstances. However, the implications of this positions are far-reaching. First, there is the link between power and knowledge. It is held that the powerful, broadly defined as those who own and control the means of production, will be in a position to dictate what is to count as valid knowledge. Secondly, by implication, that there exists a body of knowledge that is not "ideological" and which, therefore, has a greater claim to validity.

Marx never really made clear how we are to distinguish between ideology and truth (1970: 224). Although this is the case, it tends to miss the subtlety of Marx's position. Marx is saying that ideology produces a distorted view of the world, but he does not appear to claim that a "neutral" view, or "view from nowhere" is then available once ideology is transcended. Indeed, he refused to pronounce on this question and was rather dismissive of philosophical disputes over the possibility of knowledge (Marx 1974: 39–41). For Marx, "objective" knowledge was a practical question linked to the material circumstances of people in their everyday lives (Marx 1974: 121). The consciousness of bourgeois society is seen as "false" because it blinds the proletariat to the material reality of their existence. With the "goal of history" realized in communism, material conditions would allow the realization of people's "essential being". He never really tells us what this is. Yet we cannot know the characteristics of a fully developed human nature *a priori* from within the "false consciousness" of bourgeois ideology (Marx 1974: 48). In the first instance, the ideology has to be transcended:

> Only through the objectively unfolded richness of man's essential being is the richness of objective *human* sensibility either cultivated or brought into being (1977: 96. Original italics).

We can see here that Marx's concerns are ontological, rather than epistemological. Human "sensibility" can only be achieved under particular material circumstances. The material circumstances of capitalism are not conducive to its realization because the false consciousness of bourgeois ideology blinds people to their actual potential.

For Marxist inspired social researchers it follows from this that the claim to value freedom in social science is a bourgeois concept. Therefore, Surkin maintained

> that the rigorous adherence to social science methodology adopted from the natural sciences and its claim to objectivity and value neutrality function as a guise for what is in fact becoming an increasingly ideological non-objective role for social science knowledge in the service of the dominant institutions in American society (Surkin 1974: 22).

The implication is that a less ideological and more objective role is available to social science. Yet from a Marxist point of view "objectivity" begins from the premiss that bourgeois society is ideological and that this should be challenged from a critical viewpoint. In contrast to Weberian inspired research, Marxist research is firmly linked to political goals. As Marx said, "Philosophers have only interpreted the world in various ways; the point is to change it" (1970: 123).

In the past decades a considerable body of research in the Marxist tradition has been built up (for example, see Sharp and Green 1975, Willis 1977, Mayer 1994). What is it that makes such studies Marxist? Predominantly, it is the selection of theoretical categories of interest and particular groups to study. For example, studies of schooling, such as that by Sharp & Green, have been concerned to show how classroom practices and teaching methods reflect the dominant ideology, while Willis's subjects were not just "boys", but working class boys who, despite their resistance to the systems that they encountered, were still reproduced in the interests of a dominant economic imperative. These studies, though linked to Marxist analyses, are still somewhat removed from political practice. That said, some Marxist-based research has served as a springboard for political action. For instance, Cockburn's (1977) study of local government in London inspired a generation of grass-root activists.

Critical theory

Marx's early concern with ideology and alienation was a principal influence on the development of critical theory (Held 1990). Marx had emphasized the need for philosophy to serve emancipatory interests. Therefore, Max Horkheimer, the second director of the Institute for Social Research at Frankfurt, wrote in 1937:

> [Critical theory] . . . is not just a research hypothesis which shows
> its value in the ongoing business of men; it is an essential element
> in the historical effort to create a world which satisfies the needs
> and powers of men . . . the theory never aims simply at an increase
> of knowledge as such. Its goal is man's emancipation from slavery
> (Horkheimer quoted in Outhwaite 1987: 77).

This is then connected to an idea of truth:

> What decides the value of a theory is not the formal criteria of
> truth, [but more] its connection with the tasks which are under-
> taken by progressive social forces at particular historic moment
> (Horkheimer quoted in Outhwaite 1987: 77).

Adorno & Horkheimer (1979) came to see the social sciences as uncritical
and the embodiment of an "instrumental" rationality that has come to
characterize the Enlightenment. Reason and rationality have grown apart
in the service of capitalism. In contrast, their interdisciplinary goals came
to be centred around social criticism in the service of emancipation.
Towards this end, both positivism and interpretative approaches to the
study of social life were found wanting. As Horkheimer argued:

> Contemporary social philosophy, as we have seen, is in the main
> polemically disposed toward positivism. If the latter sees only the
> particular, in the realm of society it sees only the individual and
> the relations between individuals; for positivism, everything is
> exhausted in mere facts [Tatsächlichkeiten]. These facts, demonstra-
> ble with the means of analytic science, are not questioned by phi-
> losophy (1993: 7).

This led to a series of debates with those who championed the idea of science in the shadow of the Enlightenment and it is these that interest us
here. They were first represented by Adorno and Popper and then taken
up by Habermas and Hans Albert.

The debates, rather erroneously, became billed as the "positivist dispute in German sociology" (Holub 1991), but had little directly to do with
sociology (Adorno et al. 1976). More importantly, the protagonists on the

"positivist" side were, as noted in the case of Popper, actually self confessed anti-positivists. Nevertheless, for our purposes, the exchange brings sharply into focus the differences between an epistemologically focused social science and an ontologically and politically "engaged" social science. Popper rejected traditional accounts of science and emphasized the critical role of the scientific community in the guaranteeing of objectivity. As Holub describes it:

> According to this view the natural scientist is neither more or less "subjective" than his social science counterpart. All science derives its objectivity from a critical tradition that allows and fosters the criticism of dominant theories (Holub 1991: 23).

The Popperian tendency to place the ultimate court of appeal in a community of scientists clearly separates him from the positivists. This is also a position that allows for the role of social factors in the shaping of scientific decisions. Inevitably, this leads to the question of values in scientific investigations. Popper, while acknowledging that values have an important part to play, maintains there are two kinds of values: those that are purely scientific and those that are extra-scientific. The values of the community of scientists are wholly scientific. Because it is scientific values that are of importance, rather than the object of study as such, Popper does not make a methodological distinction between the physical and the social sciences. Moreover, Popper links "values" to the solution of problems. As he remarks elsewhere, "we are not students of some subject matter, but students of problems" (1989: 67). The solution of a problem suggests a value on a particular outcome, whether it be in the physical or social sphere. Though the values to which he refers here are "extra-scientific" ones, the objectivity in deciding between them is guaranteed by the adoption of a critical methodology.

Adorno disagrees with Popper on both the "unity of science" question and the focus on particular problems. He distinguishes between a quest for social science knowledge and a quest for scientific knowledge on the grounds that the former should be engaged in, among other things, reflection on the knowledge claims of disciplines such as those of the physical sciences. In other words, an important role for social science is that of "meta-critique". Popper's "naturalist" approach precludes such "objectivity". Consequently, scientific values cannot be "pure" ones, partly because, as Popper accepts, they must be guaranteed from within the political and social sphere: for example, by governments committed to the promotion of rigorous and critical science. As Holub notes, "the affirmation of objectivity or value-freedom as desirable features of scientific procedure is itself the expression of a value" (1991: 25).

For Popper, the resolution of a problem is the desired outcome. Further, if a theory becomes falsified in the light of empirical evidence, then a new theory must be sought. Adorno sees this as mistaken for, in taking problems in isolation, the social scientist can never get to grips with what she should be examining: that is, society itself. Social totality is itself contradictory because agents have a distorted view of reality. As such, "the (critical) theorist must try to grasp the thing itself, human society" (Holub 1991: 28). It is this notion of "totality" that is taken up by Habermas.

Habermas maintains that the idea of totality involves the individual in a process of self reflection. In contrast, a Popperian view of values starts with the instrumental considerations of empirical science. Habermas's contribution to the debate was complex and detailed. However, for our purposes it is enough to say that he exposed the weakness of the Popperian separation between scientific and extra-scientific values. Science, for Popper, is above all a rational procedure characterized by experience and argument. Yet a justification for this guarantee of objectivity rests on the terms of rational behaviour. Yet a rational justification for rationalism requires a prior acceptance of a rational attitude (Holub 1991: 34). Rationality, therefore, is itself a value and in these terms, critical rationalism becomes no more than a matter of faith.

Whereas Hans Albert, a disciple of Popper, did reply to Habermas, Popper himself remained virtually silent on the matter. Some commentators felt that there was more agreement between the protagonists than disagreement (Dahrendorf in Adorno et al. 1976). Perhaps, also, there was an incommensurability between the arguments of Adorno, Habermas, Popper and Hans Albert. Popper had always emphasized the need for theories to be exposed to a "reality", via rigorous testing, for the purposes of falsifiability. Allied to this, he had long opposed the idea of "historicism": that is, the attempt to predict the future course of human affairs by reference to historical "laws" (Popper 1986b). Universal statements concerning social totality are anathema to this position. In contrast, Habermas's project, like that of critical theory in general, although rejecting the possibility of defining ultimate philosophical foundations, is holistic in its view of human society. For Habermas, therefore, Popper's version of rationality is indicative of an "instrumental reason" that is concerned to control human affairs through the efficient marshalling of means in the service of ends; ends that remain without justification.

Critical theorists, right through to the extensive modification of this tradition in the work of Habermas, have retained a broadly Marxian commitment to emancipation from relations of domination and exploitation. As Nancy Fraser puts it:

> A critical social theory frames its research programme and its conceptual framework with an eye to the aims and activities of those oppositional social movements with which it has a partisan, though not uncritical, identification (1989: 113).

That noted, epistemological concerns have often returned in the form of a self examination that is central to critical theory. In the work of Adorno, this amounts to an attempt to take "the view from nowhere" by stepping outside of partial and distorted views of the world whose ultimate refuge was to become the aesthetic, rather than the scientific, dimension of human life (see Benjamin 1991). In this sense, it might be regarded as the desire to achieve a position of knowledge that is uncontaminated by the "noise" of the social world. However, this is a desire that is very different from the complacency of empiricism.

We may still observe that critical theory begins from the definition of a prior position from which knowledge may be gleaned. This is an ontological claim. From a Popperian standpoint this is illegitimate because the underlying epistemological premiss remains undeclared. The critical theorists, on the other hand, claim the opposite: that is, the Popperians base their methodological routes to knowledge on weak ontological foundations. Despite these differences, critical theory tended to retain a belief in the possibility of objectivity, but one not dependent upon value freedom that is, as noted, a value in itself. There are another group of theorists who share this view, but whose ontological starting point is quite different.

Feminist standpoint epistemologies

Feminist standpoint epistemologies share with Marxism and critical theory the view that an individual's social position will largely determine what a person may know. For Marxism, the proletariat is accorded the potential to overcome false consciousness thereby revealing the real nature of its class position. Similarly, feminist standpoint theories rest on the argument that women as an oppressed class can also come to occupy a privileged epistemic position (Rose 1983, Hartsock 1983).

The above claim is grounded in a set of arguments that are common to several feminist epistemologies (Harding 1986). First, knowledge and specifically scientific knowledge, is a social product. Secondly, society is patriarchal and therefore scientific practice is androcentric. Thirdly, material life structures and sets limits on understanding. In other words, what we do shapes and constrains what we may know. Thus, Dorothy Smith writes:

> Though women are indeed the expert practitioners of their everyday worlds, the notion of the everyday world as problematic assumes that disclosure of the extralocal determinations of our experience does not lie within the scope of everyday practices. We can see only so much without specialized investigation, and the latter should be the sociologist's special business (Smith 1987: 161).

From this it may be said that men's experiences, in the shape of domination, are distorted. As such, claims to scientific objectivity and neutrality simply reflect the limitations of those experiences. "Complete" and undistorted knowledge is simply not available to men. The idea of a "standpoint" therefore carries with it:

> the contention that there are some perspectives on society from which however well intentioned one may be, the real relations of humans with each other and with the natural world are not visible (Hartsock 1983: 285).

In contrast to this, women's knowledge comes from a position of being the subject of domination. It originates in and is tested against, a more complete and less distorted social experience that, in turn, has the potential to produce less distorted knowledge claims. Unlike empiricist and critical rationalist views, where objectivity lies in method, or in critical theory where this depends on coming to understand society in its contradictory totality, feminist standpoint epistemologies confer objectivity and epistemic privilege on a part of society – women. There is also another important distinction to be made between the positions we have discussed so far and feminist standpoint epistemologies. In general, those discussed so far are all rationalist doctrines; they entail a belief that knowledge forms a single system and that everything is, in principle, explicable. To be objective is to pursue explanations that are part of that system of knowledge. Objectivity becomes abstract, impersonal and universal. Though feminists use the term "objective" it is not meant in quite this sense.

Griffiths succinctly expresses what "objectivity" means in the context of feminist knowledge:

> The production of feminist knowledge is grounded in feeling. So far from feelings being seen as mere subjectivity, something to be overcome in the search for objectivity, they are seen to be a source of knowledge (Griffiths 1988: 135).

She goes on to consider work that has examined the physical sciences from a feminist standpoint. Here we find that:

> the kinds of rational objectivity and technical control taken to be constitutive of science are distortions introduced by unacknowledged and un-examined myths of masculinity which have their roots in typically masculine ways of feeling and which pervade scientific thought (1988: 135).

Through an examined dichotomy in social, political and philosophical thought, the rational has been defined as the male, and the emotional, the female; one presumed closer to culture and the other, to nature. As such, male notions of objectivity disregard the role of feelings and emotion in human life, as well as representing the desire to control the social and natural worlds. Mind, in Cartesian inspired philosophies, is the site of rationality whereas emotions, insofar as they are part of "mind", are brought under its control. Within this tradition of philosophy of mind, any relationship with the body, as closer to "nature", is disregarded and constructed as an object of suspicion. Mind becomes disembodied. The result is an implicit drawing upon a series of unexamined dichotomies that social life is presumed to be based on and scientific practice reflects: for example, culture versus nature; rational mind versus pre-rational body and emotions; objectivity versus subjectivity and the public versus the private (Harding 1986).

These dualisms provide for an alignment of the rational with the male, itself derived from cultures that prioritize male values. In contrast to this position, feminist epistemology resides in the "Hand, Brain and Heart" (Rose 1983). Women's experiences in childbirth, in caring and domestic labour, are far from disembodied. Most importantly, these experience take place within the context of oppression, or what Dorothy Smith (1987) calls "relations of ruling". Experiences, unlike the notion of the rational mind, are not abstract concepts. Thus, for women to "know" is to do so via the totality of their experiences. The role of experience in social life and scientific practice should not be sequestrated in the name of limited concepts of rationality.

From this point of view objectivity is not simply a value, but a male value. The world is seen as a complex set of relations that cannot be dichotomized in the straightforward manner that has been invoked in the past. Instead:

> Rather than a simple dualism [standpoint epistemology] posits a duality of levels of reality, of which the deeper level, or essence both includes and explains the "surface" or appearance, and indicates the logic by means of which the appearance inverts and distorts the deeper reality (Hartsock 1983: 285).

Though standpoint theorists insist that only women can access such a deeper reality, most point out that the desired end state is not the substitution of one set of gendered hypotheses for another, but to arrive at hypotheses that are not gendered at all.

There is an issue that remains in the formulation of feminist standpoints. The critique of male knowledge rests on the rejection of a set of dualisms. However, if male science represents a partial view of the world, then it follows that a better, or more accurate, description is available. Yet this implies a dualism between right and wrong descriptions. If particular ideas of objectivity are the product of an androcentric dualism, then women centred epistemologies will remain androcentric if objectivity, whatever its form, is still pursued.

At this point, a standpoint appears to require a realist epistemology. If women's knowledge is located in their experiences of oppression, then that knowledge is of "real" phenomena. Thus, Maureen Cain writes of the fusion of realist philosophy and standpoint epistemologies and provides guidelines for "good quality knowledge" (1990: 138–9). Similarly, the Marxist influence on Hartsock's methodology (1983: 283–5) is both realist and materialist in the invoking of "appearance and essence" and "abstract and concrete". In addition, Harding writes that, "Something out there is changing social relations between races, classes, and cultures as well as between genders" (1986: 244). Despite this, the accents of standpoint theorists are often relativistic.

Not only Maureen Cain, but also Sandra Harding is aware of the above tension. As such, she asks whether a recognition of the social nature of scientific knowledge necessarily requires feminism to embrace relativism. The very denial of an objective standpoint, or access to a real world appears "to cut off the possibility of a de-gendered science . . ." (1986: 137). Her answer to this problem is that these are "transitional" epistemologies and such conflict becomes inevitable. Just because these contradictions exist, it does not devalue the points made by standpoint epistemologies. First, a feminist society must be established before we can even begin to imagine what a feminist science might be. As she notes, trying to imagine a feminist science in a contemporary society is akin to asking a medieval peasant to imagine a theory of genetics, or the idea of a space capsule (1986: 139)!

Harding's plea for a tolerance of the apparent contradictions of "transitional" epistemologies is consistent with a project that has its starting point in a critique of the very modes of thought we employ to understand the world. If knowledge is shaped by social factors, then it is perfectly consistent to claim that some of these may arise from gender differences. However, any challenge to modes of thought influenced in this way must come from within those modes of thought themselves. For this reason, it is hardly surprising that at a superficial level they appear to be inadequate and contradictory.

Despite this, difficulties remain. If, as Harding and others rightly claim, we cannot know what a feminist science would look like, then we also do not know *a priori* if it describes the world more adequately than current scientific practice. However, this is a political question that is framed from an epistemological point of view. Quite simply, if women's voices have been marginalized from dominant culture, then this is not a desirable state of affairs. Further, it represents the absence of the perspectives and ideas of half of the population! Yet, possibilities remain. The belief that science is gendered seems to rest on a claim that "ordinary language" in its everyday use is gendered and that scientific language originates in "ordinary language" (Keller 1985). Clearly, science must make use of this in order to arrive at explanations (Harding 1986: 45). However, while "ordinary language" may well be androcentric, the language of today (and today's science) is not that of the eighteenth century. Perhaps, therefore, there is a capacity for change in language and thus change in the language of science. Conversely, of course, it could become more gendered in the future. It is this that necessitates the democratization of science, where the scientist is seen as accountable for the quality of the knowledge she produces in the name of those for whom she does so (Cain 1990).

Despite the clear relation between science and the use of ordinary language metaphors to explain the natural world, our stock of metaphors would, if this relation were a strict one, actually limit scientific discovery. What makes certain sciences, such as quantum physics, difficult to the lay person is that the level of abstraction required for understanding goes well beyond our stock of "ordinary language" metaphors. Physicists and mathematicians may sometimes use notation to obfuscate, but more usually this aids understanding of concepts to those who have learned the notation. In other words, this notation aids understanding in a way that our everyday language does not. The idea that scientific language is simply androcentric is thus problematic. Similarly, although admitting of the idea of "transitional" epistemologies, it does seem hard to abandon the notion of agreement and negation implied by dualisms. The abandonment of a duality of, say A or B, implies an interdependent relationship between A and B. Though A and B may well be interdependent, if they are to keep their identity as discrete units, then if something is A, it is not B and if something is B, it is not A. Even in continuous variables there is a need to identify and name the particular variables. Although nothing is exactly one metre long, a concept of measurement still requires that we pretend otherwise and measure in metres.

A final issue remains with standpoint epistemologies. Knowledge, it is claimed, is born out of experience. However, as Halberg (1989) notes, experience is a vague term that gives rise to two difficulties. First, the need to identify what female experiences actually are and second, to show how these are different to male experiences. In the first case, an epistemology that was based on female experiences would have to show that this was closed off to males. In the second case, it would have to demonstrate that there were experiences common to all women. Unless a recourse is made to saying that women's biology makes them different to men and produces common experiences to all women, then other possibilities present themselves. First, that different women have different experiences and secondly, some of these experiences are the result of class, ethnicity, disability, age, etc., which may also be part of men's "experiences". In other words, there exists the possibility that the desired objectivity may collapse into a relativism which is indicative of forms of postmodernism, including feminisms.

Summary

Traditionally, objectivity and value freedom were regarded as equivalent. However, the foregoing examples suggest that while it is possible to pursue objective inquiry, values will inevitably enter into the investigation at some point. Indeed, in feminist standpoint epistemologies values enter in the research process, in the form of individual subjective experiences, that actually help us to arrive at "objective" knowledge. In the traditional use of the term, the premises upon which objectivity rested were universal and abstract, but in the examples above they have become more particular.

For empiricism, objective inquiry meant the eschewing of all values. There then came the realization that this was an unrealistic goal and even logically problematic if objectivity itself was a value. In this way, objectivity has come to mean the pursuing of lines of scientific inquiry within the parameters of particular values. In other words, the premises that define objectivity have shifted from the universal to the particular. This takes different forms. These range from an awareness of one's own values and those whom one is researching, to that of an "engaged" political position where research contributes to a knowledge base that is necessary to the pursuance of specific goals: for example, inner city anti-poverty strategies (see Blackburn 1991).

Given this state of affairs, value freedom in the sense used by Mill and Durkheim is a doctrine rarely defended these days. Nevertheless, as we have seen, it is the *de facto* position of a great deal of governmental research. Instead, disputes centre upon what are, or should be, the value premises from which research commences. The examples given above are "grand", or first order, methodological positions. Most research, although often influenced by perspectives such as Marxism, feminism and liberalism, is conducted within the context of a research problem. The problem itself often dictates the methods and the methods will often shape the solutions.

Alan Bryman offers a good example of the kind of problems of objectivity generated by "second order" methodological decisions by citing

Weinstein's evaluation of research on mental patients (1980: 159–161). Qualitative research, in the form of participant observation, yielded results that pointed to apathy among patients, and furthermore, that the organization of the hospital actually served to inhibit patient rehabilitation. Conversely, a quantitative study in a similar setting, which employed an interview schedule with open-ended questions, suggested that patients did not regard hospitalization in such a negative way. Weinstein's conclusions were that the discrepancies between the results derived from methodological weaknesses in the qualitative studies. However, he was criticized for being too predisposed toward quantitative methods. Additionally, it was suggested that the qualitative and quantitative studies may have been addressing different questions, where the former were concerned with the experiences of being a mental patient, and the latter with patient attitudes.

Two points are of particular interest in this controversy. First, reviewers are often not impartial when confronted with research that draws upon different traditions. Therefore, Weinstein appears prepared to raise issues about the adequacy of the qualitative studies, but not those that relate to quantitative investigations. Secondly, there is the extent to which quantitative and qualitative studies are comparable when addressing the same issues (Bryman 1988). The implications are that the values of the reviewer, as opposed to those of the original researcher, fall under question. In addition, values in methodology can be "second order" – those which relate to predispositions towards favouring particular methods. This predisposition can be quite separate to "first order" commitments towards "grand methodological" positions. From the information we have provided so far, Weinstein could be a positivist, a realist or a Marxist. The message is clear. Quite simply, because it is possible for there to be a separation between method and philosophical commitment, values may enter the research process at the level of methods, as well as at theoretical or methodological levels.

There is also the question of incommensurability between quantitative and qualitative approaches to research. The two methods produce different kinds of answers. This suggests an important link between objectivity and validity. Both the qualitative and quantitative approaches to research on mental patients may have been objective, but this objectivity will relate directly to the respective validity claims made by each method. Thus, an objective account in qualitative research will be one that accurately reflects the meanings of those investigated. For this reason there is an emphasis upon the maximization of internal validity. On the other hand, an objective account in quantitative research will tend to be one from which generalizations can be made – the emphasis here being upon external validity. As such, the issues are philosophical, methodological and technical.

As for the question as to whether research can be value-free, the answer seems fairly clear. With Weber, we must conclude that investigations in the social sciences concern the values that people hold. Society itself seems to be constituted by values and it is this that provides social research with its relevance. Research takes place from within society and is conducted by societal members. From this point of view, it is difficult to see how societal and individual values might actually be absent from the research process. We have seen that values enter the research process at every stage: from the "grand" methodological position of the researcher; the selection of problems for research; the selection of methods appropriate to the research; the assessment of evidence and the determination of the content of conclusions, as well as its dissemination.

We need also to be aware that research is rarely inspired by inquisitiveness about the human condition. Quite simply, little financial support is now available for "pure" research of this type. Instead, it tends to be "applied" or "strategic" and is therefore linked to policy either directly or indirectly. Policy itself is located in moral values. As Putnam (1961) has remarked, we do and we must also, morally evaluate ourselves. We cannot be disinterested observers, apparently unconcerned with poverty, cruelty and oppression, whether we are researchers in the social or physical sciences. We must conclude, then, that research cannot, nor should it be, value free.

The question of the ramifications of this conclusion for objectivity are more complex. If the social sciences are moral sciences, then it is difficult to see how any form of objectivity based on universal moral values might be achieved. This has been long recognized and preoccupies, among others, the extensive writings of Jürgen Habermas (1992, 1993). Does it follow that if there are no universal moral values, there can be no objectivity? This conclusion would entail a nihilistic moral relativism, which might then preclude any form of social research. Objectivity will be linked, therefore, to particular values. Here we find that for feminist standpoint theorists, poststructuralists and postmodernists, objectivity is not simply a value, but a concept linked to a particular historical doctrine of rationalism associated with the Enlightenment project. Feminist standpoint epistemology recognizes this and for this reason attempts to avoid the relativistic conclusions of postmodernism by formulating a different concept of objectivity.

Others re-formulate the question. Marxists and critical theorists, for example, shift the emphasis from how we can know things to the basis upon which we know them. Clearly, this is a corrective to the narrowness that is implied by an exclusive epistemological focus upon objectivity. However, it appears only to postpone the knowledge issues. How can we know that the basis from which we can begin to know is the right one, or the best one, without some theories about knowledge in the first instance? More immediately, if ideology is so successful and all pervasive, how can we know whether we have transcended it? This is not to suggest that theoretical or empirical research programmes in this tradition cannot be fruitful, or are simply wrong. It is to suggest that having illuminated previously uncharted areas, simple answers to what are complex, but necessary questions, are not readily available.

Of course there remains, for want of a better characterization, the empirical approaches to objectivity. These stress either the idea of research problems (Popper), or selective objectivity (Ryan). Although in many ways Popper is far removed from Weber, there is a resonance between the policy goals of society, as stressed by Weber and the incremental, or "piecemeal" approach to research, emphasized by Popper. These approaches appear to have the advantage of recognizing the lower level objectivity problems associated with different methods of research, but in so doing, end up taking for granted wider normative assumptions. This was apparent in the Popper–Adorno debate.

Despite these difficulties, the conclusions are not pessimistic. We have seen that the debate is now more wide open than ever before in the history of science. The result is an extraordinarily diverse and rich body of thought concerned with these questions, that is continually evolving and illuminating previously uncharted areas. Also, despite the philosophical difficulties associated with values and objectivity, this has not prohibited the production of research that has done so much to advance our understanding of the social and physical worlds. This, of course, says nothing about whether, or how, such research is acted upon. This is the realm of extra-scientific values, that both scientists and social researchers cannot ignore in the later twentieth century. Scientific and non-scientific values are collapsing into one another; witness the debates over genetic and embryo research. The questions for our current times are not whether these may be separated, but how is this relationship to be considered and managed, upon what new sets of conditions might it be based and what ramifications does this have for the future of scientific practice? We are fortunate that there is a growing body of literature addressing these very questions.

Questions for discussion

1. Consider some examples of "characterizing" and "appraising" value judgements in the practice of social research. How useful is the distinction?
2. What is "value"?
3. Weber had a very particular notion of value freedom in social science. Can you think of examples of research where a Weberian description of value freedom can be said to apply?
4. How "objective" is critical theory?

Suggested reading

Griffiths, M. & M. Whitford (eds) 1988. *Feminist perspectives in philosophy.* Basingstoke: Macmillan.

Hammersley, M. (ed.) 1993. *Social research: philosophy, politics and practice.* London: Sage.

Held, D. 1990. *Introduction to critical theory: Horkheimer to Habermas.* Cambridge: Polity.

Holub, R. C. 1991. *Jurgen Habermas – critic in the public sphere.* London: Routledge.

Popper, K. R. 1986b. *The poverty of historicism.* London: Ark.

CHAPTER 6
Philosophical issues in the process of social research

In the introduction we noted that research is frequently motivated by a curiosity about the social world. Furthermore, that although philosophy is concerned to know what kinds of things exist in the world and what is our warrant for knowing them, research focuses upon their knowable properties. From this it may be said that philosophical assumptions are the explicit, or implicit, starting point for research. As such, this chapter seeks to examine how philosophy might inform the process of social investigation. We will identify some of the ways in which a philosophical perspective informs research and through the use of two case studies, examine key assumptions and implications in its conduct. At this point we should stress that this discussion is illustrative and is not intended to be exhaustive; that would require, at least, a book in itself. However, in drawing such connections we hope that the importance of the relationship between philosophy and social research is further understood.

Philosophy and social research: a dynamic encounter

The temptation exists to talk of the philosophical "content" of research as if it were an ingredient in a cake whose proportions vary according to a recipe. This is a misunderstanding of the relationship between philosophy and social research. Philosophy might have the capacity to illuminate, but it hardly dictates. At the same time, although not all philosophy is research based, we can fruitfully examine research from a philosophical viewpoint. There is a philosophical angle in all that we do that enables us to understand our actions, their assumptions and consequences. For instance, research issues will be informed by moral and ontological considerations about the social world, whereas the methods chosen will contain epistemological assumptions about the operationalization of the research question and the best means for obtaining the knowledge required. Indeed, the methods themselves may stand as a testimony to our views on how it is possible to obtain such knowledge in the first place. Finally, the process of conducting research and the completed research itself interacts with the world in which it takes place. In that sense, as we saw in the last chapter, we cannot simply claim to be detached from our work. Our considerations, therefore, are not just technical, but also moral, epistemological and ontological.

The question as to whether such considerations are explicit or implicit will largely depend on the nature of the research itself. In most cases, in order to achieve a philosophical perspective on research we are required to view it through different spectacles. Occasionally, however, the ways in which particular viewpoints inform research is more self-evident: for example, where the starting point for research is a "critical" perspective (Harvey 1990). "Critical" can be taken to mean criticism of the existing social order from, for instance, a class, race, ethnic, or feminist perspective. A critical perspective implies a standpoint that is both morally informed and politically engaged. In the case of critical theory, as we found in Chapter 5, this leads to an understanding of the relationship between knowledge and human interests (Habermas 1989). Likewise, research informed by feminist standpoint theory is overtly philosophical because it begins from a political viewpoint that has epistemological and ontological connotations. As Harvey points out, the very generation of knowledge itself might be seen as critique for it involves, "a process of moving toward an understanding of the world and of the knowledge that structures our perceptions of the world" (Harvey 1990: 3–4).

In considering the relation between knowledge and human interests, consider the work of Goldthorpe et al. (1968). Their research was conceived during the time when the theory of "embourgeoisement" was influential in the social sciences. Broadly speaking, the theory held that, following the Second World War, a growing affluence brought about by structural changes in employment from manufacturing to service industries and unskilled to skilled labour, although not producing mobility between classes, had led to the adoption of bourgeoise values and life styles in manual classes. The result was said to produce a growing middle class and hence a shrinking working class. This was said to be an era of affluence brought about by full employment through Keynesian demand management accompanied by a strong and effective Welfare State.

Collectively, these changes were said to lead to an erosion of the distinction between manual and non-manual labour, the reduction of class antagonisms and cultural homogenization. Their study set out empirically to test this idea that had mostly, up to that time, been supposition based upon popular ideology. The methods employed included surveys and observation studies. Central to its design was the idea that it should be favourable to the confirmation of the embourgeoisement thesis where detailed material on the upward mobility of workers, together with a collapse in life styles and values between the working and middles class, would be apparent. On the other hand, if the idea were disconfirmed, then it could be claimed that embourgeoisement was not taking place to any significant extent within British society (Harvey 1990: 59).

This study is replete with philosophical implications. The thesis itself sparked differences both within Marxism and between Marxists and liberals. In the "cold war" climate of the early 1960s this had far reaching political implications. In that sense, this research took place against a background that was not "neutral" in its evaluation of studies concerning social mobility. In addition, the way in which the researchers designed their work appeared to be taking this climate into consideration (Platt 1984). A dynamic fusion of scientific notions accompanied by value considerations thus took place within a highly charged ideological climate.

The above noted, not all research is so controversial or high profile. Much of the work that social researchers conduct is very routine. However, it does not follow that these are without philosophical implications or assumptions. In order further to illustrate some of these issues, let us take the process of research itself and examine some of the ways in which a philosophical perspective might sharpen our insights into its assumptions, methods and consequences.

The process of social research from a philosophical perspective

Let us start with the motivation for doing social research. It is perhaps a truism to say all research begins from a problem that is either motivated by particular funding interests or, as is increasingly more rare, those posed by virtue of curiosity within a scientific community. This difference is often characterized in terms of "strategic" and "basic" research. It is the former that often now appears to govern the idea of "scientific relevance". However, we must ask – "relevant to whom, for what reason and with what consequences?" Thus, what is often referred to as a "problem" is highly variable. Most obviously, there may be a perceived "social problem" that is seen to require a solution. Yet this problem–solution connection is not a straightforward matter. After all, as has been noted in this respect,

> social power is not evenly distributed between groups. The definition that there exists a problem will often depend on the relative power that the people who define the social problem have over those who are defined (May 1993: 36).

Policy problems will frequently be predicated upon dominant political and social values that then determine whether research is funded in the first place. This, in turn, may affect its conduct, as well as its interpretation and dissemination. These values may also be translated into official definitions that, at a more subtle level, become categories upon which measurement is then based. To then uncritically use an operationalist approach for the purposes of secondary analysis of such data reproduces these assumptions. For instance, research on ethnicity using data from the British Census is inevitably confined to the ethnic groups as defined in the census. In 1991, the concept of "ethnic group" became defined according to the categories used in the census. However, in previous censuses ethnicity was derived in other ways: for example, country of birth (Dale & Marsh 1993: 34). What "counts" as ethnicity and what may count as a research problem associated with ethnicity, will vary as a result of these definitional changes.

As we have said, not all problematics are simply governed by dominant interests. Some may begin from a theoretical problem. One such study involved an examination of the 1965 Watts riots in Los Angeles (Stark et al., cited in Menzies 1982). The concern here was less with riots as a social or political problem, than with the testing of the symbolic interactionist view on how riots might be viewed as a process of reification involving a number of distinct incidents, events and behaviours (Menzies 1982: 31–2). Symbolic interactionism, as we have noted earlier, is a theoretical position in sociology with origins in the pragmatist tradition. Therefore, what may be considered agents' conceptions of a riot may, in turn, have philosophical foundations in a pragmatist theory of truth.

The above noted, the relationship between particular social science theories and research practice is not always so straightforward. It now becomes important to distinguish between three types of approach to this question: these are "grand", "middle" and "grounded" theoretical perspectives. The first of these is often found in Marxist or structural-functionalist approaches to the study of social relations; the second in what Robert Merton (1968) has termed "theories of the middle range" and the third has its origins in the work of Glaser & Strauss (1967).

Theoretical starting points in "grand theory" are easier to examine from a philosophical perspective because they are usually more explicit in their aims and formulations. That noted, a great deal of recent research pays only lip service to, or completely denies the possibility of, "grand theory". This has received something of a boost with the advent of the "post-critiques" as we shall see in the next chapter. Merton, on the other hand, viewed middle range theory as lying between everyday working hypotheses about social phenomena and attempts to describe social behaviour in inclusive unified theories. Within this type of relationship between theory and research an examination of its philosophical assumptions and implications becomes more difficult. Finally, the methodology of grounded theory tends to follow two criteria. First, that it should "fit" the data and not be forced onto it. Secondly, that it should be meaningfully relevant to the behaviour under study (Glaser & Strauss 1967). Therefore, it has been characterized not only as an interpretivist approach, but also an empiricist programme of social investigation.

Despite these differences all research implies a position on knowledge claims about the nature of social phenomena, as well as their constitution. Thus, a researcher may take an "action" or "structure" approach to a research problem. The unit of analysis may then be the individual, relations between individuals, or the social group as a whole. The decision to take the first approach may be implicitly grounded in an individualist view of society that then denies the validity of treating social groups as "entities" with identifiable attributes. On the other hand, the researcher may adopt a holist position whereby social institutions cannot be understood by simply studying the characteristics of its constituent members.

A theoretical starting point will also have implications for the explanations and/or understandings offered in the resulting data. Studies of poverty from an individualist perspective may be more inclined to explain individual poverty in terms of individual attributes that either predispose, or determine, that people will act in particular ways. In contrast, researchers from a holist perspective would be predisposed to seek explanations of poverty that begin from the idea of social structures and proceed from there to examine their effects on individuals. In addition, explanations may invoke causes from a positivist or realist viewpoint, or they may simply draw conclusions from associations between variables thereby drawing upon a probabilistic research strategy. Alternatively, cause or association may be seen as irrelevant to interpretivist approaches that are concerned with human understanding and the interpretation of meaningful communication.

So far, philosophical implications and assumptions have been located in the identification of a research problem, the theoretical and ideological context of the research itself and the explanations that might result from implicitly or explicitly choosing from a number of strategies for knowing the social world. More specifically, philosophical commitments have a direct bearing on the manner in which research is conducted and the types of validity and reliability then obtained in its results. This, of course, relates to the generation of "truth".

A key goal for social research is to achieve validity. Because this means quite different things between approaches to research and may take different forms, the philosophical implications are complex. In particular, it is said that survey research may obtain greater external validity than qualitative approaches that concentrate on internal validity. Take an attitude scale measuring job satisfaction. This is said to have a validity beyond the setting in which it was administered. As such, it would make sense to a wider audience and would be easily replicable; a characteristic, it is sometimes said, that is at the heart of external validity. At a general level, it may therefore be subject to test within a community of scientists working on the same area of interest. It might then be argued to possess the potential to be valid, first, at the level of congruence within a scientific community and secondly, at the level of correspondence with a given set of social conditions.

This idea of validity noted, this method may fail to grasp what was really important to the workers surveyed. A bland choice of "level of satisfaction", where 1 = very dissatisfied and 5 = very satisfied, leaves the interpretation of "satisfied" open to the respondent. The irony here is an assumed congruence of meaning between what the designer intended and the ways in which it is interpreted by the respondents. From this point of view, one could say that all quantitative research assumes an ethnographic dimension to its design where the latter is characterized as being concerned with meaning construction in everyday life. A focus group, or depth interview, therefore, is said to allow the respondent(s) to construct meanings that are valid to them within their social context. Likewise, a key advantage of participant observation is that it allows the observer to understand how agents in particular settings construct meanings: that is, what is situationally rational.

The whole point of using participant observation is to understand forms of action and modes of life that can only be understood from the "inside". It follows from this that the actions considered rational within the research setting will make little sense outside it. Moreover, because the researcher cannot know what are the important meanings *a priori* within a particular setting, then she cannot know the extent to which these meanings are valid in similar situations. Of course, the meanings that give validity in these circumstances may have a limited currency beyond the particular setting. Here, one may move beyond actions to consider those underlying structures with which they interact. It is these structures that are then generalizable. However, note that one has now gone beyond the confines of so-called action theories, or research programmes, that reflect a commitment to philosophical idealism, to a realist-based form of ethnography where the idea of "truth" changes (see Porter 1993).

It will be recalled from Chapter 2 that there is an important connection between validity and truth. We noted that a statement can be valid, but is not necessarily true and vice versa. Whereas a conclusion may be valid, because there is agreement with the premiss(es), the premiss(es) themselves could be "untrue". Consider, then, the truth status of claims in social research. A correspondence theory of truth requires that for something to be true there must be agreement with the facts. However, what should count as the "facts"? In survey research there is often an implicit commitment to the correspondence theory of truth, yet the status of truth claims can be very local. While questions about sex, age, marital status, etc., are relatively unproblematic – provided the respondent does not lie, is in possession of the knowledge required, understands the question and the responses are correctly coded – this cannot be the case for attitudes. When researchers ask respondents for their opinions, then they are asking respondents to reveal what they believe to be the truth. In one sense, truth is put to one side and validity is considered to be that which is important to the respondent.

Within qualitative research based upon idealism, the commitment to a correspondence theory of truth, implicitly or explicitly, is not so frequent. Because emphasis is placed upon the meanings of those researched then what is often sought is coherence. In carrying out research on the Flat Earth Society, for example, it is the reasons that people offer for what they do and the ways in which the meanings they use make sense of their lives that are of interest, not whether the basis of their beliefs are true as such. This noted, it must be said that theories of truth are not a major preoccupation of researchers. Scan the index of most methods, or even methodology texts, and the word will be unlikely to appear. Yet a commitment to a view of "truth" is implicit in all research. A theory of truth may provide inspiration to a methodological programme, such as that of the pragmatist inspired Chicago School (Hammersley 1989), or it may underlie realist ontological claims about the reality of the social world (Sayer 1984).

Closely related to validity and truth are issues of generalization and reliability. The kind of generalizations one can make about a particular type of social situation using ethnographic approaches are often seen as limited in comparison to survey research. Whereas William Whyte's *Street corner society* (1943) is regarded as a classic piece of participant observation, his findings on street gangs may not be generalizable. As Whyte noted, "To some extent my approach must be unique to myself, to the particular situation, and to the state of knowledge when I began research" (quoted in Bryman 1988: 90). Nevertheless, relativism does not simply follow for the notion of "reasonable extrapolation" is still available (Quinn-Patton 1986). Unlike the usual meaning of the term "generalization", an extrapolation clearly connotes that one has gone beyond the narrow confines of the data to think of other applications of the findings. Extrapolations are modest speculations on the likely applicability of findings to other situations under similar, but not identical, conditions. Extrapolations are logical, thoughtful and problem-orientated rather than purely empirical, statistical and probabilistic (Quinn-Patton 1986).

We should also note that because there exists a level of intersubjective agreement between researchers, then some generalizations about commonly agreed or understood constructs can be made to similar situations. Although Whyte was cautious in terms of the applicability of his findings, it might be possible to say something about the general characteristics of gangs using, for example, Schutz's idea of typifications or Simmel's idea of formalism (Frisby 1981). Indeed, within the ethnomethodological tradition the methods that people use to categorize individuals would appear to be generalizable through invoking the notion of the structure of practical action (Atkinson & Heritage 1984, Garfinkel & Sacks 1986). However, this is emergent from within everyday life, rather than being imposed, via theoretical models, on everyday actions and utterances. Finally, it is perfectly possible to compare the findings from study X to those of study Y and seek commonalities between them.

If the findings are valid, are they necessarily reliable? If we repeat a focus group interview in a different setting, will we reach the same conclusions? In these terms we might observe that validity is a focus on the meaning and the meaningfulness of the data whereas reliability is a focus on its consistency (Quinn-Patton 1986). There may be acceptance that qualitative research is capable of producing "valid" data, but there is often doubt as to whether it can be relied upon. While validity and reliability are closely related, it is quite possible to have one without the other. A repeated measure in survey research, or experiments, may be reliable in that the same results are obtained each time, even within a wide variety of circumstances. However, the measure itself may not be valid because it does not achieve what it set out to do.

Finally, we should note that the reason for the choice of methods will vary in the research process. The decision to opt for participant observation, rather than, say, survey methods, for example, may be the result of several factors. First, it may represent a prior commitment to an interpretivist approach to knowing the social world. Secondly, it may represent a technical decision whereby participant observation is a more appropriate method with which to tackle the research question and thirdly, it may be the only way in which one may gain access to certain groups, thus reflecting a practical necessity. Whatever the reason, however, the types of validity and reliability that may then be alluded to remain to be usefully examined under the philosophical microscope.

Research issues to do with validity and reliability might be said to be at the "sharp end" of the philosophical issues we discussed in Chapter 4. While the choice of method may be ostensibly made on methodological grounds, the methods themselves will have consequences for the claims we can make based upon our research. In order to illustrate these themes, we will now move on to consider two very different examples of recent social research. The first of these we have taken as typical of the type of policy related work many researchers are routinely engaged in. The second example is very different in terms of its methodology, methods and motivations.

Philosophy and social research: two case studies

Evaluating Neighbourhood Watch schemes in London

This case study is concerned with crime reduction and attitudes towards crime in two London suburbs (Bennett 1988). Neighbourhood Watch schemes had their origins in the US in the 1970s, but made an appearance in the UK, in London, in 1983. As a result of official encouragement from the police and government, they have spread throughout Britain. Defining exactly what a Neighbourhood Watch scheme is, is not a straightforward matter. Although their activities vary, a central feature seems to be, "the notion of the public becoming 'the eyes and ears of the police'"(Bennett 1988: 242).

The research attempted to evaluate Neighbourhood Watch schemes in terms, primarily, of their ability to reduce crime and the extent to which they reduced fear of crime. In order to achieve this, a quasi experimental research design was adopted. This method involved data collection at a point before some treatment – in this case the implementation of a Neighbourhood Watch scheme – and at a point after the treatment had time to take effect. In addition, comparisons were made with an area where no Neighbourhood Watch schemes were implemented in order to serve as a "control group". Secondary socio-demographic data were used to match the sites to produce the best possible match based upon "social composition, general geographic structure and crime rate" (Bennett 1988: 244).

The process of data collection itself took the form of a survey exploring incidences and perceptions of crime. The first round of surveys was conducted between one and two months before the launch of Neighbourhood Watch programmes and the second round of surveys took place following, approximately, one year of their implementation. Overall, the study found that "victimizations" (crimes) had increased in the experimental areas, but had fallen or remained constant in the areas where no Neighbourhood Watch scheme had been implemented. However, where such schemes had been implemented, there was a reduction in the fear in relation to household and personal crime and evidence of, "improvements in social cohesion . . . and involvement with others in home protection" (Bennett 1988: 252).

At first glance, the research would appear to be straightforward and a world away from an illuminating examination from a philosophical perspective. The study is a piece of survey research, with a clearly stated hypothesis about the potential reduction of crime that might come about as a result of the implementation of Neighbourhood Watch schemes. Indeed, it is typical of a great deal of "bread and butter" commissioned policy research. Yet, we find philosophical implications at a number of levels.

We might first observe that while some would question whether the research is "positivist" or not, it is without doubt in the positivist tradition and very firmly in the naturalist camp. There is both an implicit and explicit neutrality on the benefits, or otherwise, of Neighbourhood Watch schemes and a commitment to particular "scientific standards" in the design and conduct of the research itself. As a result, the work is strangely silent on the very general issue with which it is concerned. In Chapter 5, we noted a dichotomy in the practice of research around the pathological and the normal. Nowhere is this more pronounced than in definitions of crime or deviance (see Hester & Egline 1992). This is not to say that a society can avoid such classifications, simply that they are a social product and not a pre-given category. It follows that Neighbourhood Watch schemes require some working definition of what it is that their adherents should be watching out for. It is sometimes said that crime is that with which police forces are concerned. In other words, though there are thousands of laws on the statute book, the only ones that matter are those that are enforced, or those to which police direct their attention. These are matters of social and political values that relate to the allocation of resources.

Trevor Bennett discusses the variability in resource allocation for the Neighbourhood Watch schemes and argues that this may be a factor in their success or failure. It may be that police district A emphasizes the fight against burglary and vandalism, district B is more concerned with crimes against the person and district C is preoccupied with getting the paperwork right. Each district places different priorities on different crimes. Neighbourhood Watch schemes are not only social constructions of what counts as "criminal", but the construction itself may be subject to local variability. Nevertheless, the British Home Office, in commissioning the research, does so for particular reasons. As such, we need to be aware of the possibility that researchers who are funded by such means may well be complicit in establishing and maintaining particular values.

In Chapter 5 we called into question the notion of any investigation as a value free activity. Therefore, it is hardly surprising that in our example the research may be seen to begin from a value laden position. Yet the scientific credibility of the enterprise may be seen to rest not only upon an implicit neutrality, but also on a method that is claimed to be objective. In the laboratory, the physical scientist wishes to isolate parts of the world when conducting an experiment and in doing so will hold certain things constant while manipulating other relevant factors. The effects of such intervention are often controlled for and there is a high degree of internal validity. In other words, there will be a high degree of confidence upon which conclusions may be based concerning the causal effects of one variable on another.

We should note that, relative to the above, the internal validity of the quasi-experimental method is poor. This is because the number of intervening variables, including, in this case, interviewer effects, changing perceptions of crime, changes in environmental factors, etc., can only be surmised. In some sophisticated studies what are termed "violations of assumptions" about the circumstances assumed to exist, are controlled for in statistical models (Bishop et al. 1975). Nevertheless, we could not possibly control for all of the things that might change between two time points, or might be different between places. Here, Bennett points out that:

> In order to control for differences between the samples, it is necessary to use a statistical analysis which can simultaneously control for demographic and other differences between the samples (Bennett 1988: 251).

However, we should remember that the demographic differences arise from census variables, themselves a product of social selection. Therefore, what is considered to be important is to some degree "inherited" by the research, whereas other important differences may be omitted, by default, from the evaluation.

These points noted, we should not be too harsh. The kind of problems faced here and the solutions adopted are commonplace and to some extent reflect what we have termed the "open nature" of the social world. It is thus not surprising that quantitative researchers are forced into adopting "associations" between variables in a probabilistic strategy, rather than specifying a more explicit causal chain. Furthermore, in the relation between the researcher and the sponsor of the research, it is often the case that the latter may prevent the former from fully publishing and disseminating their findings because they do not meet with their ideologically pre-given expectations. Therefore, in evaluating such work from a philosophical perspective, we should be aware that there exists a complicated relationship between the ethics and politics of research at the stages of design, data collection and the publication of findings (see Homan 1991, Punch 1986).

Finally, in a summary discussion Bennett notes that, "the changes shown were less promising than might have been hoped" (Bennett 1988: 253). He asks why an evaluation might fail to find the desired effects and cites the work of Rosenbaum (1986) in terms of it being attributable to "measurement failure", "theory failure", or "programme failure". In the first of these, "failure" is attributable to poor evaluation design or a method of statistical analysis that failed to detect a programme effect. In the second, although there is success in the implementation of a scheme and its evaluation, failure results from flaws in the theory underlying the scheme. Finally, although the theory underlying the programme might be sound, its implementation is flawed. Bennett's conclusion was that the latter was the case. As such, although the overall theory of the implementation of Neighbourhood Watches was sound, its implementation was poor and this was likely to be the result of local factors (in London) surrounding the discretion invested in senior divisional police officers to implement and resource schemes as they saw fit.

It is important to note that failure due to poor research design, or the underlying theory of Neighbourhood Watch schemes was rejected by Bennett; the first because "it is hard to believe" that the research design was so poor as to serve to conceal Neighbourhood Watch success and the second because other research shows the theory to be sound. This left him with a third possibility: that is, although the underlying theory of Neighbourhood Watch schemes was correct, the theory was poorly implemented – and in the examples used, this was the case: specifically, that the design of Neighbourhood Watch as expressed in the Metropolitan (London) police guidelines was not a good example of Neighbourhood Watch in general. From this point of view:

> There is a danger that Neighbourhood Watch throughout the country is being implemented on the basis of uncertain theoretical principles and on speculative programme design (Bennett 1988: 254).

At this point there seems to be some "over-stretching" of the findings in order to rescue the implicit theory underlying the research; this being that

Neighbourhood Watch schemes are a good thing. Such strategies, as Lakatos noted, are far from unusual in science. Scientists will deflect theory failure by reference to a complex web of assumptions, which are often untestable in themselves. In this case, the theory is "saved " by reference to the manner of implementation as opposed to the rationale and effect of Neighbourhood Watch schemes themselves. This strategy carries the advantage that its assumptions cannot be falsified. If the same results are achieved in further research, then once more poor implementation of the theory can be blamed. If, on the other hand, further research showed a scheme, or schemes, to be successful, then clearly the theory had been implemented correctly!

At this last level we can say that this research is no more ideologically motivated, nor more "scientifically" flawed, than thousands of other similar projects. We offer it as an illustration of some of the philosophical implications that arise from the value base of the research, and the methodological strategies adopted, within its design and execution.

"Doing the business" of qualitative research

Our second example of research is not offered as a contrasting virtue, but rather as a piece of social research that has a very different starting point and methodological approach to that of Bennett. This allows a comparison of both philosophical assumptions and implications. In order to achieve this, we will first provide a description of the study in terms of its contents and methods and then move on to discuss it from a philosophical vantage point.

In 1988, Dick Hobbs published a book entitled, *Doing the business: entrepreneurship, the working class, and detectives in the East End of London*. Utilizing his own biography and the techniques of participant observation, interviews and documentary research, he examined a culture that survives on the margins between illegal activity and legitimate enterprise. This is the culture whose ethos is summarized by the phrase "doing the business" and it affects the actions and perspectives of the detectives who seek to police it, as well as those who are policed by them.

The early chapters in the book are devoted to an historical contextualization, which then serves to situate the descriptions of the contemporary cultures of the East End and its policing in the second half of the book. These early chapters contain a "natural history" of British policing, with particular reference to the Metropolitan police force and the social construction of criminality within London. This was manifested, for example, by a concentration upon particular social groups who were seen to constitute a threat to the established social order. This account is also accompanied by the examination of an economy that thrived and in his study still does, on the processes of bargaining and exchange. Chapters then follow on East End gangsters, which include a discussion of the Kray twins and Richardson brothers.

The second half of the book then moves on to contemporary times with one chapter devoted to youth entrepreneurs and the ways in which they mediate the culture described earlier. The aim then changes to one of understanding adult entrepreneurship. One means by which this is achieved is to focus upon the activities taking place within a local pub where entrepreneurs and police detectives alike gather to "do their business". Through both direct experience and testimony we are given an insight into each of their worlds. For instance, there is the entrepreneur known as the "jump-up merchant" (Hobbs 1988: 154). We are told not only of his ethos, but also his *modus operandi*. His attempts, for example, to burgle a business were "thwarted by security arrangements" and all he got away with was an old ladder! The next day he became a window-cleaner, but found he was afraid of heights and so sold the ladder. A true entrepreneur! The parallels between such activities and the rhetoric of the government of the time were not lost on the author.

As for the detectives, they also met their occupational demands by using the rhetoric and strategies of this culture: for example, by "turning a blind eye" to certain activities and by nominating certain individuals to "take their turn" in order to boost police clear-up rates. However, their understandings of the "market place" were never complete, as demonstrated by the time several detectives were drinking in a pub in the early hours of the morning while above them, as the majority in the neighbourhood knew, there was a large consignment of stolen whisky!

In the postscript, the effect of the unleashing of market forces on the area are charted, the result of which is an attack on the population, "unprecedented since the blitz of the Second World War in terms of its viciousness and irrevocable damage inflicted" (1988: 218). In spending some time with those whom he researched at a holiday resort, he writes that such breaks are "crucial" in a culture "constantly besieged by bourgeois society and market trends" (1988: 234). However, for the present, it seems, people will still be "doing their business". It is here that the cultural antecedents of the East End are readily apparent in their actions.

This case study represents a rich mixture of philosophical issues and assumptions, as well as having a number of implications for the study of social life. If we consider the various strategies available to researchers for knowing the social world, as we have noted previously, they each carry with them various epistemological and ontological presuppositions. In this study we find an ontological and epistemological commitment to the research legacy of the Chicago School of sociology (Hobbs 1988: 15). Here we find a pragmatist commitment to truth that is exemplified through the need to familiarize oneself with the context in which people interact and construct the meanings that they then attribute to their social worlds. At the same time, from an ontological vantage point, the construction of the social self is viewed as a dialectical process between subject and object where self-consciousness is seen to arise in the context of social action (Mead 1964) or, in this case, the process of "doing the business".

Methodological consequences follow from this initial commitment. Overall, this represents a clear adherence to the concept of "internal validity". In order to interpret accurately the situated understandings of those social actors who were the subject of his study, the author required the twin strategies of familiarity and empathy. Thus, we find him alluding to his cultural credibility, through the utilization of his own biography, in order to substantiate his findings and interpretations:

> my status as an insider meant that I was afforded a great deal of trust by my informants, and I was allowed access to settings, detailed conversations, and information that *might not otherwise have been available* (Hobbs 1988: 15. Emphasis added).

The role of experience within the pragmatist tradition is thereby emphasized. Within this tradition the questions for science are considered to be obtained from experience itself, thus providing parallels with the empiricist tradition. In the process of social research, however, experience may be derived from a number of sources: for example, at the level of the personal; the professional in terms of exploratory research programmes; from previous research, or a theoretical sensitivity that is derived from familiarity with a body of technical literature (Strauss 1988: 12).

In the case of this study, the credibility, as opposed to the validity, of its presentation to various audiences, often rested upon personal experience. This was a study of a male culture by a researcher with a high degree of cultural authenticity that became apparent in the presentation of his initial findings to academic audiences. Rarely were his findings disputed. This occurred despite the fact that, from a quantitative point of view, the findings may not have appeared to be replicable. In addition, the earlier accounts of his research were, "naïve, loosely formulated, and theoretically vacuous" (Hobbs 1993: 49). The point is that it was his personal experience that gave this study its credibility and from there, an assumption was made concerning its validity from an "internal" viewpoint. In an account of this process that is refreshingly honest, Hobbs noted of this phenomenon that:

> people believed me, they considered what I had to say about petty crime in East London was true, and I didn't know why. Other researchers, far more experienced and technically competent than myself, would be given a tough time, yet at this early stage what I had to say was accepted (Hobbs 1993: 49).

Even so, a careful reading of the work reveals a utilization of all of the above sources of experience.

At this stage we should note the existence of a social dynamic that is illuminated more by sociology than philosophy. It is cultural authenticity that may provide the legitimacy for particular studies, but it is the culture to which one turns that is of importance in this process. Academia does consist of those whose backgrounds are not middle class. However, it is a middle-class occupation and this explains much of the success of the reception of this study of working-class culture. Therefore, when turning to some hardened community workers in the East End to disseminate the same accounts, the author's biography and accent were not enough to give the value of his findings, nor the novelty of his methods, sufficient cultural credibility (see Hobbs 1993).

Despite this observation, the overall methodological commitment in this study appears to be to "analytic induction". In *Doing the business* we find a fusion of pragmatism and induction exemplified by what has been termed "naturalistic inquiry". However, naturalism has a different sense to that which we have used before where there exists a belief in the applicability of the natural scientific model to the study of social phenomena. This sense simply exhibits, "a profound respect for the character of the empirical world" (Denzin 1979: 39). In this respect, it reflects an empiricist commitment to the production of truth in terms of the accurate representation of the social world as it appears to those who are part of it. Overall, we might argue that the desire to represent the intrinsic character of social phenomena, as opposed to the imposition of models of social reality that do not accurately represent those phenomena (the process of deduction), is reflected in the commitment to participant observation. From an ontological vantage point, the culture is seen as sufficiently open to a form of "negotiated order" analysis (Strauss 1978) whereby the individuals who are part of it construct the meanings and symbols that make sense of it. Methodologically, therefore, the researcher must become part of such a culture to understand this process.

At a socio-theoretical and philosophical level, this study appears to reflect a commitment to the fluidity of social life, as is consistent with the tradition known as symbolic interactionism (see Rock 1979). In addition, it seems to be committed to a form of philosophical idealism in terms of the idea of "free agents" who adopt different strategies in order to cope with, make sense of and survive in, their social worlds. Yet equally, particularly given the amount of the book that is devoted to historical contextualization, this could be read as a realist programme in terms of its assumptions and implications. After all, a philosophical idealist reading sits somewhat uneasily with the general tenor of the book as revealed in the quotes noted above: for example, the allusion to an "onslaught" by bourgeois culture and the damage caused by a "yuppie culture" of money and office development in the East End.

This now begins to look more like the critical realist programme of Roy Bhaskar (1975, 1989, 1993). As noted, the historical contextualization of East End culture provides a way of situating the accounts of the contemporary entrepreneurial culture. In other words, the resources that people drew upon were those given and transmitted from the past. This was action in the sense that it involved considerations and deliberations, but it was structure in the sense that it pre-existed those individuals and was reproduced by them in their daily actions. Furthermore, a dominant material culture is clearly posited in terms of its ability to affect the culture that is studied, despite the interpretations and actions of those who are a part of it. As he notes in the conclusion:

> The East End, as I have stressed throughout this book, has always had a rather peculiar relationship with capitalism, but now central government is exploiting that relationship to the full, and by direct intervention in municipal government and the manipula-

tion of crucial funding by way of fantastic levels of subsidy to private enterprise, the East End is now being used as a flagship for a "new" Great Britain Ltd (Hobbs 1988: 222).

To read this study as one of critical realism is not to suggest the replacement of a social philosophical model of free agents with those who are determined by circumstances beyond their control. That would be to set up an ontological dualism between free-will and determinism that is not recognized within this tradition. Aside from the comments we made earlier in relation to this body of work, we might simply paraphrase Marx, "people make history, but not in circumstances of their own choosing" (Marx 1980: 96). These are the same words which Anthony Giddens, whose work, some have argued, also falls within the realist tradition, uses to characterize the ontological basis of his theory of structuration (Giddens 1984: xxi). However, he takes another ethnography, only this time by Paul Willis (1977), to illustrate the methodological implications of his ideas (see Giddens 1984: 289–309).

Summary

We started this chapter by noting that our intention was to be illustrative. In seeking to achieve this, the above two case studies offer us different ways of looking at social phenomena. Clearly, these works may be read at different levels. The point is, however, that a philosophical perspective on the research process enables us to understand the basis of reasoning employed in the practice of social research, as well as the implications of the methodological commitments that social investigators bring to their studies of social phenomena. Nevertheless, we should note that they, like those whom they study, are often constrained in their choices. Consider the methods they might employ for their studies. Constraints operate in terms of the nature of the social phenomenon that is the object of their curiosity and the values of the funding bodies who enable them to conduct their research in the first instance. Research, therefore, is a mixture of both strategies and methods affected by political and social considerations, as well as informed by philosophical issues.

In relation to the work by Dick Hobbs, we noted how his own background added to the credibility of his narratives. This, of course, is not the same as the concept of validity as pursued within the correspondence theory of reality that is seen to characterize scientific endeavours. Yet there are those who see all research as narratives – even the idea of science itself. This represents a radical critique of all that has gone before us. As a result, it is deserving of our attention. It is to the post-critiques of science and social research that we now turn.

Questions for discussion

1. Compare the research of Bennett and Hobbs. What are the key differences in the philosophical assumptions held?
2. What makes us choose one methodological approach over another? To what extent do philosophical assumptions inform these choices?
3. Identify an example of recent empirical research. What kinds of philosophical assumptions and implications are entailed?
4. Dick Hobbs wrote, "Because of my background I found nothing immoral or even unusual in the dealing and trading that I encountered. However, I do not consider the study to be unethical, for the ethics that I adhered to were the ethics of the citizens of the East End" (1988: 7–8). In your opinion, is this a necessary strategic device for the enhancement of internal validity, or is it just an excuse for moral relativism?

Suggested reading

Bryman, A. 1988. *Quantity and quality in social research*. London: Unwin Hyman.
Harvey, L. 1990. *Critical social research*. London: Unwin Hyman.
Hammersley, M. & P. Atkinson 1995. *Ethnography; principles in practice*, 2nd ed. London: Routledge.
McKarl-Nielsen, J. (ed.) 1990. *Feminist research methods: exemplary readings in the social sciences*. London: Westview Press.
Marsh, C. 1982. *The survey method – the contribution of surveys to sociological explanation*. London: George Allen & Unwin.
Knorr-Cetina, K. & A. Cicourel (eds) 1981. *Advances in social theory and methodology: towards an integration of micro and macro theories*. London: Routledge & Kegan Paul.

CHAPTER 7

Poststructuralism, postmodernism and social research

This chapter has two aims. First, to examine the views of writers of both the poststructuralist and postmodernist schools of thought in relation to the philosophy of social research. Secondly, to illustrate how these ideas relate to the methodology of social research and the social sciences in general, leaving us in a better position to evaluate their implications for the practice of social research.

The post-critiques: taking aim at foundationalism

Given the sheer breadth of these topics, the aim here is one of clarification, not resolution. This is fortunate, for when it comes to postmodernism it is not possible to say the "jury is out and will soon reach a verdict"; there is not, nor can there be, any jury who might allude to universal concepts of justice upon which to base their judgements. Monolithic concepts of truth based upon universal reason are now committed to the dustbin of history. Allusions to transcendental and universal concepts of truth in the name of science have vanished into the air of relativism. No doubt as we write, the complacency of modernity, based upon Enlightenment principles, is once again being demolished by new converts to postmodernism, or questioned and subverted by a new generation of poststructuralists.

Even if our aim in this chapter is one of clarification, there is now an overwhelming body of literature relevant to this topic (for example, Lash 1990, Docherty 1993, Sarup 1993, Smart 1993 and Bertens 1995). To some this may be a good thing. At the same time, it is quite clear that the idea of a "postmodern condition" is not without considerable criticism, some of which we will outline in the summary section of the chapter. Given this state of affairs, our path will be one of attention to its arguments, as well as its implications for social research. Although the French intellectual scene, from which so much of this writing derives, has been the subject of literary derision (Bradbury 1989), we agree that in approaching the postmodern and poststructuralist literature it is not helpful to do so in the manner of either wholesale adoption or rejection. As one writer who approaches this work in such a manner suggests:

> if radical manifestos proclaiming the end of sociology and social philosophy "as we know them" seem unfounded, equally convincing is the pretence that nothing of importance has happened and there is nothing to stop "business as usual" (Bauman 1992: 105).

Perhaps the first point we should note is that critics of the Enlightenment project are not new. We have already considered the ways in which the critical theorists approached this subject. For them, the modern age is characterized as a disjuncture between reason and rationalization. As Adorno & Horkheimer wrote in 1944:

> For the Enlightenment, whatever does not conform to the rule of computation and utility is suspect. So long as it can develop undisturbed by any outward repression, there is no holding it. In the process, it treats its own ideas of human rights exactly as it does the older universals. Every spiritual resistance it encounters serves merely to increase its strength . . . *Enlightenment is totalitarian* (1979: 6. Emphasis added).

Compare this quote to one of the leading figures of the postmodernist movement – Jean-François Lyotard. Here we find that claims to speak for "reality" and society as a "whole" are firmly laid to rest. For this reason, the scientific aim of generalization is not viewed as part of the path towards greater knowledge. On the contrary:

> The nineteenth and twentieth centuries have given us as much terror as we can take. We have paid a high enough price for the

nostalgia of the whole and the one . . . Under the general demand for slackening and for appeasement, we can hear the mutterings of the desire for a return of terror, for the realization of the fantasy to seize reality. The answer is: Let us wage war on totality; let us be witnesses to the unpresentable; let us activate the differences (Lyotard 1993: 46).

Jürgen Habermas (1992) argues that the openings of postmodernism in Western thought may be found in the writings of the German philosopher Friedrich Nietzsche (1844–1900). In Nietzsche's writings we can find him espousing the doctrine of perspectivism: that is, there is no transcendental vantage point from which one may view truth, and the external world is interpreted according to different beliefs and ideas whose validities are equal to one another. References to postmodernism may also be found in 1930s literary criticism, while in North America during the 1960s there was a postmodernist movement in art, "constituted as a potentially avantgardist cultural configuration" (Smart 1993: 19). Its roots may also be traced in dance, art, film, photography, as well as architecture (Bertens 1995). In this sense, we may characterize postmodernism as a general cultural movement associated with the epoch known as postmodernity. The characteristics of this age include the rise of the information society (Lyotard), the triumph of production over consumption (Baudrillard), coupled with general denunciations of meta-narratives of explanation, totalizing politics and homogeneous and invariant concepts of social identity.

In a classic work, *The sociological imagination*, originally published in 1959, Mills writes of the changing notions of "reason" and "freedom". He notes how social science has inherited terms that, even though they are outdated, are still rooted in their practice. These "categories of thought", if generalized to contemporary situations, "become unwieldy, irrelevant, not convincing" (1970: 184). Given this state of affairs:

We are at the ending of what is called the Modern Age. Just as Antiquity was followed by several centuries of Oriental ascendancy, which Westerners provincially call the Dark Ages, so now The Modern Age is being succeeded by a *post-modern period*. Perhaps we may call it: The Fourth Epoch (1970: 184. Emphasis added).

157

If this "Fourth Epoch" is a search for new values, identities and ways of life, it is not surprising that we can range, in reaction to postmodernism, from those immersed in the cosy slumbers of the "nothing has changed" group, to those convinced by its arguments. These tensions have opened up new fields of inquiry. It has led to a desire, for example, to understand social identity, feelings, emotions, sexuality and the "body" – not simply an epiphenomena of the mind as represented in Cartesian rationalism (see Featherstone & Turner 1995). This has been undertaken through the use of forms of research that are often regarded as "unscientific", in terms of their being rooted in art and subjectivity, as opposed to "science": for example, biography, autobiography and photography. Accompanying this process has been the breaking down of disciplinary barriers between, for instance, literature, art and science. In these terms, we might view social research as part of the search for new values and ways of life. It could be characterized, perhaps, as simply another form of representing the desire, motivated by Michel Foucault's injunction to write, in order, "to become someone other than who one is" (quoted in Miller 1993: 33).

Although not a new concept, the sheer scale of the postmodern assault on the social sciences is a more recent phenomenon. At an epistemological level, converts to postmodernism regard it as doing nothing less than pulling the rug from under the feet of traditional scientific foundations. Although there remains definitional ambiguity over the term, for our purposes postmodernism may be viewed as a critique of the values, goals and bases of analyses that, from the Enlightenment onwards, have been assumed to be universally valid. Its theoretical base is therefore pluralist and anti-reductionist. This results in a celebration of difference and diversity, rather than similarity and uniformity. Methodologically, the alternative to the complacent foundationalism of modernism becomes the maxim, apparently favoured by Feyerabend (1978), that "anything goes". Given this, it provokes established scientific beliefs. As the postmodern philosopher Jean Baudrillard puts it, "there is always an element of provocation in what I write. It is a sort of challenge to the intellectual and the reader that starts a kind of game" (Baudrillard in Gane 1993: 153–4).

Foundations and representation in question

In reaction to these critiques we could take the "middle ground" by rejecting the complacency of modernism and methodological anarchism. We might simply say that postmodernism has reinforced the idea that truth is contingent and nothing should be placed beyond the possibility of revision. However, elements of these critiques go further than this. At an individual level, they constitute a direct challenge to the expert status of the researcher. Consider, for instance, the consequences of Jacques Derrida's deconstructionist project. Science may be seen from this point of view as a form of rhetoric that serves to obfuscate more than it illuminates. Behind every technical argument there lurk values and it is these that should be exposed by the process of deconstruction.

Derrida's overall strategy is to expose what he calls the "disingenuous dream" of Western philosophy. So far, we have discussed this in terms of the attempt to find a transparent language that might represent the world as it "really" is. The history of science can thus be read as the attempt to legislate for what is to constitute valid knowledge. As we have seen, this goal attained its credibility with the Cartesian notion that a transcendental standard against which truth could be objectively measured, independent of the objects of scientific inquiry, was possible. In Kant's work, we found the fusion of reason and empiricism. According to this view, the material world causes sensations, but it is our mental apparatus that orders them. Reason becomes a universal capacity from which arose a whole new mode of thought:

> Rational mastery of nature and society presupposed knowledge of the truth, and the truth was universal, as contrasted to the multi-fold appearance of things or to their immediate form in the perception of individuals. This principle was already alive in the earliest attempts of Greek epistemology: the truth is universal and necessary and thus contradicts the ordinary experiences of change and accident (Marcuse 1969: 17).

Methodologically we have seen that this required representation and reality to correspond to each other in the process of rational scientific inquiry. If accepted, then once *the method* is found, we then discover *the reality*. This leads to a claim of objectivism defined as:

> the basic conviction that there is or must be some permanent, ahistorical matrix or framework to which we can ultimately appeal in determining the nature of rationality, knowledge, truth, reality, goodness, or rightness (Bernstein 1983: 8).

However, is the world not characterized by chance, accident and difference that science attempts not to represent, but to control in the name of limited concepts of ontology and epistemology?

In the unfolding history of epistemology, the Kantian notion was challenged through the argument that rationality, the guarantor of this process, is historically and sociologically constituted and not some ahistorical objective reality. The argument that this is relativistic, from a Cartesian perspective, is met by the counter-claim that we "progress", in terms of our knowledge base, as we move from one age to the next. However, for the post-critiques, even this historicist move does not go far enough. Why? Because George Hegel (1770–1831), the first European thinker to consider knowledge in these terms, was still committed to two cornerstones of scientific endeavour: objectivity and truth (Sayers 1989). Reason, in other words, may still be mobilized in defence of "science", which claims for itself the role of an arbitrator of progress.

The implications of the undermining of this argument are far reaching. Quite simply, once we move beyond Cartesian and historicist claims, the concepts that underpin scientific practice become confined to the epistemological toilet and with this, the security of the scientific practitioner's expert status, as well as that of their discipline in general. This is where Nietzsche steps in; a thinker who has been so influential on such diverse thinkers as Derrida, Baudrillard, Deleuze and Kristeva.

This strand of thought, as it applies to the history of social science, is also argued to be present in the work of Michel Foucault. It comes as no surprise that Richard Rorty, a contemporary "anti-foundationalist" thinker, should pursue this line of thinking in his interpretation of Foucault:

> To see Foucault as a Nietzschean enemy of historicism rather than one more historicist enemy of Cartesianism, we need to see him as trying to write history in a way which will destroy the notion of historical progress (1987: 47).

Chance and chaos, not the discovery of "truth" and "progress", now enter research endeavours. In an historical manner, rather than Derrida's philosophical approach, the very "background thinking" (Gouldner 1971) of the researcher and philosopher is exposed under this critical gaze. Even the attempt to break free of this historical legacy, according to Foucault, leads us into the building of other forms of constraint as we search, in vain, for universals that might demarcate between the "true" and the "false". In these circumstances, the best that a social researcher might hope for is to act as an interpreter, but certainly not the legislator of truth (Bauman 1987).

How did this all happen in the history of epistemology? It starts from the recognition that we are structured by history and even the forces of nature. Despite this, an apparent anthropological constraint was turned into a strength. In this process, scientists became the legislators of what was to count as "valid" knowledge. From the Enlightenment onwards, this has involved a move away from an analysis of representations, towards what Foucault calls an *analytic*:

> From Kant on, an analytic is an attempt to show on what grounds representation and analysis of representations are possible and to what extent they are legitimate (Dreyfus & Rabinow 1982: 28).

Foucault (1992) terms this the "analytic of finitude". It represents the desire to achieve a correspondence between reality and a language (scientific) that can describe that reality. However, Foucault added to this in two ways. First, through a critique of transcendental reason and the corresponding desire to find a universal, ahistorical and normative basis for a "way of life". In practice, this came to mean that differences between ways of life could be judged according to reason, whereas the "authenticity" of such a dialogue is based upon the participants' abilities to reach a particular standard; a standard set by limited notions of Western rationality. One of the implications of this critique is that research cannot then adjudicate, on a normative basis, between ways of life, but may only describe them relative to time and place.

Secondly, there are Foucault's (1980) arguments on the inseparability of knowledge and power. This undermines the ideal of knowledge as liberation, as well as the practice of human sciences as being separate from the operation of power. Thus, where power is exercised, knowledge is also produced. In this respect, the human sciences, by producing knowledge, affect social and institutional practices. The knowledge they generate about relations and practices between individuals in societies has an effect on the regulation, or discipline, of those societies:

> there is no power relations without the correlative constitution of a field of knowledge, nor any knowledge that does not presuppose and constitute at the same time power relations (Foucault 1977: 27).

We have become both the subjects and objects of knowledge. The human sciences appeared not as the result of some scientific problem that demanded analysis, nor as the result of some "pressing rationalism"; the decision to include people among the objects of science "appeared when man constituted himself in Western culture as both that which must be conceived of and that which is to be known" (Foucault 1992: 345). If we now view the human sciences as implicated in the operation of power for the purposes of the classification and regulation of the population, we can understand the problems of arriving at concrete and scientific classification systems that, by default, assume that knowledge may be separated from the exercise of power. Instead, according to Foucault, to base social science upon Enlightenment reason leaves us with a legacy of inherent instability and conflict. On the one hand, research is justified through the positivistic findings it produces. On the other hand, it is critical insofar as it constantly reflects upon the possibilities for producing such knowledge in the first instance. In the process, reason becomes its "iron cage" and its practice and findings act not as a source of liberation, but as part of a continual process of the inextricable link between power and knowledge.

Prediction, explanation, generalization and classification have become the guiding principles of scientific enquiry. They are, in turn, linked to the idea of controlling the social world. Unitary bodies of theory create hierarchies through which truth is filtered. Therefore, the scientific authority to arbitrate between truth and falsehood is predicated upon an appeal to objective knowledge and an access to truth enabled through the formulation of procedural rules (Bauman 1987). It is this desire to universalize, and the foundations upon which it is based, that postmodernist thinkers take as the focus of their critiques. It results in a denial of difference and diversity among peoples who are then judged according to dominant standards of Western reason. Attempts to generalize across social contexts are thus seen as not simply inaccurate but, as noted in the earlier quote from Lyotard, totalizing and even despotic.

For Lyotard (1984) there are no universal explanations based on metanarratives, nor the allusion to some universal that lies outside the sphere of scientific competence. He is also opposed to the idea of validating different types of knowledge according to the dominant standards of Western reason. As such, there is no constant standard of *reason*, but there are *reasons*. This would seem to be problematic in terms of the general tenor of this book. We have suggested, along with others before us (Gjertsen 1989), that science has needed to ground itself in a discourse that is itself not "scientific". That discourse is philosophy. This, according to Lyotard, has occurred in two ways. First, through the idea of progress in terms of the pursuit of truth and secondly, in terms of education as being a healthy condition for the purposes of liberation. However, these narratives have lost their credibility. How has this occurred?

Influenced by Wittgenstein's idea of language games, Lyotard calls for the abandonment of the search for "hidden" meanings and "depth" explanations, in favour of the "play" of language games. Broadly speaking, science has always distinguished itself from narrative. Narrative flows through society and individuals may participate in a manner that does not require justification in terms of reference to some grand, legitimating narrative. Any person may therefore occupy the place of the "speaker". Science, on the other hand, is a single language game with a very different logic. It allows only denotative statements whereby competence is required on the part of the speaker, not the listener. As such, an understanding of an existing body of scientific knowledge is required for its legitimation where the rules of the language game are understood by its participants. It appears not to require narrative for this purpose. Instead, science "progresses" through the approval of others within the same field of expertise. Add to this idea the "age of information" and we can see how, as the complexity of scientific work increases and with that the types of proof required to test theories, technological innovation becomes bound up with scientific enterprise. More complicated computer programmes, for example, are needed in order to routinely conduct scientific work.

The result of this process is what Lyotard (1984) calls "performativity". Technology allows a scientist to achieve maximum output for a minimum input, but one that costs more and more money in terms of the technology required for its performance. While, as Popper had already noted, ideas and discoveries may take place in the absence of such funding, most science is now conducted on this basis. The result is a scientific language game where wealth, truth and efficiency combine, not the idealized concept of the disinterested pursuit of knowledge. Our earlier question "what is science?" is now answered in terms of science being a self-referential language game where money and truth are bound as one, without the possibility of allusion to a meta-narrative (philosophy) in order to justify its methods, insights, procedures and conclusions. This non-foundationalist thinking lays scientific quests for foundational "truth" firmly to rest.

Taking aim at the subject

What we have generally termed the "post-critiques" do not simply reside in epistemology. Ontological assumptions that draw upon humanism also find themselves questioned by these traditions. We have seen that Anthony Giddens shuns the possibility of drawing up a set of predetermined epistemological principles for his inquiries. Instead, he argues that social theory should seek to overcome a set of dualism's through an ontological concern with, "conceptions of human being and human doing, social reproduction and social transformation" (Giddens 1984: xx). When it comes to the subjects of modernity and social identity, his concerns are thus focused upon ontological security and existential identity (Giddens 1991).

Giddens recognizes the absence of a unified subject upon which to base social theory and social science in general, but he still conceives of history in terms of the actions of individuals. However, the concept of a unified and autonomous subject falls under the critical gaze of both postmodernism and poststructuralism and with that, the ideas of this influential sociologist. The key concept here is "humanism". In this context, we can take it to refer to the centrality of human subjects as the source of knowledge, accompanied by a stress on human agency as deployed in social explanations and understandings:

> From Descartes's *cogito*, to Kant's and Husserl's transcendental ego, to the Enlightenment concept of reason, identity is conceived as something essential, substantial, unitary, fixed, and fundamentally unchanging (Kellner 1993: 142. Original italics).

It has become yet another "foundation" upon which social science has been able to proceed.

Poststructuralism was not the first school of thought to subject this idea to critical scrutiny. Marxists have emphasized a dialectic between agency and material circumstances, and structuralists, such as Lévi-Strauss, sought an underlying unity in what were divergent surface meanings. Structure and culture, meaning and causally motivated behaviour, and explanation and understanding, all became dualisms in the process of debates around these issues and form the intellectual and cultural legacies that, as Mills noted, we have now inherited. In the poststructuralist camp, Foucault did not abandon the significance of meaning in human relations, and returned to the concept of the "subject" in his later work (Dews 1989). However, he did react to the influence of Sartre and existentialism in French intellectual life and subjected this humanist tradition to a radical critique (see Miller 1993). The same may be said for the psychoanalyst Jacques Lacan (1901–83). Lacan, in his interpretations of Freud, held that we were "de-centred" subjects who only came to recognize ourselves through language that, as we shall see, is a system of differences in terms of the arbitrary relations that exist between the signifier and signified. Once again, this offended the humanist tradition with its concept of a homogeneous ego. Along with Derrida, Lacan has influenced the works of Hélèle Cixious, Luce Irigaray and Julia Kristeva whose writings have been labelled "postmodern feminism" (Tong 1989).

It is these strands in poststructuralist thought that often provoke a deep hostility in those who emphasize agency in understanding human conduct. These arguments and their implications can be followed via a brief examination of the ideas of Jacques Derrida whose deconstructionist project, as noted, entails the exposing of what is referred to as the "disingenuous dream" of Western philosophy. Accompanying this is the breakdown of the distinction between what are often and somewhat oddly called, the "hard" and "soft" sciences. This distinction has enabled a simple dualism to be drawn between reality and fiction. How has this occurred?

We have seen that science might be characterized as the desire to achieve a correspondence between the language used to describe reality and reality itself. Now, the structuralists, such as Ferdinand de Saussure (1857–1913), maintained that signs are divided into two parts: the signifier (the sound) and the signified (the idea or concepts to which the sound refers). The meanings of terms are thus fixed by language as a self-referential system, leaving Saussure to consider the relationship between thought and language via a comparison with a sheet of paper:

> thought is the front and the sound the back; one cannot cut the front without cutting the back at the same time; likewise in language, one can neither divide sound from thought nor thought from sound . . . Linguistics then works in the borderland where elements of sound and thought combine; *their combination produces a form, not a substance* (Saussure in Easthope & McGowan 1992: 7. Original italics).

The signifier and signified thereby relate. However, Derrida does not accept this connection. For Derrida, the relationship between words and thoughts or "things", never actually connects. Instead, what we arrive at are structures of differences where the production of meaning is not achieved through a correspondence arriving at the final signified, but only through the different significance that is attached, by speakers, to words themselves. As such:

> when we read a sign, meaning is not immediately clear to us. Signs refer to what is absent, so in a sense meanings are absent, too. Meaning is continually moving along on a chain of signifiers, and we cannot be precise about its exact "location", because it is never tied to one particular sign (Sarup 1993: 33).

The implication is that meaning can never be fixed, nor readily apparent. We are left with an inability to decide based upon the idea of *différance*: that is, fixed meanings always elude us because of the necessity of clarification and definition. This process requires more language for its production, but language can never be its final arbiter. In other words, signs can only be studied in terms of other signs whose meanings continually evade us.

This philosophical conundrum was recognized by philosophers who, to put it in the language of the post-critiques, sought an area of certainty for their formulations. For some this came in ontology. One of the more famous examples of this move took place in the work of Martin Heidegger (1889–1976) who moved Husserl's phenomenological focus from epistemology to ontology. It was Heidegger who, along with Nietzsche, recognized the limitations of Western reason in his critique of, among others, Kant. He argued that we are not just external observers of the social and natural worlds, but are also "beings" who exist in time. Therefore, we are part of, not separate from, the world. However, for Derrida, he also sought a *logos*: that is, a foundational basis for beliefs exemplified in either an essence of being (ontology) and/or grounds for knowing (epistemology). This may be seen in Heidegger's attempts to overcome the falsehood of the Enlightenment by returning to an original state of "Being". Here, language and experience would become one. Nevertheless, for Derrida this is not a satisfactory answer because, once again, it rests upon the desire to find an unmediated truth about the world by smuggling into its formulation what he calls a "transcendental signified".

As a result, "Heideggerian thought would reinstate rather than destroy the instance of the logos" (Derrida in Kamuf 1991: 35). Unmediated scientific truth, therefore, is simply not attainable.

The idea of the "real", and the methods for reaching this, provide scientists with an existential security. In this way, social selves and scientific endeavours act in a symbiotic manner that, according to the post-critiques, is a false relationship. We desire to "discover" the social world through observations, experiments, textual analysis, questionnaires, videos or other methods that are employed towards this end. In so doing, the right to know or understand is proclaimed. Contrary to this, the post-critiques see us as implicated in the production of knowledge. In poststructuralist terms, there is complicity in perpetuating a "metaphysics of presence" (Derrida) or, in a more historical than philosophical vein, the relationship between power and knowledge in discourses that produce "truth" (Foucault). In postmodernist terms, science is a self-referential language game that can no longer appeal to meta-narratives (Lyotard), nor make judgements regarding the differences between the real and the imaginary, for ours is an age of what has been termed "hyperreality" (Baudrillard). Whether or not one argues that poststructuralists work within modernity to expose its limits and postmodernists seek to overcome it, it remains the case that science in general and social science in particular, may no longer speak with the authority that its predecessors once enjoyed.

The post-critiques and the practice of social research

In this section we will consider the relationship between the above ideas and social research. Our intention is only illustrative given the aims of this book and the space available to us. We also note that, for some, we can apparently expect little else of the following narrative. Connections and possibilities are thus suggested in terms of the writings and researches of those who have attempted to apply the above ideas in their studies of societies and social relations.

Derrida and deconstruction

Let us start with Derrida's poststructuralism and its methodological consequences. It was noted earlier that science may be read as a form of rhetoric:

> Deconstruction refuses to view methodology simply as a set of technical procedures with which to manipulate data. Rather, methodology can be opened up to readers intrigued by its deep assumptions and its empirical findings but otherwise daunted by its densely technical and figural findings (Agger 1991: 29–30).

Once again, we are left with the idea of science as obfuscation, not liberation through illumination. The idea, as Agger notes, albeit with a modified critical theory in mind, involves questioning the underlying assumptions of science that may then be open to question through the revealing of the values and interests that inform its practices. However, the result is not enlightenment for even a "deconstructed science" may not attain the truth, merely expose it as another form of rhetoric that, more than others, can bury its presuppositions away from the gaze of those who have not served its apprenticeships. We cannot, of course, allude to language to solve this problem for Derrida's principle of "undecidability" will always obtain.

Despite this latter insight, Derrida argues that there is still a "metaphysics of presence" in Saussure's work because he prioritizes speech over writing. Whereas Saussure challenges the idea of the subject before language and sees the subject produced by language, he still sees a link between sound and sense in the prioritization of what is known as "self-present speech" (Norris 1987). The result is that he, as with Western thought in general, becomes committed to a metaphysics of presence: that is, the existence of a unified speaking subject. Derrida seeks to correct this bias. After all:

> If writing is the very *condition* of knowledge – if, that is to say, it can be shown to precede and articulate all our working notions of science, history, tradition etc. – then how can writing be just one object of knowledge among others? (Norris 1987: 94. Original italics).

From this we can say that it is writing, not the speech-act of the subject, that should be the subject of social inquiries within a deconstructive mode.

Armed with this insight, deconstructionist researchers may descend upon the social world to examine the presuppositions that are buried in the texts produced in the course of its everyday activities. The idea of questioning the metaphysics of presence affects social research practice in terms of, for example, its use of "consciousness" and "intentionality" as explanatory frameworks in the study of human relations. As a result, the task of social research becomes the deconstruction of texts in order to expose how values and interests are imbedded within them and how the social world is fabricated through what is known as "intertextuality". In the process, how the social world is represented becomes more important than the search for an independent "reality" described by such texts. There are certainly ethnographers who have examined the implications of this idea in terms of the process of representations through description (Atkinson 1990, Fontana 1994).

This links into the debate on the subject and humanism in its implications that we both read and are *written by* texts. This is not necessarily assumed to be a conscious process, but an unconscious one. Ann Game, whose book is devoted to arguing for a "deconstructive sociology", notes how this idea goes right to the core of so much social science reasoning. She starts her study by noting that, "The idea that reality is fictitious and fiction is real does not find favour with sociologists" (Game 1991: 3). The focus of social inquiry now moves towards "how" meanings are produced, not that to which it finally refers. If this epistemological move is not sufficient to debunk common claims and arguments, then those who base their claims on ontology are also taken to task. Game argues that Giddens prefers the idea of the subject as being characterized by "consciousness" over that of the "unconscious". A metaphysics of presence thus pervades his work and sociology in general:

> The idea that we write and read culture *is* incompatible with the sociological conception of human agency; they are based on fundamentally different assumptions about the subject and meaning. One of the concerns of this book is to argue for the significance of the unconscious to an understanding of cultural processes (Game 1991: 6. Original italics).

From this starting point the fact–theory relation is taken to be a "writing practice", not one upon which the process of validation is achieved through the correspondence theory of truth. Difference is celebrated and the Cartesian mind–body duality is debunked in favour of seeing the human body as a site of representation, identity and action. Drawing upon the work of, among others, Irigaray, Derrida, Freud, Barthes and Saussure, questions of the "essential" nature of women (a fixed ontological claim) are then abandoned in favour of the mode through which they are defined and represented by texts. Texts are seen as social practices and observations become acts of writing, not the reporting of an independent reality.

Social research is now implicated in and part of, the production of reality itself. Social research is an activity that forms conceptions of social reality and so opens up the question of, "how research texts might be written in an open and reflexive way" (Game 1991: 32). We are then left with the notion that no single text is to be authorized and then theorized in terms of being open to test against some empirical reality. It may only be viewed in terms of other stories or accounts of social life. Armed with these insights she then analyzes films, photographs, texts on English Heritage and the idea of "urban strolling". We will briefly illustrate how this deconstructive research programme is conducted by using one of her studies.

Using transcripts of interviews, Ann Game conducts an interview with a "boss" on "boss–secretary relations"; the discourses of the boss are compared to those of the secretary in order to ask, "Do they tell the same story? And if not, what does this suggest about multiplicity?" (Game 1991: 116). The result is a series of differences that are posited in their accounts in terms of how the relations between boss and secretary are considered, managed and enabled. Office spatial arrangements, roles, tasks, the notion of both having particular attributes that are then seen to enable effective functioning in terms of the division of labour between them, the separation of public and private lives, all add up to "social positionings". Game does not, as is consistent with her methodological prescriptions, separate herself from this process noting how, as an "outside" academic, she tended to identify with the boss more than the secretary. This is seen as, "symptomatic of a general unease about the power relations of research and the constitution of the other to the subject of research" (1991: 127).

THE POST-CRITIQUES AND THE PRACTICE OF SOCIAL RESEARCH

Foucault: discourses, objects and subjects

When it comes to the implications of poststructuralism in the work of Foucault we find, despite differences between his work and that of Derrida (see Boyne 1990), similarities in terms of the critique of the subject–object distinction. A number of researchers, albeit not uncritically, have found analytic mileage in his work for the study of different social phenomena (for example, see Jones & Porter 1994, Law 1994, May 1994, Weeks 1991). As Barbara Townley writes in her study of Human Resource Management (HRM) in the organization of work relations:

> To illustrate the relevance of his work for personnel, we must follow his recommendation to question the self-evident and return to the basic building block on which personnel practices are premised: the employment relationship. Central to this relationship is the indeterminacy of contract, the naturally occurring space between expectation and deliverance of work. The "gap", or space, between what is promised and what is realized, inevitably exists in a transaction between the parties. In the employment relationship, this gap is between the capacity to work and its exercise (1994: 13).

This provides a way in which she is able to analyze the methods through which everyday practices, as part of the discourse of HRM, inform so many people's working lives: for example, evaluations, rankings, performance indicators, self- and peer-assessments, etc., all of which create employees as both subject and object within their working environments. "Quality circles", "attitude surveys", "testing" of candidates for jobs and the work of "Assessment Centres" are just some of the techniques she analyzes in order to develop her insights.

To analyze discourses in this manner means insisting upon the idea that the social world cannot be divided into two realms: the material and the mental. What we see, once again, are the concepts of consciousness and intentionality, among others, being questioned in the process of a form of social inquiry that seeks to overcome the dualisms so often associated with the history of social thought and the practices of the social sciences. Discourses are seen to provide the limits to what may be experienced, the meanings attributed to those experiences, as well as what might be said and done as a result (Purvis & Hunt 1993). As Mitchell Dean

171

(1994) puts it in his study of Foucault's methods, social researchers are presented with the possibility of examining the conditions under which representation itself actually takes place, as well as the generation of ideas and knowledge. In these terms, a social researcher would examine what Foucault (1991) has termed the "form of appropriation" of the discourse, as well as its "limits of appropriation".

As part of this overall strategy, the notion of "eventalization" sees the singularity of an event not in terms of some historical constant or anthropological invariant. Instead, the use of Foucault's methods provides for a subversive strategy that breaches the apparently self-evident nature of an event to show that "things" might have been otherwise. This is said to allow for a series of possibilities without the allusion to some guarantee in terms of either ontology or the inevitable unfolding logic of history as found, for example, in the works of Marx and Hegel. To attempt to impose some unilinear development on history, as is the case in evolutionary schemas, or to reduce social change to mono-causal explanations is anathema to Foucault's methodology. For him, there is no external certainty or universal understanding beyond history and society. Instead, the social researcher is required to "rediscover"

> the connections, encounters, supports, blockages, plays of forces, strategies and so on which at a given moment establish what subsequently counts as being self-evident, universal and necessary. In this sense one is indeed effecting a sort of multiplication or pluralization of causes (Foucault 1991: 76).

As in Townley's study, discourses may be analyzed in terms of how they appropriate subjects and turn them into objects, as well as the limits that exist to their forms of appropriation. In so doing, this strategy demonstrates the ultimate "arbitrariness" of the discourses themselves and provides for the possibility of alternative modes of organizing social life, "So my position leads not to apathy but to hyper- and pessimistic activism" (Foucault 1984: 343). With the relationship between power and knowledge and these points in mind, Foucault wrote of his study *Madness and civilisation* (1971):

> if, concerning a science like theoretical physics or organic chemistry, one poses the problem of its relations with the political and economic structures of society, isn't one posing an excessively

complicated question? . . . But, on the other hand, if one takes a form of knowledge (*savoir*) like psychiatry, won't the question be much easier to resolve, since the epistemological profile of psychiatry is low and psychiatric practice is related to a whole range of institutions, economic requirements and political issues of social regulation? (Foucault 1980: 109).

Baudrillard: simulation and the end of the social

There are those who have drawn upon the above ideas and labelled their works "postmodernist". It is at this point that one sees an affinity and overlap between these different authors in terms of the rejection of metanarratives. This then entails the study of the social world from the point of view of multiple perspectives rather than, say, the monoliths of race, gender, class and ethnicity. Presuppositions are, as noted, to be distrusted, while foundations are, within postmodernism at least, to be dismissed as epistemologically untenable, ontologically groundless and ultimately, politically unacceptable. Relativism, it appears, is unproblematic. On the contrary, it is to be celebrated.

In considering the work of Baudrillard within this genre and its implications for the practice of social science, we might first observe that we live in an information age where the media have proliferated to such an extent they are now part of our everyday lives:

> The combination of verbal and visual elements to constitute texts is becoming increasingly important in our society, and advertising is at the forefront of it. Television as a medium produces only such composite texts, but advertisements in printed materials also give greater emphasis to them. And the visual element is progressively becoming the more important in advertising. The salience of the image has been taken to be one of the *main characteristics* of contemporary "postmodern" culture (Fairclough 1989: 208. Emphasis added).

In this work, Norman Fairclough accepts the idea of media saturation but seeks to develop a "critical linguistics" based upon its potential for emancipation. As such, it is anathema to the work of Baudrillard (1983a) who, while arguing that media images are now the most fundamental part of the contemporary world, would reject such emancipatory goals.

Media and cultural sources in general are now so involved in the simulation of reality that, under the condition of what he terms "hyperreality", we are no longer able to distinguish between reality and its representation. This is particularly so in the case of America (Baudrillard 1993). Following the implications of his argument through, the postmodern condition means that signs no longer have any depth to them, nor any meaningful referent. Although this leaves something of an opening for cultural studies (see Inglis 1993), our contemporary age may be characterized by a "nostalgia" for a return to the link between representation and reality that was once found in politics and history (Gane 1991). However, this is a by-gone age and so becomes a fruitless gesture.

For Baudrillard, the result is that the political realm may no longer be viewed as autonomous, while the social realm is now so saturated with media images that is has become "anonymous". It follows that the supposed meaningful referents that are continually invoked in social research – class, gender, etc. – now disappear with the collapse of the "social". With that also collapses the possibility of social science. Instead, we are left with an undifferentiated "mass". Quite simply, where the sign no longer refers to the "real", social science concepts are no longer tenable for the real has been overrun by the "hyperreal". However, what then occurs, in the absence of any expression by the masses that may link itself with social or political reality, is a process of statistical representation, using social surveys and opinion polls, directed at what is often referred to as the "silent majority" (Baudrillard 1983b):

> Here, there is no system of polarities, no differentiation of terms, no flow of energy, no field or flow of currents. The mass is born short-circuited in "total circularity". What seems to occur he argues is a circulation around simulation models, and a collapse of the complex system into itself . . . For no-one, no organisation, as has been the case previously can any longer speak with confidence "for" the mass (Gane 1991: 136).

The resulting "simulacra" or models of social science thus have no grounding in anything but their own "reality" which becomes self-serving. There may be jobs for opinion pollsters, but their work has no validity in terms of appealing to some correspondence with reality.

In an era where the real no longer exists, "codes" of the original appear.

They enable a state of simulation to ensue that by-passes the process of production. This reflects Baudrillard's rejection of Marxism, in order to characterize the current age in terms of reproduction. In the condition of postmodernity, the state is achieved whereby the real and its representation become erased and everything is either, or has the potential to become, simulacra. As such, the ability to decide, for example, between ideas, aesthetics and political persuasions, now collapses. In these terms, precedence is now given to the object over the subject. Social "needs", for example, are not given nor can they be "researched" in the traditional sense, but are overtaken by the politics of seduction. The once revolutionary class are no longer subjects who, to paraphrase Marx, may become from a class in itself, a class for itself, but give themselves over to fascination and ecstasy. They live the postmodern condition; unlike the intellectuals who despair and simply desire an era through which history has passed. For this reason, the masses may be venerated for such a recognition, but from a rather different point of view to that of traditional Marxist or critical social research programmes more generally. These, of course, would seek to uncover the ideological mechanisms that distort understanding in the first instance.

According to the above view, we are exhorted to examine the ways in which reality is increasingly the object of the process of simulation. Take, for example, research on organizations. Here, we might wish to examine how organizations participate in the manufacture of images. To remain faithful to Baudrillard's position, we would posit neither a reality, nor unreality, but instead consider the ways in which organizations play upon their definitions of reality; hence the topic of our research would be their participation in the politics of seduction. More specifically, in considering organizational culture, we would seek to understand the practices and symbols within the cultural domains that make up organizations. This would require the entry of the researcher into what has been described as a, "vortex of symbols and symbol transformation" (Turner 1992: 58). In addition:

> Looking backwards, attempting to codify and to classify, we can identify those elements of the culture of an organization which have been embodied in training or set out in official handbooks. But once a culture is imposed in this way, it is already a collection of worn metaphors, a sedimented symbolism . . . These impositions already represent a simulation and a seduction of the reality of organizational culture (Turner 1992: 58).

Of course, in Baudrillard's epoch of postmodernity, there is no transcendental position from which one may view this process, nor pronounce upon its "truth". The best we might achieve is to be a spectator in the process of seduction.

Rorty: science and the art of persuasion

Finally in this section, we turn to the implications for the practice of social science in the writings of Richard Rorty. Despite his reservations on aspects of French postmodernism (Rorty 1993), we find similar arguments being expressed in his work (Rorty 1989, 1992). Rorty, like Lyotard, is influenced by Wittgenstein, but he also inherits the tradition of American pragmatism and regards Heidegger as one of the leading philosophers of this century.

For Rorty, to abandon the correspondence theory of reality is not to replace it with a thoroughgoing idealism such that "things" are not asserted to exist until they are given a name. However, any appeal to "reality", separate from such naming, is not possible in cases where definitions of reality are subjected to dispute. For this reason, attempts at delineating some pre-linguistic form of suffering, as in Marx's materialist project, are doomed to failure. It follows that scientific standards cannot arbitrate in cases where reality itself is the subject of dispute. Instead, if scientists are to justify their findings in such instances, they must resort to interpersonal skills. They must persuade people of their definitions of reality and from there, reach some sort of consensus based upon these abilities; even if this means resorting to a dogmatic assertion of their interests (Rorty 1992). This is an idea of truth based upon the general notion of "warranted assertability" (Bhaskar 1993: 216). This aims at an entire corpus of philosophical discourse which, as a narrative, has underpinned much of scientific endeavour. As Rorty puts it:

> The reason we anti-representationalists bother to hold the controversial philosophical views we do is that we think that this idea that some descriptions get at the *intrinsic* nature of what is being described brings the whole dreary Cartesian problematic along with it, and that this is a problematic that nobody needs – the result of being held captive by a picture that it was in Descartes' interest to paint, but not in ours (1992: 42. Original italics).

The implications of this position are that the social sciences and sciences in general, should come to accept that philosophers have been complicit in imposing a "truth" upon the population. Their practices, based upon arguments from the Greeks onwards, are open to the charge of "truth imposition". In contrast to this, liberal democracy, based on conversation, is the only possible way forward. Feminist practice, for example, should co-opt familiar words and use them in unfamiliar ways in order to create the "logical space" in which a new language, to describe women's feelings and sense of identity, might then emerge (Rorty 1991). In this formulation, we find no allusions to a universal category of "woman", nor a general theory of oppression in order to justify feminist insights. Instead, we find a gradualist approach to feminism in which new moral identities would emerge that, over time, "may gradually get woven into the language taught in our schools" (Rorty 1991: 9). As such, we should now come to appreciate, as Norris puts it in his summary of Rorty's position:

> that rhetoric (not reason) is the bottom line of liberal-democratic truth; that metaphors (not concepts) are the linguistic coin in which shared social interests typically achieve their best, most creative expression; and that belief (not truth) is the sole court of appeal in any genuinely working participant democracy (1993: 284).

According to this line of argument, feminist social research would contribute to the production of a new language, but not from the vantage point of scientific authority. Objectivity should give way to relativism. The abandonment of the former, with its allusion to universals, is outweighed by the benefits that come from the adoption of the latter (Rorty 1991). The search for truth is now placed to one side in favour of the desire to achieve solidarity. Social research must, in other words, break free from the shackles of any privileged epistemological position.

Summary

In reviewing the above we find, not surprisingly, that the direct translation of the implications for social research of postmodernist ideas are at their most problematic. When one reads the results of social research by those who have sought to employ postmodernist ideas, a modification of the insights of its central protagonists appears a usual feature of their narrative and, some would argue, an inevitable feature of attempting such an incorporation. In this sense, it appears to have operated as a corrective to the grander claims that science, and social science, have made for themselves and requires a re-specification of their aims and values (Simons & Billig 1994). For instance, for some authors, to admit of the role of narrative in science, as Lyotard has argued, is not to abandon its practice to fiction. It is, however, to recognize the tradition in which one works and the ways in which it authorizes its practitioners. It calls, therefore, for a, "conscious and reflective creation of a specific genre" (Czarniawska-Joerges 1995: 28), as opposed to the non-reflexive complacency of positivism and empiricism. For others, to adopt a postmodernist perspective represents both a refusal of the master narratives that construct particular images, as well as a demand for recognition (Young 1990).

On the other hand, we find Kantian elements in the work of both Foucault and Derrida. Perhaps it is this which, in part, has enabled us to draw links between their ideas and the implications for the practice of social research. For instance, Norris argues that the concentration on writing in Derrida's ideas represents a Kantian move. Why? Because it is a transcendental move insofar as we seek to understand and explain the presuppositions of our knowledge in the texts that we produce. Thus, writing becomes, "the precondition of all possible knowledge" (Norris 1987: 95). We might say, therefore, that Derrida and Foucault work as protagonists within Enlightenment discourse. This enables them to both utilize its basis while exposing its limits and limitations. They remind us that science cannot, by itself, legislate over "truth". In the case of Foucault, at least, this does not mean a denial of the concept of validity (Visker 1992).

Baudrillard, on the other hand is, by his own admission, an *agent provocateur*. He seeks to debunk all that we take for granted and dismiss the social and hence, social science while, it should be noted, at the same time refusing the label "postmodernist" (see Gane 1993). Yet, if the link between sign and referent is past, so too is natural science particularly given that it has, as Popper himself admitted, an important social and psychological dimension to its practice. However, Baudrillard, as with postmodernism in general, has met with considerable criticism (for example, see Habermas 1992, Harvey 1992, Norris 1993, Kellner 1994, O'Neill 1994). Yet even he can act as something of a sounding board for the complacency of contemporary practices without accepting, wholesale, some of his more extreme arguments (see Rojek & Turner 1993).

With these comments and qualifications in mind, the following are intended to characterize the choices that we seem to face when considering the post-critiques. It is these that we leave you with in order that you have the basis upon which to build your own views on this subject and its relation to the philosophy, methodology, theory and the practice of social research.

First, you can simply ignore the ideas altogether! Although this does not, taking the constraints of one's own time into consideration, seem to be in the spirit of committed scholarship. Secondly, it is possible to consider and then refute their insights from established theoretical paradigms that are argued to have been wrongly characterized (Callinicos 1991, Walby 1992). Thirdly, following a consideration of the post-critiques, you can modify your existing arguments and research practices accordingly. In terms of modifying an existing research programme, the following have been considered: an encounter with symbolic interactionism with its roots in American pragmatism (Denzin 1992); an encounter with a feminist research programme that still retains a commitment to social, economic and political change (Fraser & Nicholson 1990, Sawicki 1991) and finally, an encounter with critical theory in general (Agger 1991). Finally, postmodernity itself is turned into a research topic. In order to achieve this there must be an accompanying refutation of the claim that there is a collapse of the "social" and with that, the social sciences. This involves a revised project through the rejection of a postmodern social science in favour of, for example, a sociology of postmodernism (Bauman 1988, Featherstone 1991).

Questions for discussion

1. Do you consider Lyotard's notion of "performativity" to be an accurate characterization of contemporary scientific research?
2. What are the potential insights that Baudrillard's work might have for social research, or does it simply represent its negation?
3. If we can no longer allude to the subject as an explanatory device, what implications does this have for the methodology and methods of social research?
4. How might one go about analyzing the effects and properties of discourses?

Suggested reading

Dean, M. 1994. *Critical and effective histories: Foucault's methods and historical sociology*. London: Routledge.

Dickens, D. R. & A. Fontana (eds) 1994. *Postmodernism and social inquiry*. London: University College of London Press.

Poster, M. 1990. *The mode of information: poststructuralism and social context*. Cambridge: Polity.

Simons, H. W. & M. Billig (eds) 1994. *After postmodernism: reconstructing ideology critique*. London: Sage.

CHAPTER 8
Conclusion

We have problematized, clarified and illustrated, but not resolved as such. This is hardly surprising, for the former represent those themes that, we argued, are part of the positive relationship that can exist between social research and philosophy. From this point of view, one cannot expect philosophical discourse to represent a final court of appeal. As we noted in Chapter 1, we find illumination in examining science from a philosophical point of view, but not all philosophical problems are translated into scientific questions. Similarly, while social research yields systematic information on the social world, the question as to what to do with this information, in terms of its application, becomes a matter for societal values and political relations. However, that is not to suggest that the practice of science and social research is separate from such issues – this much has been clear from our prior discussions.

In terms of the positive potential of this relationship, we deliberately started with the taken-for-granted question, "what is science?". Once placed under the philosophical microscope, we saw how and why it may be claimed that particular work is characterized as "scientific". At this point, we entered the realms of ontology and epistemology. These were expressed in terms of the grounds for knowing what things exist in the social and natural worlds and what properties they possess. Here we found two traditions that approached these questions, both of which had consequences for the conduct and nature of scientific endeavour. These were the traditions of empiricism, as exemplified in the work of Hume and the tradition of rationalism, as found in the work of Descartes. An attempted fusion between these two approaches then occurred in the work of Kant.

These abstract debates appear, on first glance, to be far removed from the daily business of science. Yet when we begin to consider the search for *a* method that would prove to be *the* unifying factor in the process of scientific discovery, we can see how they relate directly to scientific endeavours. Empiricism, for example, grounds its basis of knowledge in experience as derived through the senses. This, in turn, may be translated into induction as a characteristic of scientific procedure where everything rests upon specific observations from which are derived general principles concerning the uniformity of nature. In the work of Kant, however, his critique of empiricism and fusion with rationalism, leads to the insight that the material world may cause our sensations, but it is our mental apparatus that then orders these stimuli. The mind thus provides the concepts through which people understand and explain their experiences.

The implications of this latter position were then traced in the following manner. The object world, with which empiricism is concerned, does not have an existence that is independent of our thoughts. The point is that if we are to come to have reliable and valid knowledge concerning the natural or social worlds, then it rests upon the exercise of reason as a universal capacity of the human mind. At this point, we noted that Kant differentiated between synthetic and analytic statements. The latter were found to rely upon deductive logic whereby the truth of a conclusion is contained within the premises of an argument. This philosophical abstract notion then fed into the idea of science proceeding upon the basis of deductive, not inductive logic, with attention to the instruments with which we measure the social and natural worlds becoming paramount.

The logical positivists took these ideas on board, yet with the empiricist implication that science should reflect the world as it appears to us and cannot, with any legitimacy, get at what the world is beyond that appearance. All other endeavour was thereby reduced to metaphysical speculation. Karl Popper, once associated with the "Vienna Circle", found these conclusions to be too harsh and contrary to the procedures of deduction. After all, they not only ruled out the realm of metaphysics, but also that of theory. The simple separation, held by the logical positivists, between a language that describes reality and the conceptual language which is then used to explain that reality, does not hold. The idea of verification as a characteristic of science, in this tradition, must be predicated upon a separation of these two languages. According to Popper, however, this was not possible. Given this, he maintained that theories can never be proved correct, and that science must be open to the idea of falsifying them according to a rigorous set of tests and procedures. Science was now characterized as the systematic search for "disconfirming instances" of particular theories, which themselves must be open to falsification. In other words, the elimination of untruth is said to lead us closer to the truth.

Popper's work also allowed for the role of subjective criteria in the formulation of theory. This may be taken a step further to say that not only the theories, but also the procedures of science, have a central social dimension to their practice. Science, therefore, is not a disembodied activity whose practitioners float freely over the social and natural landscapes unfettered by the context of their work. Kuhn thus examined the actual practice of science in terms of what he called "paradigms". Assumptions were found to be held to be true within a hermetically sealed scientific community. These standards set what was to constitute "normal" science; until, that is, a revolution in thought took place that directly challenged these assumptions. Science may now be characterized, as it has been by a particular group of sociologists of science, as a process informed by social and psychological factors. This perspective, informed by empirical studies of science, may lead us to conclude that there is no systematic difference between the social and natural sciences in terms of the methods, procedures and theories that they generate and employ. Given this potential end point to Chapter 2, it became of importance to consider the status of the social sciences. Do they, or should they, reflect the same methods as used in the physical sciences, or are they different from, but not inferior to, these sciences? We examined these questions in Chapter 3.

From an historical viewpoint, it was perhaps inevitable that the social sciences should attempt to replicate the methods of the natural sciences; evolving as they did in their shadow. The positivism of those such as Comte, Durkheim and Mill certainly represented this position, where the differing subject matter of the disciplines was said to have no relation to the search for a unity of method. The assumptions of this position were that we may justifiably study social life by examining the "external regularities" of human behaviour. This then follows the natural scientific model that explains an event by considering it as *the effect of a cause* (Strasser 1985: 2. Original italics). This approach, however, left us with problems. After all, human meaning and consciousness are central features of the social world; hence, there is an ontological distinction to be made with the natural world. As such, some reference to the "inner mental states" of human beings is required in order to understand, as opposed to explain, social relations. This process involves, "understanding what

183

makes someone tick" or how they "feel or act as a human being" (Taylor 1981: 30).

This latter observation took us in the direction of what we characterized as interpretivist approaches to the study of social life. These took several forms from hermeneutics, via a Weberian synthesis of explanation and understanding, through to phenomenology. For instance, in Dilthey's neo-Kantian move, he argued that we cannot know the world in itself, but we can come to know the human consciousness that represents that world. Following Hegel, this world could be known through what was termed the objective mind which, as part of the history into which we are all born, enables us both to understand our environments and to act within them. The implication is that we should seek to understand the social world from the "inside", not explain it from the "outside" by reference to natural scientific models of cause and effect.

Weber then emerged as something of an iconoclast in his fusion of causality and meaning. The social sciences should seek to understand social action while explaining it in terms of the relations of cause and effect. Did this synthesis, within the tradition of German idealism, hold? Not so from the perspective of phenomenology. This tradition was represented by the work of Husserl and following him, the sociological phenomenology of Schutz. Here we return to the idea of social reality being constituted by human consciousness. On this occasion, however, it was manifest in the idea that people, in a taken-for-granted manner, draw upon a "natural attitude" in everyday life. In Schutz's work this became a pre-reflexive world which is constituted of common sense ideas that enable us to attribute meaning to, and communicate within, the social environments that we inhabit. In order to achieve validity, therefore, the theories of the social sciences must reflect this stock of common sense knowledge if it is accurately to reflect everyday life. The practice of social science must then obey what Schutz (1979) called the "postulate of subjective adequacy": that is, there should not be a disjuncture between the social scientific and everyday world of "theorizing".

Phenomenology was also to take a more ontologically inspired course that was to be found in the work of Heidegger. This involved a critique of Kant in that he did not attempt to "solve" the relationship between a perceiving subject and an object world, because he moved the whole question of human existence to an examination of "being-in-time". This ontological basis found its outlet in the works of Gadamer who argues that a text may be read as indicative of a particular epoch. Similarly,

Ricoeur, in seeking a bridge between the traditions of explanation and interpretation, argues that whereas intentionality may be present in speech, it is not present in a text whose existence is as a power for the purpose of disclosing something about a particular world to the reader via the act of appropriation (Ricoeur 1982). Hermeneutics had moved us away from a unidirectional preoccupation with method, as in the concept of *verstehen*, to being indicative of a general way of life. At this level, the implications for social research lie in terms of "belonging" to a social world and "encountering" a world that may be alien to the researcher.

The general trend up to this point was a move away from a correspondence towards a coherence theory of truth. Nevertheless, we were still left with a central issue in the interpretivist tradition, that is, if the understanding of human meaning is a goal of social investigation, then how can we know other minds? It thus became necessary to examine this and other questions posed in Chapter 3 by considering particular views on social reality, together with the strategies that researchers adopt in generating their knowledge about the social world. This was a division between ontological and epistemological positions that we made for the purposes of enhancing an understanding of these important debates. Yet it was, as we noted in Chapter 4, one that ultimately collapses.

We divided ontological claims regarding social reality into two broad camps: those of the idealists and the realists. The former hold social reality to be mind dependent, while the latter consider social reality to consist of real phenomena that are not simply reducible to acts of perception. The adoption of one or other of these perspectives clearly had implications for the methodological strategies thought appropriate for the discovery of social phenomena. For instance, working within the traditions of neo-Kantian idealism, Weber's methodology involved the use of "ideal types". These serve as heuristic devices predicated upon the idea that we can never come to know reality itself, but instead must sharpen the instruments through which we observe it. This, in turn, required a degree of congruence between the concepts used by the investigator and those of the investigated, given that social science was concerned with the constitution of meaningful behaviour. The route taken for this purpose was to employ notions of the rationality of social action in order, to link to our earlier discussion, that cause and meaning were both appropriate to the conduct of social science.

You will recall that for Schutz the imposition of scientific models of social reality onto everyday life leads to reification of social phenomena and hence a resultant reduction in accurate representation. This critique had some parallels with the linguistic turn in social investigation insofar as meanings in everyday life became a topic, rather than a resource, for the social sciences. The important difference here, however, was that any reference to inner consciousness – one of the problematics with which we left Chapter 3 – was no longer required for the process of social investigation. Instead, we should focus upon publicly available language games, themselves indicative of forms of life, where the concept of a "private language" became redundant. In other words, we needed to expunge what some who work within this tradition of ordinary language philosophy have called the "phenomenological residua" in social thought (Coulter 1979).

An influential translation of Wittgenstein's ideas on language games, which overlooks the centrality of praxis in his work (see Rubinstein 1981), was to enter the social sciences via the work of Peter Winch. Now, if we accept that social reality is dependent upon language for its constitution, then we might look to the rules of language through which people attribute meanings to situations, activities and utterances in everyday life. These same rules would then also apply to the societies of which they are a part. Therefore, we not only jettison the need to refer to inner consciousness in our studies of social relations, but also the applicability of cause and effect to its study. Furthermore, in order to understand forms of life it is necessary to do so from the "inside", only this time through reference to language use.

Despite the considerable criticisms of Winch's ideas – in particular, that they were relativistic and still required notions of truth and falsehood in the study of language – this linguistic movement found its outlet in the work of the ethnomethodologists. Together with the work of Schutz and Parsons as their intellectual antecedents, the focus of social inquiry was to move from questions of why to those of how. In other words, to take the topic of social science as the everyday methods through which people produce social reality. Here we witnessed the jettisoning of epistemological and ontological concerns, to the adoption of a methodological strategy for understanding the social world.

Questions still remained in this empiricist programme of social investigation. These revolved around the exact relationship between language games and the role of the interpreter. More specifically, how do ethnomethodological analysts apparently float free from their own language games in order to interpret those of others? To explicate this process would require a resort to the concept of a hermeneutic encounter between different cultures. This is a notion that is conspicuous by its absence in a tradition where relativism, if not always explicitly celebrated, is implied in its procedures for the uncovering of the practical structures of everyday actions. Furthermore, as Winch (1990) notes in his more recent reflections, the idea of the applicability of cause will not simply disappear from the study of social life. Indeed its meaning is clearly more broad than his earlier work, which drew rather narrowly upon the legacy of Mill, had allowed for. This is where realism made its entry into our accounts on the study of social phenomena.

For our purposes, one of the central tenets of realism is the proposition that although there is a clear relationship between the development of scientific knowledge and the objects that it describes, the latter are regarded as "existentially intransitive" (Bhaskar 1994: 549) in order that, a priori, any form of scientific investigation can take place. As such, it becomes necessary to posit the existence of a world that is, to some degree, independent of human consciousness in order to justify the title "scientific". It follows that to study the social world simply in terms of intersubjective meaning production is highly limited. Social science should now also concern itself with those structures that underpin our actions and may exist independently of our perception of them.

Given the problems of identifying necessary and sufficient conditions in open systems, realists employ the notion of "tendencies". A sophisticated methodology was thus required so that a link might be established between the intransitive objects of social reality and the transitive objects that exist within social science. However, whereas realists were naturalists, they were not reductionists. With this in mind we found ontology driving their ideas and, given that the social world is constituted by the actions and meanings of people, social structures are not viewed as simply existing independently of those actions. Given this, structures are seen to produce people, as well as being reproduced by their actions. This "transformative capacity" was found to be represented not only in the work of Bhaskar but also, to some degree, within the social theory of Anthony Giddens.

An empiricist might object to the above insofar as structures are not directly available to the senses. Instead, for realists, they are an object of explanation, not empirical examination as such. However, we noted earlier that Popper was critical of the logical positivists on the grounds that they believed reality and descriptions of reality possess some strict demarcation point. This opens up questions regarding the strategic consequences of critical rationalism, our next port of call, for scientific study. Two issues, in particular, were of importance at this stage. First, the limitations of falsification as a characteristic of scientific procedure and secondly, the consequences of the entry of social and psychological criteria into the scientific process. These were found to be linked.

Lakatos noted that, from a strategic point of view, scientists will hold onto the central theoretical elements of their research programmes. Around these sit what might be characterized as satellite hypotheses that are subject to falsification, rejection or modification. As long as this provides novel insights, programmes are maintained. On occasion, however, even the core theoretical elements will be damaged by scientific discoveries. Now, while this provides a corrective to naïve falsificationism and allows for the role of social factors in scientific work, Lakatos's concerns were entirely with the physical sciences. The hard core of Marxism, for example, is more difficult to disprove on these terms quite simply because it contains a scientific element, and also informs praxis: that is, practical conscious activity. Therefore, as long as it appears to make sense of society for particular groups of people and informs their actions, it cannot be simply "falsified". Ironically, there exists a degree of idealism in what many regard as this materialist theory that scientific "tests" will neither capture, nor refute.

One way round this in the practice of science is not to get preoccupied with the appropriateness of tests for concepts, but instead link them directly into concerns of operationalization. The result is a correspondence between a concept and measure, where the latter is seen as constitutive of the former. Concepts require empirical indicators and these are operationalized to produce a series of measurements, for example, the proposition that, "IQ is what IQ tests measure". However, we are back to the problems we have encountered before. As Rom Harré noted, this is a positivist programme whereby the only permitted objects in science are those that are observable. This is problematic also because it says nothing of the relationship between the observer and the observed. In addition, given the number of concepts which surround our ideas of, say, class, this strategy cannot render justice to these given the instrumentality of the approach.

We were then left with three more ways in which we might seek to understand the process of science from the point of view of strategic knowledge production. They were: probability theory, network theory and pragmatism. Probability was noted to be the opposite of critical rationalism insofar as it was inductive. It becomes the suspension of cause in favour of statistical inference. Expressed in these terms we find an enormous amount of market and social science research proceeding on this very basis. Here we found a distinction to be made between objective and subjective probability. The first operated more in terms of closed than open systems that, as we have argued, characterize the social world. In terms of the latter, Bayesian theory sought to account for social life as an iterative process whereby we learn from our environment and adjust our behaviours accordingly. While this allows for the social dimension of knowledge accumulation, a difficulty remains in terms of identifying, *a priori*, the relationship between new and prior knowledge in order to understand this process.

Probability theory was then found to be associated with network theory in terms of the relationship between classes. Network theory, in the Duhem–Quine thesis, holds that scientific theories form an interconnected web. From this it followed that we could not be sure that it was our entire background thinking that was not being falsified, according to Popperian ideas, by our scientific tests. This allows, once again, the entry of a particular group of sociologists of science onto the terrain of explaining scientific strategy. The theoretical language that describes reality now became a centre of inquiry. This language is formed within a social network that has a self-referential character. Given this, it does not refer to a set of external conditions, as maintained by the correspondence view of truth, but on the contrary, to the network of which it is a part. We thus travel back to coherence theory as a characteristic of scientific endeavour. However, it does not follow from this that all theories may be considered as possessing equal validity. To consider this question we might propose, for example, that all utterances pre-suppose a particular claim to validity. As such, claims to validity might be settled within a scientific community whose ideal is that of "truth-seeking". This is where pragmatism entered our considerations.

In the pragmatist tradition, which we chose to present as one characterization of scientific procedure, we noted a rejection of the subject–object dichotomy in social and philosophical thought. In its place, we find an adaption to the environment accompanied by the production of meanings that orientate our conduct. Now, within this tradition, the possibility existed for the focus of inquiry on meaning production to exceed that of truth-seeking as an ideal that orientates the conduct of scientists. This is where James stepped in, to view knowledge production as the satisfaction of indigenous needs and interests. Knowledge production thereby became judged by its "usefulness", rather than its "truth". We found this leading to an instrumentalism to which Peirce reacted, referring to his work as 'pragmaticism' in order to differentiate it from such formulations.

From the discussion in Chapter 4 we concluded that the social dimension to scientific knowledge production would not leave our picture. If we accept this link, the questions are begged as to what extent such work might be considered "objective". This, as we noted, is usually defined in terms of science being a value-free enterprise. However, what if we reversed this taken-for-granted notion and posit, instead, that valid social science is only produced through being informed by values? It was arguments around this issue that we sought to illuminate in Chapter 5 where our first step was the clarification of what is often called the "is–ought" question or, as we expressed it, the relationship between facts and values. For clarity of exposition, we then translated this into four positions that exist within the social science literature. Once again, our aim was not to exhaust what is a considerable body of literature, but to illustrate the ways in which social scientists have approached this important issue.

Our first stop, perhaps not surprisingly given the history of the social sciences, was to examine the positivist approach. Durkheim's holist and structuralist approach to the study of society, in contrast to atomism, permitted an objectivity at the level of the study of aggregate social phenomena. However, the very naming that is part of the process of classifying social phenomena is a normative act. Weber, on the other hand, noted the existence of social values in the determination of ends. Yet it did not follow from this observation that the social sciences could not be value-free endeavours for we cannot deduce an "ought" from an "is". Social science, therefore, cannot, "partake of the contemplation of sages and philosophers about the meaning of the universe" (Weber in Gerth & Mills 1948: 152). The division of labour between social science and philosophy, in terms of the separation between means and ends, was clear. Nevertheless, we argued that the contemporary resonance of Weber's writings actually derive from their being informed by values. From this observation we noted that knowledge is situated; as we put it, it is a view from somewhere. The debate now shifted to an examination of that social space and the positions that we inhabit in the formulation of our ideas, as well as our practices. This forms part of the armoury of a reflexive social science, where the tools of social inquiry are turned back on themselves in order to examine the conditions under which knowledge is produced in the first instance (Steier 1991, Bourdieu & Wacquant 1992).

From this starting point both Marxism and neo-Marxism consider the relationship that exists between facts, values and ideology. We now have to consider the role of power in the construction of truth. This we found to be based upon an ontological view that there existed a true state of consciousness that was masked by prevailing economic, social and political conditions. Value-freedom in such a context would be symptomatic of a desire to mask the truth. Hence, this view inverted the standard conception of objectivity as the disinterested pursuit of knowledge. This then translates itself, for example, into a programme of social research that generates a series of insights into the aims of social movements who oppose the prevailing social order. The value of such work is not then measured by positivist conceptions of truth, but by its ability to contribute to a more enlightened state that might free people from the constraints of ideological control.

The nature of this contention, particularly from those scholars associated with the Frankfurt School of Social Research, led to a debate with Popper who took a more instrumental view on the practice of science: that is, a problem-oriented perspective. This led to a distinction between scientific and extra-scientific values. However, for those such as Habermas this was a distinction, predicated upon rationalism, that ultimately broke down. Furthermore, it led to a positivist conception of knowledge as exemplified by the desire for a technical-instrumental control of the social and natural worlds. These opposing views often centred upon the difference between an epistemological and ontological position where the latter was exemplified, at least in the writings of critical theorists up to, but not including Habermas, in philosophical anthropology. It was at this point that we considered the arguments of feminist standpoint theorists.

Standpoint feminism has its starting point in the idea of women as the "other". We find the idea of the dominant culture being male, from which women are excluded. This discrimination is then turned into an advantage for it forms a privileged epistemic position from which to view social relations. Add to this a series of unexamined dichotomies on which our thinking has based itself and we have new grounds for knowledge from a feminist perspective. In the process, dominant conceptions of objectivity are defined as being symptomatic of male values.

Tensions within standpoint feminism were examined in terms of its potential towards relativism. However, it is at this point that the separation of scientific and non-scientific values becomes of importance once again. It is the social, political and economic conditions under which science proceeds that, inevitably, affect its conduct. Therefore, as with such debates within Marxist circles, to imagine a feminist standpoint science in a feminist society lies beyond our current comprehension. We were left, once again, with an orientating principle that informs scientific practice, whose ends may be those towards which we strive in the hope that we will ultimately reach them. Feminist standpoint science may thus be characterized as possessing an ethos, informed by an ethic, ultimately orientated towards a set of political goals: that is, a change in the structure and relations of society.

Our conclusion to this chapter was a play on its content: social science is not, nor ought it to be, a value-free endeavour. To this we might also add the natural sciences. Instead, we should be vigilant about the ways in which values inform our activities in the conduct of research. This issue and some of those we had examined in previous chapters were then taken into consideration when examining the research process in Chapter 6. Here we could not exhaust our discussions, but merely serve to illustrate some of the ways in which a philosophical reading of the research process helps to sharpen our insights into its practice. In a sense, this is exactly what Chapter 7 continued to do only this time from a philosophical angle associated with postmodernism and poststructuralism.

The post-critiques aim, to differing degrees, at the very heart of the assumptions of scientific practice that have a long historical pedigree. It was for this reason that we took the critiques of epistemology and ontology as the focus of the first part of this chapter. Starting with Kant, we find the centring of the individual in terms of knowledge production. Reason was the guarantor of scientific objectivity and generalization. In contrast to this view, some post-critiques celebrated relativism and severed the link between knowledge and liberation. Indeed, any form of generalization in the name of reason was regarded as tyranny. This nihilist position was evident in the writings of a number of authors within these traditions.

When it comes to the translation of their work into a programme of social research, it is clear that a number of people have found inspiration in the post-critiques. However, we argued that it was not without significance that those ideas that have appeared to have the most impact on social research, particularly those originating from Foucault and Derrida, may be read from a Kantian vantage point. Baudrillard's "play" with ideas results in the collapse of the social and with that the idea of the social sciences. It is here perhaps that we find nihilism at its height, despite Baudrillard's assertion that he is not a postmodernist. To this extent, we concluded that for those who have sought to employ the post-critiques in the service of social research, these have acted as "sounding-boards" against which to measure the grander claims of a modernist-based science. The question for some then becomes how to re-frame the status of critique following the postmodern onslaught (Simons & Billig 1994).

So we reach the end of our journey. This has been a complex one but also, we hope, illuminating. Interestingly, this parallels the way in which we would characterize the whole relationship between philosophy, social research and science. Indeed, scientific endeavours themselves are now more open to contestation, while systems in the physical world are seen to be more open; a long acknowledged characteristic of the social world. Ontologically, therefore, the principal difference between the subject matter of the physical and social sciences may now be the order of complexity. From a political point of view, in considering the issues surrounding science and the environment, what Popper termed "extra-scientific values" have entered the terrain of inquiry to such an extent that any simple demarcation between the means and ends of research has become increasingly untenable. In these instances, politics so informs the evaluation and conduct of research that allusions to scientific values become more of a means of gaining some degree of autonomy from such considerations, than serve as an accurate characterization of the process of scientific inquiry itself. For the postmodernists, of course, these allusions would be based on faulty premises drawn from Enlightenment discourse.

Perhaps at this late stage we might just outline our position on these arguments. Of course the demarcation between scientific and extra-scientific values has always been a hard one to maintain and even, in some instances, undesirable. However, this hardly means the adoption of the nihilism of some postmodernist discourses as a corrective to what is often seen as complacent modernism. To this extent, hermeneutic investigations of science have revealed how interpretation is as much a part of the conduct of the physical as social sciences. Nevertheless, to accept this, together with the observation that science and politics are interrelated, is not then to abandon the quest for explanations. As James Robert Brown puts it in his discussion of these issues in terms of the works of Rorty:

Knowing why particular political strategies worked (or failed) is of obvious vital interest. The same can be said for science. I'm

193

happy to join Rorty in lumping science and politics together, but let's try to explain the successes (or failures) of both, rather than turn our backs on them (1994: 3).

We would concur with this argument. There is now evidence of a renewed dialogue in the philosophy of science and social science that is reconsidering the relationship between and nature of these disciplines. New views in philosophy abound, the result being that not only does such philosophical discourse permit us to see our endeavours in a new light, but that account must be taken of the daily practices that make up scientific work. Perhaps, then, we will not find it necessary to view the relationship between philosophy and research in terms of a simple dichotomy: for example, philosophy as "abstract" and the daily business of research as "technical". Instead, we will learn that all of our decisions, however informed, have philosophical implications, whilst philosophy, if it is to have an impact upon practices, needs at least to recognize the contexts in which scientists and social scientists work.

Key definitions

Action   Relates to the "doings" of purposive agents. A key preoccupation of philosophy of social science is the explanation of human action either through antecedent causes or reasons. Accounts of social behaviour that privilege agency over structure explain the existence of the social as resulting from the actions of individuals.

Ad hominem **argument**   A fallacious argument whereby the character of a person is cited as a reason to reject their argument or the value of what they say.

Analytic   An analytic statement is one where the truth of the conclusion is contained within the premisses, e.g. "All men are mortal, Socrates is a man, therefore Socrates is mortal." Compare with Synthetic.

A priori   Literally "from what comes before". In philosophy it is used to refer to conclusions reached on the basis of reasoning from self-evident propositions.

Axiom   A self-evident, or wholly accurate statement. Principally used in mathematics. In social science there are few, or no, statements that are considered as axiomatic, though some have claimed that statements such as "individuals seek to maximize pleasure and minimize pain" are of this type.

Bayes's theorem   A method of evaluating the conditional probability of an event. Bayesians argue that many methodological puzzles stem from a fixation upon all or nothing beliefs and that these may be resolved by applying "degrees of belief" to a hypothesis.

Conventionalism   The view that the adoption of one scientific theory over another is simply a matter of convention.

Critical theory   Originally a diverse strand of Marxism, but with origins in Hegelian philosophy. It has since drawn on a number of other influences including systems theory and psychoanalysis. A characteristic of humanity is rational thought that allows us the potential to create or transform our environment. Moreover, our capacity for rational thought provides us with standards by which we can criticize existing societies. A term originally associated with the Frankfurt School and more recently with the modifications of this tradition in the work of Habermas.

Deduction   An argument is said to be deductive if the conclusion can be deduced from the premiss. Compare with Induction.

Dependent/independent variable   In research, changes in the "dependent variable" are explained by reference to the influence of the "independent variable". For example, educational achievement (dependent variable) may be linked to social class, location, etc. Which variables are treated as dependent or independent will depend on the theoretical framework of the research.

Determinism/deterministic   A doctrine that claims all events are determined by prior events and the operation of natural laws. Thus, it is held that if such causes can be uncovered then it is possible to predict the future with accuracy. In its extreme form it has had few adherents in social science and with the advent of quantum physics and non-linear mathematics, deterministic models of the physical world are taken less seriously.

Dualism   A theory which holds that phenomena are either physical or mental and cannot be reduced to each other. Descartes was possibly its most famous exponent (I think, therefore I am) in his separation of the thinking thing from that which is being thought. Compare with Monism.

Ecological fallacy   An error of reasoning where conclusions about individuals are wrongly derived from premisses about groups. For example, aggregate data about factors associated with poverty cannot be used to draw conclusions about the cause of poverty in individuals.

Empiricism   The doctrine that all knowledge about the world is derived from sense experience. In some very influential forms, especially in the work of Hume, it takes a "psychologistic" form whereby that which we describe as experience is really a description of the contents of our mind. Although usually contrasted with idealism, in this form it might be regarded as collapsing into idealism.

Epistemology   A branch of philosophy concerned with how we know what we know and our justification for claims to knowledge.

Ethnomethodology   A form of sociology "invented" by Harold Garfinkel. Its influences are principally those of phenomenology, the ideas of the American sociologist Talcott Parsons and ordinary language philosophy. It is an attempt to empirically explain how agents ("members") produce meanings in social practices. It is held that all knowledge, including ethnomethodology itself, is a social creation.

Falsification   To show something to be false. Popper argued that although theories can be conclusively falsified they can never be conclusively verified. For him, falsification was the criterion of distinction between science and non-science. Compare with Verification.

Fallacy (e.g. genetic, ecological, gambler's)   In everyday life, fallacy is equated with error, but in its logical form it is an argument that involves invalid reasoning. There are many kinds of fallacy and they have important consequences in social science. For example, see Gambler's fallacy, Ecological fallacy.

Functionalism   Functional explanations have a long history in social science and are said by some to be unavoidable when explaining the actions of groups. Its origins were in biology where a particular organ is explained by its function. In sociology, functional explanation involves explaining the role of individuals, or smaller groups, through the function they perform in maintaining larger groups or society as a whole. It is a controversial doctrine criticized on a number of fronts. A particular

197

philosophical criticism is that it is "teleological" in that it explains a process by its end state, thus reversing cause and effect.

Gambler's fallacy   Makes the mistake of treating independent events as though they were dependent. For example, if when tossing a coin you reason that the more times it comes up heads, the more you increase the chances of it coming up tails next time, this is to commit the Gambler's fallacy.

Hermeneutics   A term imported from theology mainly through the work of Dilthey. It is concerned with the investigation and particularly the interpretation of human action as essentially intentional. It is particularly concerned with the content as well as the form of what is being interpreted.

Heuristic device   An artificial construct that is used to assist in understanding. Weber's "ideal types" can be seen as a heuristic device in sociology.

Historicism   Used principally and pejoratively by Karl Popper and his followers to describe an approach to social investigation that sees historical prediction as its goal. Popper claims human history is, in principal, unpredictable for human actions constitute "open systems". New knowledge cannot be predicted, because to predict it one would already have to possess it. Social science concerned with grand historical prediction, however, is no longer fashionable and Popper's critique of historicism may be regarded as something of a "straw person".

Hypothetico-deductive model   Though there are variations, the hypothetico-deductive model in science is one where hypotheses are derived from a theory. These are then tested via observation.

Hypothesis   An untested statement of the relationship between concepts within a particular theory. In some accounts, they are logically equivalent to a theory in that a theory itself is, in principle, never completely proven. A hypothesis is then simply that part of the theory subject to empirical test.

Idealism   A doctrine that takes many forms, but has a common theme whereby what we call the external world is a creation of mind. This does not mean that idealists claim that there is no "real" world, but that we can never directly perceive the "real" world. Contrast with Realism.

Ideal type A heuristic device associated with Max Weber. It is neither an average type, nor a description of the most common features of a social phenomenon. It is, instead, a conceptual type that can be used as a category, or concept, to guide research.

Ideology A system of ideas or norms that direct social or political action. Often associated with Marxism where the "dominant ideology" of a society is seen to derive from the material dominance of one class over another.

Induction Induction begins from observations of particular phenomena from which generalizations about wider phenomena are then made. Although, unlike deduction, the truth of the conclusion is not entailed by the premisses, it is said that sufficient evidence from observations constitute good reasons for accepting something as true. Thus, that the sun has risen every morning is reason enough to conclude it will rise tomorrow. The difficulty arises in deciding what constitutes sufficient evidence to reach such conclusions.

Instrumentalism A view in the philosophy of science that holds that theories are simply instruments, calculating devices or tools used for deriving predictions from data. An alternative meaning in social philosophy, which derives from William James, is that ideas or practices only have value in that they help us achieve a desired end state.

Interpretivism Approaches to social sciences that prioritize the meanings and actions of agents are collectively described as interpretivist.

Isomorphic Having a structure or form equivalent to something else. It is sometimes said that prediction and explanation are isomorphic because one logically entails the other.

Metaphysics The branch of philosophy concerned with matters that go beyond our existing knowledge, such as questions about the existence of god, the nature of "reality" or the origins of the universe. Although criticized by many empiricists as simply speculation, it remains that, at a mundane level, such speculations, or assumptions about the world, are the basis of theories that should be testable.

Methodological individualism/holism Methodological individualism and methodological holism are opposites. The former doctrine holds that all social explanation is, in principle, reducible to statements about individuals, whereas the latter argues that social "wholes" such as classes, ethnic groups, etc., have a factual existence that is not reducible to the characteristics of individual agents.

Naturalism In the philosophy of the social sciences, this is the doctrine that human beings should be considered as part of nature. Thus, the subject matter of the social sciences is continuous with that of the physical sciences and that with appropriate adaptation, the methodological approach of the latter is appropriate to the study of the former. This should not be conflated into positivism. Confusingly, "naturalism" is also used to describe an approach in interpretivist sociology that aims to study social phenomena in their natural setting.

Necessary/Sufficient condition In causal analysis, a necessary condition is where a variable, or event, must be present for another variable, or event, to occur. A necessary condition may not be sufficient to bring about that event. Conversely, a sufficient condition is where a variable, or event, is enough on its own to bring something about.

Normative A normative statement is one about what is right or what is wrong, desirable or undesirable, in a society. Therefore, it is a value judgement made from a particular political or moral perspective.

Occam's razor A philosophical view which holds that theories or explanations should be as streamlined as possible. In research it takes the form of the most parsimonious model, theory or equation.

Ontology The branch of philosophy concerned with existence and the nature of those things that exist. Compare with epistemology.

Paradox of enquiry The paradox of enquiry is summed up by Socrates when he asks how can we seek something if we don't know what it looks like and if we already know why would we seek it?

Phenomenology A philosophical method of enquiry involving the systematic investigation of the objects of consciousness. Principally associated with Brentano and Husserl and in social science, with Alfred Schutz.

Premiss In logic, this is one of the statements from which another statement (the conclusion) can be deduced. In a deductive argument, the conclusion should follow from the premiss, but that is no guarantee that the premiss is itself true.

Probability The likelihood that a particular relationship or event will occur. Values for a statistical probability range from 1.0 (always or certain) to 0 (never). Though probability is a complex and controversial topic, it is sometimes said that the absence or paucity of laws in the social world gives social science a "probabilistic" character. In other words, though we are much less certain of an event occurring in the social world than the physical world we can, nevertheless, often assign a probability value to its occurrence.

Rationalism Post Enlightenment philosophy has been dominated by two major "schools" of thought – those of empiricism and rationalism. Rationalism begins by asserting that it is possible to obtain by reason alone a knowledge of the nature of what exists and that everything is, in principle, explicable. Thus, unlike empiricism, knowledge is not linked wholly to sense data. Some forms of rationalism emphasize the deductive character of knowledge, whereas "critical rationalism" combines this with the empiricist assertion that sense data are the final court of appeal.

Realism Realism takes many forms, though each shares the view that physical objects exist independently of our perception of them. In social science, the question for realists is what is the ontological status of social phenomena? Some, like Marx and Bhaskar, argue that they have a "real" existence whereas others are prepared to allow that the physical world has a real existence, but the social world depends for its existence on its being perceived. Anthony Giddens has tried to bridge this gap by accrediting social phenomena with having what he calls a "virtual reality".

Reductionism In general, a reductive strategy is one that attempts to explain the complex to the simple. In social science, it is usually an attempt to reduce sociology to psychology and the latter to biology. In some respects, reductionism is a valid strategy in the elaboration of a concept, but often its advocates miss the point. It is as pointless to reduce sociology to psychology and the latter to biology as it is to reduce engineering to quantum description!

Refutation To refute something is to do more than deny it. Instead, a refutation requires that sufficient reason is provided for believing that what is denied is actually false. To refute a research finding is not to disagree with it, but to show it to be wrong.

Relativism It is possible to be a relativist about knowledge, cognition or value. The relativist emphasizes the importance of the environment in determining what is, or what ought to be the case. Secondly, the diversity of social environments is emphasized. It is summed up in Pascal's comment that what is truth on one side of the Pyrenees may be error on the other. Different kinds of relativism produce different arguments, but one difficulty besets all types of relativism. If it is asserted that there are no objective values, or objective knowledge, then such an assertion must have the same status as those things it pronounces upon!

Solipsism A solipsist holds that they alone exist and that what is called the outside world exists only in the conscious mind. It has been of interest to philosophers mainly because it is a view very hard to refute! Nevertheless, we work on the metaphysical assumption that it is wrong and the description "solipsistic" is nowadays often reserved for extreme forms of idealism where the possibilities of intersubjectivity are denied or minimized.

Significance Though often used as a synonym of importance, in social science it usually taken to refer to statistical significance: that is, whether a value is larger, or smaller, than would be expected by chance alone. However, though something may be statistically significant, it does not mean that it will be of substantive or practical significance.

Structuralism In a general sense, this refers to social scientific approaches that regard social structure as more important than social action. However, more recently it has come to be used to describe a diverse movement in sociology motivated by the idea that underneath the changing and unstable appearance of social reality underlying structures located in rules and/or language can be discerned. Associated with Saussure, Lévi Strauss and Althusser.

Theory   A statement, or group of statements, purporting to describe how a part, or parts of the world, work. A theory will go beyond that which is apparent to the senses, but it is usually held that a theory should be testable to be of research value. Compare with hypothesis.

Theory laden   Any concept or word that can only be understood within the context of a particular theory. For example, the concept of the "super-ego" can only be understood within the context of Freudian psychology. Many recent philosophers of science have influentially argued that all descriptive terms must be understood in the context of a theory – all terms in science are theory laden.

Validity   In logic, an argument is valid if there is agreement between the premisses and the conclusion. However, in research a measure or test is considered to be valid if it measures the property it claims to measure.

Value freedom   Traditionally science, and social science, were claimed to be free of personal or normative values. However, value freedom, even if it could be obtained, would be simply the substitution of the values of science for other values. Few would disagree nowadays that all disciplines begin from a set of values, though this need not prevent investigators from being objective.

Verification   A procedure carried out to determine whether or not a statement (usually a hypothesis) is true or false. Thus, a hypothesis that could be shown to be true is verifiable. The verification principle was at the heart of logical positivism, but repudiated by Popper who attempted to replace it with falsification. Compare with falsification.

Verstehen   A German word used by Dilthey, but especially Weber, broadly meaning "understanding". *Verstehen* is a method of interpreting social action by placing oneself in the position of the person whose actions one wishes to interpret.

Voluntarism Emphasis is placed on the individual action. Often used to denote theories that place too much emphasis on the freedom and the ability of individual agents to shape the social world.

Bibliography

Abrahamson, M. 1981. *Sociological theory, an introduction to concepts, issues and research*. Eaglewood Cliffs, NJ: Prentice-Hall.

Adorno, T., H. Albert, R. Dahrendorf, J. Habermas, H. Pilot, K. R. Popper 1976. *The positivist dispute in German sociology*. Translated by G. Adey & D. Frisby. London: Heinemann.

Adorno, T. & M. Horkheimer 1979. *Dialectic of enlightenment*. Originally published 1944. Translated by J. Cumming. London: Verso.

Agger, B. 1991. *A critical theory of public life: knowledge, discourse and politics in an age of decline*. Brighton: Falmer Press.

Althusser, L. 1979. *For Marx*. London: New Left Books.

Anderson, I., P. Kemp, D. Quilgars 1993. *Single homeless people*. London: Department of the Environment/HMSO.

Appleyard, B. 1992. *Understanding the present*. London: Pan-Macmillan.

Ashmore, M., R. Woofitt, S. Harding 1994. Humans and others, agents and things. *American Behavioral Scientist* 37, 733–40.

Atkinson, J. M. & J. C. Heritage (eds) 1984. *Structures of social action: studies in conversation analysis*. Cambridge: Cambridge University Press.

Atkinson, P. 1990. *The ethnographic imagination: textual constructions of reality*. London: Routledge.

Ayer, A. 1982. *Philosophy in the twentieth century*. London: Unwin.

—1987. Introduction. In *The logic of the moral sciences*, J. S. Mill. London: Duckworth.

Barnes, S. B. (ed.) 1972. *Sociology of science*. London: Penguin.

Barnes, S. B. 1974. *Scientific knowledge and sociological theory*. London: Routledge & Kegan Paul.

—1977. *Interests and the growth of knowledge*. London: Routledge & Kegan Paul.

Barrett, M. & A. Phillips (eds) 1992. *Destabilizing theory: contemporary feminist debates*. Cambridge: Polity.

Baudrillard, J. 1983a. *Simulations*. New York: Semiotexte.

—1983b. *In the shadow of the silent majorities*. New York: Semiotexte.

—1993. Hyperreal America. Translated by David Macey. *Economy and Society* 22(2), 243–52.

Bauman, Z. 1987. *Legislators and interpreters: on modernity, post-modernity and intellectuals.* Cambridge: Polity.

—1988. Is there a postmodern sociology? *Theory, Culture and Society* 5, 2–53, 217–37.

—1992. *Intimations of postmodernity.* London: Routledge.

Bell, C. & L. Roberts (eds) 1984. *Social researching: politics, problems, practice.* London: Routledge & Kegan Paul.

Benjamin, A. (ed.) 1991. *The problems of modernity: Adorno and Benjamin.* London: Routledge.

Bennett, T. 1988. An assessment of the design, implementation and effectiveness of Neighbourhood Watch in London. *Howard Journal of Criminal Justice.* 27(4), 241–55.

Bernstein, R. 1983. *Beyond objectivism and relativism: science, hermeneutics and praxis.* Oxford: Basil Blackwell.

Bernstein, R. J. 1976. *The restructuring of social and political theory.* London: Methuen.

Bertens, H. 1995. *The idea of the postmodern.* London: Routledge.

Bhaskar, R. 1975. *A realist theory of science.* Leeds: Leeds Books.

—1979. *The possibility of naturalism.* Brighton: Harvester.

—1989. *Reclaiming reality – a critical introduction to contemporary philosophy.* London: Verso.

—1993. *Dialectic: the pulse of freedom.* London: Verso.

—1994. Realism. In *The Blackwell dictionary of 20th century social thought,* W. Outhwaite, T. Bottomore, with E. Gellner, R. Nisbet, A. Touraine (eds). Oxford: Blackwell.

Bishop, Y. M., S. Fienburg, P. Holland 1975. *Discrete multivariate analysis.* Cambridge, Mass.: MIT Press.

Bittner, E. 1967. The police on skid row: a study of peace-keeping. *American Sociological Review* 32, 699–715.

Blackburn, C. 1991. *Poverty and health: working with families.* Buckingham: Open Unversity Press.

Blaikie, N. 1994. *Approaches to social enquiry.* Cambridge: Polity.

Blake, J. A. 1979. Ufology: the intellectual development and social context of the study of unidentified flying objects. In *On the margins of science: the social construction of rejected knowledge,* R. Wallis (ed.). Keele: University of Keele.

Blalock, H. M. & A. B. Blalock 1971. *Methodology in social research.* New York: McGraw Hill.

Bloor, D. 1976. *Knowledge and social imagery.* London: Routledge & Kegan Paul.

Bohman, J. 1991. *New philosophy of social science.* Cambridge: Polity.

Bourdieu, P. & L. J. Wacquant 1992. *An invitation to reflexive sociology.* Cambridge: Polity.

Boyne, R. 1990. *Foucault and Derrida: the other side of reason.* London: Unwin Hyman.

Bradbury, M. 1989. *Mensonge.* London: Arena.

Bramley, G. 1988. The definition and measurement of homelessness. In *Homelessness and the London housing market,* G. Bramley et al. (eds). Bristol: School for Advanced Urban Studies.

Bramley, G., K. Googan, P. Leather, A. Murie, E. Watson (eds) 1988. *Homelessness and the London housing market*. Bristol: School for Advanced Urban Studies.

Brannen, J. (ed.) 1992. *Mixing methods: qualitative and quantitative research*. Aldershot, Hants.: Avebury.

Brown, J. R. 1989. *The rational and the social*. London: Routledge.

—1994. *Smoke and mirrors – how science reflects reality*. London: Routledge.

Bryman, A. 1988. *Quantity and quality in social research*. London: Unwin Hyman.

—1992. Quantitative and qualitative research: further thoughts on their integration. In *Mixing methods: qualitative and quantitative research*, J. Brannen (ed.). Aldershot, Hants.: Avebury.

—1995. *Disney and his worlds*. London: Routledge.

Bryman, A. & D. Cramer 1990. *Quantitative data analysis for social scientists*. London: Routledge.

Buchanan, D. R. 1992. An uneasy alliance: combining quantitative and qualitative research methods. *Health Educational Quarterly* 19, 117–35.

Buck, N., J. Gershuny, D. Rose, J. Scott (eds) 1994. *Changing households: the British household panel survey 1990–1992*. Essex: University of Essex Centre for the Study of Micro-social Change.

Burchell, G., C. Gordon, P. Miller (eds) 1991. *The Foucault effect: studies in govermentality*. London: Harvester Wheatsheaf.

Bynner, J. & K. Stribley (eds) 1979. *Social research: principles & procedures*. Milton Keynes: Open University Press.

Cain, M. 1990. Realist philosophy and standpoint epistemologies or feminist criminology as a successor science. In *Feminist perspectives in criminology*, L. Gelsthorpe & A. Morris (eds). Milton Keynes: Open University Press.

Callinicos, A. 1991. *Against postmodernism: a Marxist critique*. Cambridge: Polity.

Carnap, R. 1969. *The logical structure of the world and pseudoproblems in philosophy*. Berkeley: University of California Press.

Chalmers, A. 1982. *What is this thing called science?* Milton Keynes: Open University Press.

—1990. *Science and its fabrication*. Milton Keynes: Open University Press.

Cicourel, A. V. 1973. *Cognitive sociology: language and meaning in social interaction*. Harmondsworth: Penguin.

Clifford, J. & G. E. Marcus (eds) 1986. *Writing culture: the poetics and politics of ethnography*. Berkeley: University of California Press.

Coakley, J. (ed.) 1992. *The social origins of nationalist movements*. London: Sage.

Cockburn, C. 1977. *The local state*. London: Pluto.

Collins, H. M. 1975. *Changing order: replication and induction in scientific practice*. London: Sage.

Coulter, J. 1979. *The social construction of mind: studies in ethnomethodology and linguistic philosophy*. London: Macmillan.

Czarniawska-Joerges, B. 1995. Narration or science? Collapsing the division in organization studies. *Organization* 2(10), 11–33.

Dale, A., S. Arber, M. Procter 1988. *Doing secondary analysis*. London: Unwin Hyman.

Dale, A. & C. Marsh (eds) 1993. *The 1991 Census users' handbook*. London: HMSO.

Dale, A., M. Williams, B. Dodgeon 1996. *Housing deprivation and social change*, London: Office of Population, Census and Survey. In press.

Davidson, D. 1994. Actions, reasons and causes. In *Readings in the philosophy of social science*. M. Martin & L. McIntyre (eds). Cambridge, Mass.: MIT Press.

Dean, M. 1994. *Critical and effective histories: Foucault's methods and historical sociology*. London: Routledge.

Dennett, D. 1991. *Consciousness explained*. London: Penguin/Allen Lane.

Denzin, N. K. 1979. The logic of naturalistic inquiry. In *Social research: principles and procedures*, J. Bynner & K. M. Stribley (eds). Milton Keynes: Open University Press.

—1992. *Symbolic interactionism and cultural studies: the politics of interpretation*. Oxford: Basil Blackwell.

Dews, P. 1989. The return of the subject in the late Foucault. *Radical Philosophy* 51, 37–41.

de Vaus, D. A. 1991. *Surveys in social research*, 3rd edn. London: UCL Press.

Dickens, D. R. & A. Fontana (eds) 1994. *Postmodernism & social inquiry*. London: UCL Press.

Docherty, T. 1993. *Postmodernism: a reader*. London: Harvester Wheatsheaf.

Dreyfus, H. & P. Rabinow 1982. *Michel Foucault: beyond structuralism and hermeneutics*. Chicago: University of Chicago Press.

Durkheim, E. 1983. *Pragmatism and sociology*. J. B. Allcock (ed.). Translated by J. C. Whitehouse. Cambridge: Cambridge University Press.

Easthope, A. & K. McGowan (eds) 1992. *A critical and cultural theory reader*. Milton Keynes: Open University Press.

Edwards, D. 1994. Imitation and artifice in apes, humans, and machines, *American Behavioral Scientist* 37, 754–71.

Elster, J. (ed.) 1986. *Rational choice*. Oxford, Blackwell.

Emmett, E. R. 1964. *Learning to philosophize*. Harmondsworth: Penguin.

Eysenck, H. J. 1953 *Uses and abuses of psychology*. Harmondsworth, Penguin.

Fairclough, N. 1989. *Language and power*. Harlow, Essex: Longman.

Featherstone, M. 1991. *Consumer culture and postmodernism*. London: Sage.

Featherstone, M. & B. Turner 1995. Body and society: an introduction. *Body and Society* 1(1), 1–12.

Ferris, T. 1988. *The coming of age in the Milky Way*. London: Bodley Head.

Feyerabend, P. K. 1978. *Against method*. London: Verso.

Fisher, N., S. Turner, R. Pugh, C. Taylor 1994. Estimating numbers of homeless and homeless mentally ill people in north east Westminster by using capture-recapture analysis. *British Medical Journal*, (January) 308.

Fontana, A. 1994. Ethnographic trends in the postmodern era. In *Postmodernism and social inquiry*, D. R. Dickens & A. Fontana (eds). London: UCL Press.

Foreman, P. 1971. Weimar culture, causality and quantum theory. In *Historical studies in the physical sciences III*, R. McCormack (ed.). Philadephia, Penn.: University of Pennsylvania Press.

Foucault, M. 1971. *Madness and civilization*. London: Tavistock.

—1977. *Discipline and punish: the birth of the prison*. London: Allen Lane.

—1980. *Power/knowledge, selected interviews and other writings 1972–1977*. C. Gordon, Brighton: Harvester Press.

—1984. *The Foucault reader.* P. Rabinow (ed.). Harmondsworth: Penguin.

—1991. Questions of method. In *The Foucault effect: studies in governmentality*, G. Burchell, C. Gordon, P. Miller (eds). London: Harvester Wheatsheaf.

—1992. *The order of things: an archaeology of the human sciences.* Originally published in 1970. London: Routledge.

Fraser, N. 1989. *Unruly practices: power, discourse and gender in contemporary social theory.* Cambridge: Polity.

Fraser, N. & L. Nicholson 1990. Social criticism without philosophy: an encounter between feminism and postmodernism. In *Feminism/Postmodernism*, L. J. Nicholson (ed.). London: Routledge.

Freund, J. 1968. *The sociology of Max Weber.* London: Penguin.

Frisby, D. 1981. *Sociological impressionism: a reassessment of Georg Simmel's social theory.* London: Heinemann Educational.

Frost, P., L. Moore, M. Louis, C. Lundberg. J. Martin (eds) 1991. *Reframing organizational culture.* Newbury Park, Calif..: Sage.

Frost, P. J. & R. Stablein 1992. *Doing exemplary research.* Newbury Park, Calif.: Sage.

Gadamer, H. G. 1975. *Truth and method.* Originally published in 1960. London: Sheed & Ward.

Game, A. 1991. *Undoing the social: towards a deconstructive sociology.* Milton Keynes: Open University Press.

Gane, M. 1991. *Baudrillard: critical and fatal theory.* London: Routledge.

— (ed.) 1993. *Baudrillard live.* London: Routledge.

Garfinkel, H. 1967. *Studies in ethnomethodology.* Englewood Cliffs, N. J.: Prentice-Hall.

— (ed.) 1986. *Ethnomethodological studies of work.* London: Routledge & Kegan Paul.

Garfinkel, H. & H. Sacks 1986. On formal structures of practical actions. In *Ethnomethodological studies of work*, H. Garfinkel (ed.). London: Routledge & Kegan Paul.

Gelsthorpe, L. & A. Morris (eds) 1990. *Feminist perspectives in criminology.* Milton Keynes: Open University Press.

Gershuny, J., D. Rose, J. Scott, N. Buck 1994. Introducing household panels. In *Changing households: the British household panel survey 1990–1992*, N. Buck, J. Gershuny, D. Rose, J. Scott (eds). Essex: University of Essex, Centre for the Study of Micro-social Change.

Gerth, H. & C.W. Mills (eds) 1970. *From Max Weber: essays in sociology.* London: Routledge & Kegan Paul.

Giddens, A. (ed.) 1972. *Emile Durkheim: selected writings.* Cambridge, Cambridge University Press.

—1976. *New rules of sociological method: a positive critique of interpretive sociologies.* London: Hutchinson.

—1984. *The constitution of society: outline of the theory of structuration.* Cambridge: Polity.

—1991. *Modernity and self-identity.* Cambridge: Polity.

Ginn, J. & P. I. Duggard 1994. Statistics a gendered agenda. *Radical Statistics* **58**, 2–15.

Gjertsen, D. 1992. *Science and philosophy: past and present.* Harmondsworth: Penguin.

Glaser, B. & A. Strauss 1967. *The discovery of grounded theory.* Chicago: Aldine Publishing.

Goldthorpe, J. H., D. Lockwood, F. Bechhofer, J. Platt 1968. *The affluent worker: industrial attitudes & behaviour.* Cambridge: Cambridge University Press.

Golub, R. & E. Bruce 1990. *The almanac of science and technology.* Orlando, Fla.: Harcourt Brace Jovanovich.

Gouldner, A. 1971. *The coming crisis in Western sociology.* London: Heinemann.

Griffiths, M. 1988. Feminism, feelings and philosophy. In *Feminist perspectives in philosophy*, M. Griffiths & M. Whitford (eds). Basingstoke: Macmillan.

Griffiths, M. & M. Whitford (eds) 1988. *Feminist perspectives in philosophy.* Basingstoke, Macmillan.

Guba, E. G. 1985. The context of emergent paradigm research. In *Theory and inquiry: the paradigm revolution*, Y. Lincoln (ed.). Los Angeles: Sage.

Habermas, J. 1972. *Knowledge and human interests.* London: Heinemann.

—1989. *Knowledge and human interests.* Originally Published in 1968. Translated by J. J. Shapiro, Cambridge: Polity.

—1992. *The philosophical discourse of modernity: twelve lectures.* Cambridge: Polity.

—1993. *Justification and application: remarks on discourse ethics.* Translated by C. Cronin. Cambridge: Polity.

Hage, J. & B. Foley-Meeker 1988. *Social causality.* London: Unwin Hyman.

Halberg, M. 1989. Feminist epistemology: an impossible project. *Radical Philosophy* 53, 3–7.

Hammersley, M. 1989. *The dilemma of qualitative method: Herbert Blumer and the Chicago School.* London: Routledge.

—(ed.) 1993. *Social research: philosophy, politics and practice.* London: Sage.

Hammersley, M. & P. Atkinson 1995. *Ethnography; principles in practice*, 2nd edn, London: Routledge.

Harding, S. (ed.) 1976. *Can theories be refuted? Essays in the Duhem–Quine thesis.* Dordrecht: Reidel.

—1986 *The science question in feminism.* Milton Keynes: Open University Press.

Harding, S. & M. Hintikka (eds) 1983. *Discovering reality: feminist perspectives on epistemology, metaphysics, methodology and philosophy of science.* Dordrecht: Reidel.

Harré, R. 1970. *The principles of scientific thinking.* Chicago: University of Chicago Press.

—1972. *The philosophy of science: an introductory survey.* Oxford: Oxford University Press.

—1986. *Varieties of realism: a rationale for the natural sciences.* Oxford: Blackwell.

Harré, R. & P. F. Secord 1972. *The explanation of social behaviour.* Oxford: Blackwell.

Hartsock, N. 1983. The feminist standpoint: developing the ground for a specifically feminist materialism. In *Discovering reality: feminist perspectives on epistemology, metaphysics, methodology and philosophy of science*, S. Harding & M. Hintikka (eds). Dordrecht: Reidel.

Harvey, D. 1989. *The condition of postmodernity: an enquiry into the origins of cultural change.* Oxford: Basil Blackwell.

Harvey, L. 1990. *Critical social research.* London: Unwin Hyman.

Held, D. 1990. *Introduction to critical theory – Horkheimer to Habermas.* Cambridge: Polity.

Hempel, C. G. 1994. The function of general laws in history. In *Readings in the philosophy of social science*, M. Martin & L. McIntyre (eds). Cambridge, Mass.: MIT Press.

Hempel, K. 1965. *Aspects of scientific explanation*. New York: Free Press.

Heisenberg, W. 1989. *Physics and philosophy*. London: Pelican.

Heritage, J. 1984. *Garfinkel and ethnomethodology*. Cambridge: Polity.

Hesse, M. 1974. *The structure of scientific inference*. London: Macmillan.

Hester, S. & P. Egline 1992. *A sociology of crime*. London: Routledge.

Hobbs, D. 1988. *Doing the business: entrepreneurship, the working class and detectives in the East-End of London*. Oxford: Oxford University Press.

—1993. Peers, careers and academic fears: writing as fieldwork. In *Interpreting the field: accounts of ethnography*, D. Hobbs & T. May (eds). Oxford: Oxford University Press.

Hobbs, D. & T. May (eds) 1993. *Interpreting the field: accounts of ethnography*. Oxford: Oxford University Press.

Hollis, M. 1970. The limits of irrationality. In *Rationality*, B. Wilson (ed.). Oxford: Blackwell.

Hollis, R. 1994. *The philosophy of social science*. Cambridge: Cambridge University Press.

Holub, R. C. 1991. *Jürgen Habermas – Critic in the public sphere*. London: Routledge.

Homan, R. 1991. *The ethics of social research*. London: Longman.

Honneth, A. 1993. The Frankfurt School. In *The Blackwell dictionary of 20th century social thought*, W. Outhwaite & T. Bottomore (eds). Oxford: Blackwell.

Horkheimer, M. 1993. *Between philosophy and social science: selected early writings*. Translated by G. F. Hunter, M. S. Kramer, J. Torpey. Cambridge, Mass.: MIT Press.

Hospers, J. 1967. *An introduction to philosophical analysis*. London: Routledge.

Howson, C. & P. Urbach 1989. *Scientific reasoning: the Bayesian approach*. LaSalle, Ill.: Open Court.

Hoy, D. C. (ed.) 1986. *Foucault: a critical reader*. Oxford: Basil Blackwell.

Hughes, J. A. 1990. *The philosophy of social research*, 2nd edn. Harlow: Longman.

Hume, D. 1911 *A treatise of human nature*. London: Dent.

Hutson, S. & M. Liddiard 1994. *Youth homelessness – the construction of a social issue*. London: Macmillan.

Inglis, F. 1993. *Cultural studies*. Oxford: Blackwell.

Jewson, N., D. Mason, C. Lambkin, F. Taylor 1992. *Ethnic monitoring policy and practice: a study of employers' experiences*. Leicester: Ethnic Minority Employment Research Centre, University of Leicester.

Joas, H. 1993. *Pragmatism and social theory*. Chicago: University of Chicago Press.

Johnson, T., C. Dandeker, C. Ashworth 1984. *The structure of social theory*. Basingstoke: Macmillan.

Jones, C. & R. Porter (eds) 1994. *Reassessing Foucault: power, medicine and the body*. London: Routledge.

Kamuf, P. (ed.) 1991. *A Derrida reader: between the blinds*. London: Harvester Wheatsheaf.

Keat, R. & J. Urry 1975. *Social theory as science*. London: Routledge & Kegan Paul.

Kellas, J. G. 1992. The social origins of nationalism in Great Britain. In *The social origins of nationalist movements*, J. Coakley (ed.). London: Sage.

Keller, E. F. 1985. *Reflections on gender and science*. New Haven, Conn.: Yale University Press.

Kellner, D. 1993. Popular culture and the construction of postmodern identities. In *Modernity and identity*, S. Lash & J. Friedman (eds). Oxford: Blackwell.

—(ed.) 1994. *Baudrillard: a critical reader*. Oxford: Blackwell.

Knorr-Cetina, K. D. 1981. Social and scientific method or what do we make of the distinction between the natural and the social sciences? *Philosophy of the Social Sciences* 11, 335–59.

Knorr-Cetina, K. & A. Cicourel (eds) 1981. *Advances in social theory and methodology: towards an integration of micro and macro theories*. London: Routledge & Kegan Paul.

Kraus, L. 1989. *The fifth essence – the search for dark matter in the universe*. London: Vintage.

Kuhn, T. 1970. *The structure of scientific revolutions*, 2nd edn, Chicago: Chicago University Press.

—1977. *The essential tension*. Chicago: Chicago University Press.

Lakatos, I. 1987. *The methodology of scientific research programmes*. J. Worrall & G. Currie (eds). Cambridge: Cambridge University Press.

Lakatos, I. & A. Musgrave (eds) 1970. *Criticism and the growth of knowledge*. Cambridge: Cambridge University Press.

Lash, S. 1990. *The sociology of postmodernism*. London: Routledge.

Lash, S. & J. Friedman (eds) 1993. *Modernity and identity*. Oxford: Blackwell.

Laudan, L. 1977. *Progress and its problems – towards a theory of scientific growth*. London: Routledge & Kegan Paul.

Law, J. 1994. *Organizing modernity*. Oxford: Basil Blackwell.

Law, J. & P. Lodge 1984. *Science for social scientists*. London: Macmillan.

Layder, D. 1988. The relation of theory and method: causal relatedness, historical contingency and beyond. *Sociological Review* 36, 441–63.

Lincoln, Y. (ed.) 1985. *Organization theory and inquiry: the paradigm revolution*. Los Angeles: Sage.

Long, N. & A. Long (eds) 1992. *Battlefields of knowledge*. London: Routledge.

Losee, J. 1980. *A historical introduction to the philosophy of science*. Oxford: Oxford University Press.

Lukes, S. 1994. Some problems about rationality. In *Readings in the philosophy of social science*, M. Martin & L. McIntyre (eds). Cambridge, Mass.: MIT Press.

Lyotard, J. F. 1984. *The postmodern condition: a report on knowledge*. Originally published in 1979. Manchester: Manchester University Press.

—1993. Answering the question: what is postmodernism? In *Postmodernism: a reader*, T. Docherty (ed.). London: Harvester Wheatsheaf.

McCormack, R. (ed.) 1971. *Historical studies in the physical sciences III*. Philadephia, Penn.: University of Pennsylvania Press.

Macdonald, S. (ed.) 1993. *Inside European identities*. Oxford: Berg.

McKarl-Nielsen, J. (ed.) 1990. *Feminist research methods: exemplary readings in the social sciences*. London: Westview Press.

McLellan, D. 1986. *Ideology*. Milton Keynes: Open University Press.

Manicas, P. 1987. *A history and philosophy of social science*. Oxford: Blackwell.

Marcuse, H. 1969. *Reason and revolution: Hegel and the rise of social theory*. London:

Routledge & Kegan Paul.

Marsh, C. 1982. *The survey method – the contribution of surveys to sociological explanation.* London: Allen & Unwin.

Martin, M. & L. McIntyre (eds) 1994. *Readings in the philosophy of social science.* Cambridge, Mass.: MIT Press.

Marx, K. 1976. *Preface and introduction to a contribution to the critique of political economy.* Peking: Foreign Languages Press.

—1977. *Economic and philosophic manuscripts of 1844.* Moscow: Progress.

—1980. Preface to a contribution to the critique of political economy. In *Selected works in one volume*, K. Marx & F. Engels. London: Lawrence & Wishart.

Marx, K. & F. Engels 1970. *The German ideology.* London: Lawrence & Wishart.

—1980. *Selected works in one volume.* London: Lawrence & Wishart.

May, T. 1993. *Social research: issues, methods and process.* Buckingham: Open University Press.

—1994. Transformative power: a study in a human service organisation. *Sociological Review* **42**(4), 618–38.

— 1996. *Situating social theory.* Buckingham: Open University Press.

Mayer, T. 1994. *Analytical Marxism.* London: Sage.

Mead, G. H. 1964. *Selected writings: George Herbert Mead.* A. J. Reck (ed.). Chicago: University of Chicago Press.

Menzies, K. 1982. *Sociological theory in use.* London: Routledge.

Merton, R. 1968. *Social theory and social structure.* New York: Free Press.

Mill, J. S. 1987. *The logic of the moral sciences.* London: Duckworth.

Miller, J. 1993. *The passion of Michel Foucault.* London: Harper Collins.

Miller, P. & T. O'Leary 1987. Accounting and the construction of the governable person. *Accounting, Organizations and Society* **12**, 235–65.

Mills, C. W. 1970. *The sociological imagination.* Originally published in 1959. Harmondsworth: Penguin.

Monk, R. 1990. *Ludwig Wittgenstein: the duty of genius.* Vintage: London.

Nagel, E. 1961. *The structure of science.* London: Routledge & Kegan Paul.

Nagel, T. 1986. *The view from nowhere.* Oxford: Oxford University Press.

Natanson, M. (ed.) 1963. *Philosophy of the social sciences.* New York: London House.

Neurath, O. 1973. *Empiricism and sociology.* Dordrecht: Reidel.

Newton-Smith, W. H. 1981. *The rationality of science.* London: Routledge & Kegan Paul.

Nicholson, L. J. (ed.) 1990. *Feminism/postmodernism.* London: Routledge.

Norris, C. 1987. *Derrida.* London: Fontana.

—1993. *The truth about postmodernism.* Oxford: Blackwell.

O'Neill, J. 1994. *The poverty of postmodernism.* London: Routledge.

Outhwaite, W. 1975. *Understanding social life: the method called verstehen.* London: Allen & Unwin.

—1987. *New philosophies of social science – realism, hermeneutics and critical theory.* New York: St. Martin's Press.

Outhwaite, W. & T. Bottomore (eds) 1993. *The Blackwell dictionary of 20th century social thought.* Oxford: Blackwell.

Papineau, D. 1978. *For science in the social science.* Basingstoke: Macmillan.

Parkin, F. 1982. *Max Weber.* London: Tavistock.

Penrose, R. 1989. *The emperor's new mind*. Oxford: Oxford University Press.

Platt, J. 1983. The development of the "participant observation" method in sociology: origin myth and history. *Journal of the History of the Behavioral Sciences* **19**, 379–93.

—1984. The "affluent worker" re-visited. In *Social researching: politics, problems, practice*, C. Bell & H. Roberts (eds). London: Routledge & Kegan Paul.

—1986. Functionalism and the survey: the relation of theory and method, *Sociological Review* **34**, 501–36.

Popper, K. R. 1966. *The open society and its enemies*. London: Routledge & Kegan Paul.

—1979. *Objective knowledge*. Oxford, Clarendon.

—1983. *The logic of scientific discovery*. Originally published in English 1959. London: Hutchinson.

—1986a. *Unended quest – an intellectual autobiography*. Glasgow: Collins.

—1986b. *The poverty of historicism*. London: Ark.

—1989. *Conjectures and refutations*. London: Routledge.

Porter, S. 1993. Critical realist ethnography: the case of racism and professionalism in a medical setting. *Sociology* **27**(4), 591–609.

Poster, M. 1990. *The mode of information: poststructuralism and social context*. Cambridge: Polity.

Pratt, V. 1978. *The philosophy of the social sciences*. London: Methuen.

Punch, M. 1986. *The politics and ethics of fieldwork*. London: Sage.

Purvis, T. & A. Hunt 1993. Discourse, ideology, discourse, ideology, discourse, ideology . . .. *British Journal of Sociology* **44**(3), 473–99.

Putman, H. 1961. *Meaning & the moral sciences*. London: Routledge & Kegan Paul.

Priemus, H., M. Kleinman, D. Maclennan, B. Turner 1994. Maastricht Treaty: Consequences for national housing policies. *Housing Studies* **9**(2), 163–82.

Quine, W. v O. 1953. *Two dogmas of empiricism*. Cambridge, Mass.: Harvard University Press.

Quinn-Patton, M. 1986. *Utilization – focused evaluation*. London: Sage.

Rabinow, P. & W. Sullivan 1979. *Interpretive social science: a reader*. Berkeley, University of California Press.

Rae, J. 1986. *Quantum physics: illusion or reality?* Cambridge: Canto.

Ray, L. & M. Reed (eds) 1994. *Organizing modernity: new Weberian perspectives on work, organization and society*. London: Routledge.

Reed, M. & M. Hughes (eds) 1992. *Rethinking organisation; new directions in organisation theory and analysis*. London: Sage.

Rex, J. 1974. *Sociology and the demystification of the modern world*. London: Routledge & Kegan Paul.

Ricoeur, P. 1982. *Hermeneutics and the human sciences*. Edited and Translated by J. B. Thompson. Cambridge: Cambridge University Press.

Riley, G. (ed.) 1974. *Values, objectivity and the social sciences*. Reading, Mass.: Adison-Wesley.

Rock, P. 1979. *The making of symbolic interactionism*. London: Macmillan.

Rojek, C. & B. Turner (eds) 1993. *Forget Baudrillard?* London: Routledge.

Rorty, R. 1987. Foucault and epistemology. In *Foucault: a critical reader*, D. C. Hoy (ed.). Oxford: Basil Blackwell.

—1989. *Contingency, irony and solidarity*. Cambridge: Cambridge University Press.
—1991. Feminism and pragmatism. *Radical Philosophy* 59, 3–14.
—1992. We anti-representationalists. *Radical Philosophy* 60, 40–2.
—1993. Cosmopolitanism without emancipation: a response to Lyotard. In *Modernity and identity*, S. Lash & J. Friedman (eds). Oxford: Blackwell.
Rose, H. 1983. Hand, brain and heart: a feminist epistemology for the natural sciences. *Signs* 9, 73–90.
Rosenbaum, D. P. 1986. *Community crime prevention: does it work?* London: Sage.
Rosenberg, A. 1988. *Philosophy of social science*. Oxford: Clarendon.
Rubinstein, D. 1981. *Marx and Wittgenstein: social praxis and social explanation*. London: Routledge & Kegan Paul.
Rudner, R. 1966. *Philosophy of social science*. Englewood Cliffs, N. J.: Prentice-Hall.
Russell, B. 1980. *The problems of philosophy*. Milton Keynes: Open University Press.
—1984. *History of Western philosophy and its connection with political and social circumstances from the earliest times to the present day*. London: Unwin Hyman.
Ryan, A. 1970. *The philosophy of the social science*. Basingstoke: Macmillan.
Sarup, M. 1993. *An introductory guide to post-structuralism and postmodernism*, 2nd edn. London: Harvester Wheatsheaf.
Sawicki, J. 1991. *Disciplining Foucault: feminism, power and the body*. London: Routledge.
Sayer, A. 1984. *Method in social science :a realist approach*. London: Hutchinson.
—1992. *Method in social science: a realist approach*. 2nd edn. London: Routledge.
Sayers, S. 1989. Knowledge as social phenomenon. *Radical Philosophy* 52, 34–7.
Schutz, A. 1972. *The phenomenology of the social world*. Originally published in 1932. Translated by G. Walsh & F. Lehnert. Introduction by G. Walsh. London: Heinemann.
—1979. Concept and theory formation in the social sciences. In *Social research: principles and procedures*, J. Bynner & K. Stribley (eds). Milton Keynes: Open University Press.
Scott, J. 1990. *A matter of record: documentary sources in social research*. Cambridge: Polity.
Scriven, M. 1994. A possible distinction between traditional scientific disciplines and the study of human behaviour. In *Readings in the philosophy of social science*, M. Martin & L. McIntyre (eds). Cambridge, Mass.: MIT Press.
Scruton, S. 1982. *Kant*. Oxford: Oxford Paperbacks.
Shapin, S. 1975. Phrenological knowledge and the social structure of early 19th century Edinburgh, *Annals of Science* XXXII, 219–43.
Sharp, R. & A. Green 1975. *Education and social control: a study in progressive primary education*. London: Routledge & Kegan Paul.
Shore, C. 1993. Ethnicity as revolutionary strategy: communist identity construction in Italy. In *Inside European identities*, S. Macdonald (ed.). Oxford: Berg.
Silitoe, K. 1987. Questions on race/ethnicity and related topics for the Census. *Population Trends* 49, 5–11.
Simons, H. W. & M. Billig (eds) 1994. *After postmodernism: reconstructing ideology critique*. London: Sage.
Singer, P. 1983. *Hegel*. Oxford: Oxford University Press.
Singleton, J. R., B. Straits, M. Straits, R. McAllister 1988. *Approaches to social research*.

New York: Oxford University Press.

Smart, B. 1993. *Postmodernity*. London: Routledge.

Smith, D. E. 1987. *The everyday world as problematic: a feminist sociology*. Milton Keynes: Open University Press.

Smith, J. K. & L. Heshusius 1986. Closing down the conversation: the end of the quantitative–qualitative debate among educational enquirers. *Educational Researcher* **15**, 4–12.

Spybey, T. 1995. *Globalization and world society*. Cambridge: Polity.

Steier, F. (ed.) 1991. *Research and reflexivity*. London: Sage.

Stillwell, J. C. H., P. H. Rees, P. Boden (eds) 1992. *Migration processes and patterns volume 2: Population redistribution in the United Kingdom*. London: Belhaven Press.

Strasser, S. 1985. *Understanding and explanation: basic ideas concerning the humanity of the human sciences*. Pittsburgh, Pa.: Duquesne University Press.

Strauss, A. 1978. *Negotiations, varieties, contexts, processes and social order*. San Francisco: Josey-Bass.

—1988. *Qualitative analysis for social scientists*. Cambridge: Cambridge University Press.

Strauss, L. 1963. Natural right and the distinction between facts and values. In *Philosophy of the social sciences*, M. Natanson (ed.). New York: Random House.

Surkin, M. 1974. Sense and nonsense in politics. In *Values, objectivity and the social sciences*, G. Riley (ed.). Reading, Mass.: Addison-Wesley.

Sutton, R. I. & A. Rafaeli 1988. Untangling the relationship between displayed emotions and organizational sales: the case of convenience stores. *Academy of Management Journal* **31**, 461–87.

Taylor, C. 1981. Understanding in human science. *Review of Metaphysics* **4**, 25–38.

Thomas, W. I. & F. Znaniecki 1958. *The Polish peasant in Europe and America*. New York: Dover.

Tong, R. 1989. *Feminist thought: a comprehensive introduction*. London: Unwin Hyman.

Townley, B. 1994. *Reframing human resource management: power, ethics and the subject at work*. London: Sage.

Townsend, P. 1979. *Poverty in Britain*. Harmondsworth: Penguin.

Travers, M. 1994. The phenomenon of the radical lawyer. *Sociology* **28**, 245–9.

Trigg, R. 1985. *Understanding social science*. Oxford: Blackwell.

Tudor, A. 1982. *Beyond empiricism: philosophy of science in sociology*. London: Routledge & Kegan Paul.

Turner, B.A. 1992. The Symbolic understanding of organisations. In *Rethinking organisation; new directions in organisation theory and analysis*, M. Reed & M. Hughes (eds). London: Sage.

Tyler, S. A. 1986. Post-modern ethnography: from document of the occult to occult document. In *Writing culture: the poetics and politics of ethnography*, J. Clifford & G. Marcus (eds). Berkeley: University of California Press.

Verschoor, G. 1992. Identity, networks, and space. New dimensions in the study of small scale enterprise and commoditization. In *Battlefields of knowledge*, N. Long & A. Long (eds). London: Routledge.

Visker, R. 1992. Habermas on Heidegger and Foucault: meaning and validity in the philosophical discourse of modernity. *Radical Philosophy* 61, 15–22.

Von Mises, R. 1951. *Positivism*. London: Constable.

Walby, S. 1992. Post-post-modernism? Theorizing social complexity. In *Destabilizing theory: contemporary feminist debates*, M. Barrett & A. Phillips (eds). Cambridge: Polity.

Wall, R. 1990. *English and French households in historical perspective*. LS Working Paper 67. London: City University.

Wallis, R. (ed.) 1979. *On the margins of science: the social construction of rejected knowledge*. Keele: University of Keele Press.

Ward, C. & A. Dale 1991. *Geographical variation in female labour force participation*. LS Working Paper 71. London: City University.

Weber, M. 1949 *The methodology of the social sciences*. Translated and edited by E. A. Shils & H. A. Finch. Glencoe, Ill.: Free Press.

—1958 *The Protestant ethic and the spirit of capitalism*. New York: Scribners.

—1974. "Objectivity" in social science and social policy. In *Values, objectivity and the social sciences*, G. Riley (ed.). Reading, Mass.: Addison-Wesley.

—1985. *The Protestant ethic and the spirit of capitalism*. Originally published in 1930. London: Unwin.

Weeks, J. 1991. *Against nature: essays on history, sexuality and identity*. London: River Oram Press.

Weinstein, R. M. 1980. The favorableness of patients' attitudes toward mental hospitalisation. *The Journal of Health and Social Behavior* 21, 397–401.

Whyte, W. F. 1943. *Street corner society*. Chicago: Chicago University Press.

—1991. Comments for the SCS critics. In *Reframing organizational culture*, P. Frost et al. (eds). Newbury Park, Calif.: Sage.

Willis, P. 1977. *Learning to labour*. Farnborough: Saxon House.

Wilson, B. (ed.) 1970. *Rationality*. Oxford: Blackwell.

Winch, P. 1970. The idea of a social science. In *Rationality*, B. Wilson (ed.). Oxford: Blackwell.

—1990. *The idea of a social science and its relation to philosophy*. Originally published in 1958. London: Routledge.

Wolheim, R. 1971. *Freud*. London: Fontana-Collins.

Woolgar, S. 1988. *Science – the very idea*. London: Tavistock.

Woolgar, S. W. & B. Latour 1979. *Laboratory life: the social construction of scientific facts*. London: Sage.

Young, A. 1990. *Femininity in dissent*. London: Routledge.

Index

Printed in the United Kingdom
by Lightning Source UK Ltd.
106770UKS00001B/91